THE PRICE WATERHOUSE PERSONAL FINANCIAL ADVISER

Price Waterhouse LLP

IRWIN
Professional Publishing®
Chicago • London • Singapore

Irwin Book Team
Executive editor: *Amy Hollands Gaber*
Senior marketing manager: *Tiffany Dykes*
Production supervisor: *Bob Lange*
Assistant manager, desktop services: *Jon Christopher*
Project editor: *Susan Trentacosti*
Senior designer: *Heidi J. Baughman*
Jacket designer: *Image House, Inc.*
Compositor: *Precision Graphic Services, Inc.*
Typeface: *11/13 Garamond*
Printer: *R. R. Donnelley & Sons Company*

Times Mirror
Higher Education Group

Library of Congress Cataloging-in-Publication Data

The Price Waterhouse personal financial adviser / Price Waterhouse
LLP
      p.   cm.
    Includes index.
    ISBN 0-7863-0461-8
    1. Finance, Personal.   I. Price Waterhouse (Firm)
HG179.P736   1996
332.024—dc20   95-22720

Printed in the United States of America
1 2 3 4 5 6 7 8 9 0 DOC 2 1 0 9 8 7 6 5

DEDICATION

T oday Price Waterhouse LLP is a leader in providing personal financial planning due in large part to the vision and determination of Stanley H. Breitbard. While National Director of the Personal Financial Services practice from 1983 to 1994, Stan recognized that providing investment advice was integral to delivering this service. That was radical thinking in those days. Today we realize it was visionary.

Primarily, as a result of Stan's efforts, Price Waterhouse became the first Big Six accounting firm to register with the SEC as investment advisers. This allowed us to identify winning investment strategies for our clients *and* to implement them as well. That point of differentiation helped catapult Price Waterhouse Personal Financial Services to its leadership position.

Stan's dedication to the profession, understanding of human nature, and love of people was evident in the leadership he provided to our firm and to the industry as the first chairman of the American Institute of Certified Public Accountants' personal financial planning executive committee. Many concepts that the profession today considers fundamental were articulated by Stan and a small group of individuals on the committee more than 10 years ago.

Many of the philosophies explored in this book were pioneered by Stan. Concepts such as achieving lifetime financial equilibrium, life event planning, and asset allocation strategies all have Stan's strong imprint on them. Stan believes that one should first prepare for life events, then deal with tax and financial planning matters; life events, after all, give shape, form, and meaning to the technical aspects of personal finance. And, that overriding theme sets this book apart from others.

We're confident that as you read this book all of the ideas will seem simple, rational, and most important *doable.* That's no accident; one of Stan's gifts is the ability to take abstract, complex concepts and render them easily understandable by breathing life into them.

At Price Waterhouse Stan has been a leader in the true sense of the word. Without Stan this book never would have been written. In addition, most of us in Price Waterhouse's Personal Financial Services practice would not be providing the high level of sophisticated services our clients have come to expect. No doubt, individuals tackling financial planning on their own or with the help of advisers would be less-informed consumers. It is for those reasons, and many more not articulated here, that we dedicate this book to Stan Breitbard.

Thank you.

Carol Caruthers
National Director
Price Waterhouse LLP
Personal Financial Services

Price Waterhouse's Personal Financial Services provides corporate executives, business owners, board members, retired executives, and high net worth individuals with comprehensive financial planning services, including compensation, investment, retirement, estate, tax, and insurance planning. Registered with the Securities and Exchange Commission, Price Waterhouse's Personal Financial Services performs proactive investment counseling to help executives identify and implement winning investment strategies. Close personal attention and implementation assistance are the hallmarks of this service. For other individuals and employees of all income levels we use a combination of personalized analyses, workshops, and interactive software to help them develop savings habits and investment strategies aimed at achieving their financial goals.

Price Waterhouse LLP, with 14,000 men and women in 106 U.S. offices, provides ideas, information, and advice to help clients make better decisions for business and personal success. It is part of the worldwide network of Price Waterhouse firms, which offers accounting, auditing, tax, and consulting services to corporations, individuals, and government agencies in 118 countries and territories.

Price Waterhouse partner Carol Caruthers is national director of Personal Financial Services. Based in St. Louis, Ms. Caruthers is a Certified Public Accountant and on the Executive Committee of the Personal Financial Planning Division of the American Institute of Certified Public Accountants. You will find Ms. Caruthers quoted extensively in nationally renowned financial publications.

Price Waterhouse's National Personal Financial Services telephone number is (314) 425-0581.

Personal Financial Services Practice leaders include:

Atlanta	Charles Paul
Buffalo	Mark Bonner
Century City	Robert Wagman

Chicago	Meloni Hallock
	Roger Hindman
	Kevin McAuliffe
Dallas	Richard Joyner
Hartford	Mark Carley
Houston	Clark Blackman
Los Angeles	Allan Jacobi
New York	Richard Kohan
	Kevin Roach
Philadelphia	Paul Bracaglia
Pittsburgh	Larry Brown
San Francisco	Michael van den Akker
St. Louis	Joan Hamilton
	Becky Whitmore
Washington, D.C.	Bonnie Orleans

ACKNOWLEDGMENTS

We want to acknowledge the important contributions of many Price Waterhouse professionals, including the Personal Financial Services Practice leaders, the Tax Technical Services group, and the Tax Marketing group.

Special thanks go to Chris Foster, who managed the project from drafts to manuscript to book form; to Bob Casey, our editorial consultant, for his patience and skill; to Stuart P. Tobisman, Esq. of O'Melveny & Myers for his review of Chapter 10; and to Amy Gaber, our editor at Irwin, for her encouragement from beginning to end.

Price Waterhouse LLP

P R E F A C E

Over the years, Price Waterhouse has guided thousands of corporate executives, professionals, small business owners, and many others on the road to achieving financial equilibrium. Now we are able to bring our approach to an even wider audience through the *Personal Financial Adviser*. Along the way, we discuss many ideas: the choices life requires of us, many of them involving financial trade-offs, and financial planning, which is really the process of managing those trade-offs throughout your life. As such, this book represents more than just an exercise in number-crunching to anticipate future needs or a sermon on setting aside the resources required to meet those needs.

More important, what you encounter here are practical, *doable* suggestions for getting your financial life into balance, of managing risk, of living within your means, and of being ready for those challenges life invariably presents. As you will see, we firmly believe that benefits of financial planning extend beyond financial well-being. In other words, getting your financial life into balance will help you balance other aspects of your personal life as well—your emotional life, your family life, your career. That is what Price Waterhouse means by financial equilibrium.

A key word here is *personal*. To many people, financial planning means little more than reducing income taxes or finding a stockbroker. To us at Price Waterhouse, personal financial planning begins with the personal and family aspects—care of children and aging parents, for instance. It involves many aspects of personal finance, including saving, investing, and setting specific financial goals relative to key life events—education funding, planning for retirement, disability, and providing for your survivors in the case of premature death.

Finally, we recognize that seeking financial equilibrium is an ongoing process, one that changes as your life changes. To that end, we offer solid advice not only on how to reach equilibrium, but also how to stay on course as the road twists and turns.

Now is the best time to get started.

C O N T E N T S

BEGINNING THE PROCESS

BEGINNING THE PROCESS

LIFE EVENT PLANNING

INTEGRATING YOUR PLANS

SAVING AND INVESTING

TOWARD PERSONAL FINANCIAL EQUILIBRIUM

Myth vs. Reality

Myth: Financial planning is for people with a lot of money.

Reality: No matter what your means, a financial plan will help you keep your personal goals in synch with your money. People with modest resources can't afford not to plan.

Myth: Financial planning takes more time and effort than it is worth.

Reality: Financial planning encourages you to (1) set important financial goals, (2) identify choices you need to make about the future, and (3) come to agreement with family and loved ones about how financial resources will be used. These are all significant accomplishments and well worth the time you will spend on them.

Myth: Once I've come up with a financial plan, I'll never have to worry about it again.

Reality: To keep pace with the changes in your life, you will need to revisit your financial plan periodically. Otherwise, you may fall short of your retirement goals or find yourself unable to meet other future needs along the way.

Understanding and Managing Life's Financial Trade-offs

Life presents each of us with a seemingly endless series of choices. Even something as ordinary as the beginning of a routine workday offers many options. You can choose to get up early, arise at your customary hour, or sleep late. Your choice, once made, closes some options but opens new ones. The early riser trades sleep for an array of possibilities. What to do, and in what order? Exercise vigorously? Read the morning paper? Take a long walk? Go to work early? Shower? Watch TV news? Eat breakfast? Here the choosing becomes harder. Some activities can be done simultaneously (watching TV news and eating breakfast). Others cannot (taking a long walk and reading the morning paper), so trade-offs are required. Some are best carried out in a particular sequence (exercising vigorously, then showering). Other activities are mutually exclusive (going to work early and taking a long walk)—you can choose one but not both.

As the day goes on, the choices multiply, and so do the trade-offs you must make. In addition to these routine daily decisions, there are less frequent but bigger choices to be made concerning careers, friends, personal values, marriage, family, religious beliefs, lifestyles, and many more. All choices, large or small, help give us a sense of freedom that enhances our lives. Yet each one carries a consequence because it requires a trade-off: selecting option A means you will consume some resource (your time or emotional energy, for example) that otherwise could have been spent on option B.

Often the resource involved is money, and at first glance, money trade-offs seem as straightforward as any. Children learn that the same 50 cents cannot buy both a candy bar and a soda. It will purchase only one of those items, so a choice must be made. Many parents give their children weekly allowances to acquaint them with this reality and afford them experience in making their own financial trade-offs. By adulthood, you know too well the choices imposed by money. The dollar amounts may be bigger—you may, for example, be deciding between a new kitchen and a new car, each costing $20,000—but the nature of the trade-off still seems the same as candy vs. soda.

On closer examination, however, financial trade-offs turn out to be much more complex and challenging than the simple money choices made by children. Let's look at some reasons for this.

Financial trade-offs reach into the future. The choices you face now are never solely between alternate ways to spend your money *today*.

Whether you realize it or not, as part of the bargain you are also trading off among various ways to spend money *in the future*. Thus, the choice is not simply between using $20,000 to buy a new kitchen or a new car today. A third alternative, for example, is to use the $20,000 to pay for three or four years' worth of basic living expenses when you are retired. Someone age 40 or so can accomplish that goal with a fair degree of confidence by investing $20,000 now. A fourth alternative is to spend half the $20,000 fixing the kitchen today and use the rest to pay for a round-the-world trip in

Making money trade-offs without a financial road map may leave you out of gas and far short of your destination. The road map you need is a financial plan.

five years, again by investing the remaining portion. Of course, there are countless other potential present/future trade-offs when any money decision is being made.

Financial trade-offs involve uncertainty. That's because they reach into the future and the future is unknown. Tomorrow may turn out as you expect, with things following the general direction they are now headed; or it may veer off on an unforeseen course. This uncertainty raises the risk involved in any financial trade-off.

For example, you may decide today that you can comfortably commit $20,000 to a new kitchen because those three or four years of retirement expenses will be covered by your company pension; then six months from now you may be a victim of corporate "downsizing," lose your job, and see your employer's pension contributions stopped. Your mistake, if it could be called one in retrospect, came in choosing to spend money on a current extra (the kitchen) instead of a future necessity (basic living expenses).

Yet this type of miscalculation is inevitable. You can't know with certainty what your future necessities will be, or what resources you will have available to meet them. Different people, at different times in their lives, may have widely varying views on what expenses are essential; one person's extras may be another person's necessities. All you can know for sure is that a dollar used to meet current expenses today will not be available to meet future expenses tomorrow.

Financial trade-offs are influenced by emotions and personality. While money may not be the root of all evil, it is a factor in many emotional

LIFE'S FINANCIAL TRADE-OFFS

You Make Choices to Use Your Resources Either for

CURRENT LIFE EXPENSES   **OR**   **FUTURE LIFE EXPENSES**

Spend Now, Forgo Later   vs.   Save Now, Spend Later

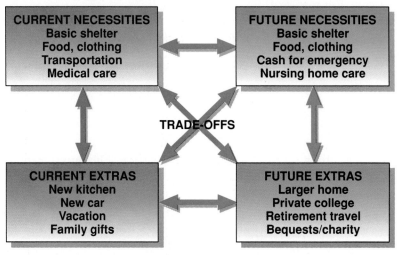

CURRENT NECESSITIES
Basic shelter
Food, clothing
Transportation
Medical care

FUTURE NECESSITIES
Basic shelter
Food, clothing
Cash for emergency
Nursing home care

TRADE-OFFS

CURRENT EXTRAS
New kitchen
New car
Vacation
Family gifts

FUTURE EXTRAS
Larger home
Private college
Retirement travel
Bequests/charity

and personal conflicts. Such conflicts can color your judgment where money is concerned. For example, emotional ups and downs may make you feel richer or poorer, causing you to spend more or less, even though your financial condition and future needs have not changed. Personality also comes into play. People who feel particularly compelled to spend money, or to hoard it, have trouble making trade-offs between current spending and future spending. Spenders may derive a sense of self-worth from owning the latest styles in clothing or high-status luxury goods; some may feel compelled to consume even if it leads to financial problems. Or perhaps they are encouraged to spend by an overwhelming self-confidence about their own future financial prospects. Tomorrow's needs will be taken care of, they believe, so why not consume all your income today? Hoarders may feel their own compunction, many of them saving from fear of losing personal financial security. Their sense of self-worth, too, may be tied to money, not the spending of it but the feeling of independence or accomplishment that comes from possessing it. For them, satisfaction is a bigger bank balance, not a bigger car.

Financial trade-offs are family matters. Couples with differing priorities or feelings toward money may find themselves at odds when trying to make financial trade-offs. One spouse may want to retire at age 60 and feel a pressing need to save, while the other plans to work until 70 and would rather spend money now on a new house. Many parents find themselves addressing painful decisions regarding college costs. They are torn between the desire to send their children to the best colleges possible and the reality of paying for it. If the kids attend high-cost schools, the parents will be broke; if they select lesser schools for financial reasons, the

To achieve financial equilibrium, you must be able to strike a balance between your financial resources and your spending goals.

parents will feel guilty. Decisions about money often turn out to be most difficult when loved ones are involved.

Financial trade-offs need the guidance of a financial plan. Let's say you were leaving on an extended auto trip. You wouldn't jump in the car and proceed from one intersection to the next, each time making a new decision whether to turn or not. That approach might lead you in the wrong direction, wasting time and gasoline. Instead, you would have a road map showing your destination and the best route to get there. The same holds true for your financial life. Making money trade-offs without a financial road map may leave you out of gas and far short of your destination.

The road map you need is a financial plan. It should list your goals—your financial destinations—and lay out a strategy to achieve those goals. For example, you may decide you want to retire at age 65 with a certain income in today's dollars. Your financial plan will show you what you need to save each year to accomplish that, and thereby guide you in making the financial trade-offs between current spending and future needs. Your plan won't predict the future or guarantee that you will reach your goal. But it will help you deal with the uncertainty involved in making trade-offs that reach into the future. Just knowing your destination can serve as a kind of guidepost for prioritizing financial decisions.

And like a good road map, your plan can help you get back on the highway when a detour such as a medical disability forces you to temporarily divert retirement savings to meet current needs. No step you can take will be more important in enabling you to manage life's financial trade-offs than preparing your own financial plan.

Financial Equilibrium

In physics, equilibrium is a state of complete balance between opposing or conflicting forces. Financial equilibrium represents the same type of harmony where money and lifestyle are concerned. To achieve financial equilibrium, you must be able to strike a balance between your financial resources and your spending goals. You must also successfully make the trade-offs shown in the accompanying chart between life's current expenses and those that will need to be borne in the future. If you can accomplish those things, getting your financial life into balance will do more than just improve your personal finances. It will help you bring

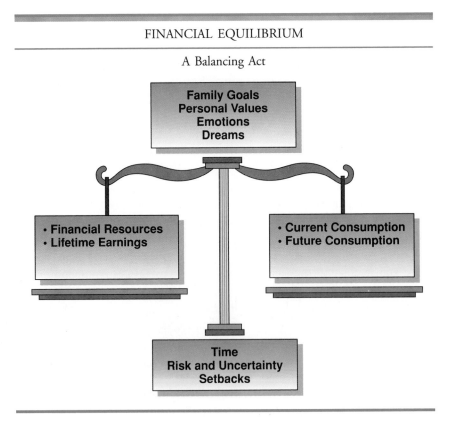

FINANCIAL EQUILIBRIUM

A Balancing Act

Family Goals
Personal Values
Emotions
Dreams

• **Financial Resources**
• **Lifetime Earnings**

• **Current Consumption**
• **Future Consumption**

Time
Risk and Uncertainty
Setbacks

balance to other aspects of your life as well: your emotional life, your family life, and your career or business life.

To have reached a state of financial equilibrium is to be reasonably prepared for whatever curves life will throw at you. That may require you to seek some risk protection. Some events in life are unpredictable and highly unlikely to occur, but when they do occur their effect can be devastating. For example, the likelihood that you will die before retirement age is statistically very low. But the financial impact on the family and dependents of a wage earner who dies prematurely can be overwhelming. That's why you need life insurance if you have dependents and don't own sufficient assets to support your loved ones in the event of your death. Likewise, the probability of being disabled before retirement is low and the financial consequences high. That speaks for disability income insurance that can provide living expenses not just for your dependents but also for you during your disability. By adequately protecting yourself against these risks, you can help ensure that you and your dependents enjoy the balance of financial equilibrium.

Other life events may also pose large financial consequences but are highly predictable. These costs you should expect to pay for out of your own invested assets. If you have young children, for example, and you expect that they will attend college, you can estimate today the amount of money needed to pay tuition bills and even predict the dates when

---

LIFE EVENTS: WILL YOU BE FINANCIALLY READY FOR THEM?

The Biggest *Personal* Events in Your Life
Are Also the Biggest *Financial* Events in Your Life

- Temporary Disability   - Marriage
- Birth of Children   - Paying for College
- Remarriage   - Second Home   - Aged Parents
- Home Purchase   - Divorce   - Retirement
- Job Loss   - Death of Spouse
- Starting a Business   - Children Get Married
- Relocation   - Serious Illness   - Premature Death

Time ⟶

INCOME AND EXPENSES MAY BE PERIODICALLY OUT OF SYNCH

Financial Planning Can Prepare You to Meet Expected and Unexpected Needs

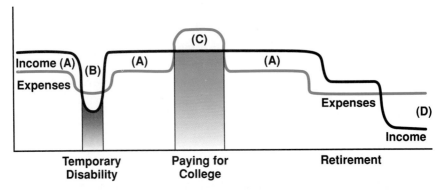

A = **Income exceeds expenses, resulting in saving and accumulation of assets.**

B = **Income falls below expenses because of disability, even after expenses have been reduced. The difference between income and expenses must be met by liquidating investment assets, borrowing, or from disability income insurance benefits.**

C = **Expenses exceed income because of college costs. The difference is met by liquidating assets or borrowing.**

D = **Expenses exceed income in later retirement years because of the declining purchasing power of a fixed pension. The difference is met by liquidating assets.**

those bills will arrive. Much the same can be said of retirement. While it may carry a huge expense, greater than that of any other life event, retirement won't sneak up on you. Both its approximate cost and date of onset can be estimated, affording you plenty of time to get ready.

Achieving Financial Equilibrium

Financial equilibrium is a lifelong concept. In the short term, however, income and outgo may be out of synch at different times in your life and for different reasons. Households typically go through a cycle of financial deficit and surplus, first borrowing to finance a home and cars, later paying down those debts and eventually accumulating investment assets out of surplus income. This life-cycle money mismatch is explained by the fact that younger workers typically have low incomes but high spending needs because of costs associated with household formation and child rearing. When the kids have left home and the mortgage gets paid off, households typically are able to increase their savings to help fund retirement needs. They may find, nonetheless,

Saving and investing will be key elements in any financial strategy you adopt, and they will provide the means to help you achieve financial equilibrium.

that too much spending on current life expenses over the years has seriously narrowed the range of financial options available to them as they grow older.

If you are out of balance, consuming too much today and short-changing your future goals, how do you move toward financial equilibrium? One step is to reduce current expenses. For many of us, a relatively small cutback in consumption translates into a big increase in savings. Let's say you now save 5 percent of your after-tax income and spend the rest. Shrink spending by five percentage points—from 95 percent to 90 percent of your income—and you are reducing consumption by only one-nineteenth, a tiny fraction. Odds are that cutting back by such a small amount will be relatively painless. If you can do it, the results will be impressive: You will increase your rate of savings by 100 percent and be moving at a much faster pace toward meeting your goals.

Another step is to improve your investment returns. If you stick to cash equivalents such as bank savings accounts, Treasury bills, or money market funds, you will be less likely to achieve your long-term financial goals. Those types of investments have average returns of less than 4 percent a year, compared to average returns for stocks of 10 percent. Invest in stocks, in other words, and your money can be expected over the long term to grow two-and-a-half times faster than if you invested in cash equivalents.

Combine these two steps—double your saving rate and boost your investment returns from the expected rate earned by cash equivalents to the expected rate earned by stocks—and you increase the amount of money you will accumulate over time by a factor of five. (Example: $1,000 saved every year at 4 percent would return $43,000 after 25 years, while $2,000 saved annually at 10 percent would amount to $216,000.)

Saving and investing will be key elements in any financial strategy you adopt, and they will provide the means to help you achieve financial equilibrium. We will return to those subjects later. For now, let's take a closer look at financial planning and see what's involved in formulating your own goals and developing strategies to achieve them.

THE IMPORTANCE OF FINANCIAL PLANNING

This chapter describes the activities involved in preparing a financial plan. To set the stage, it will introduce and formally describe the planning process. Also included is an overview of the financial planning profession and advice on choosing and working with a financial planner. The chapter will advise you how to manage the planning process, what you can expect to get for the fees you pay, and how you can be a better client to be sure you get full value for your money. The goal is to prepare you either to develop your own plan or to be able to work more effectively with a professional planner to prepare your plan.

Myth vs. Reality

Myth: Preparing a financial plan will show how deep in the hole I am as far as money is concerned and just make me depressed.

Reality: If you are down about your financial future, the "reality check" of a financial plan will show you the way to turn things around. That's going to be good news, not bad news.

Myth: Financial planning is too expensive.

Reality: Odds are that you will get your money's worth if you hire a professional financial planner. However, you may be able to prepare a financial plan yourself. One of the goals of this book is to help you understand the process so that you can plan on your own or have a more cost-effective relationship with a financial planner.

Myth: All financial planners are the same.

Reality: There is considerable variation in the professional background and training of financial planners. The scope of their practices differs as well. Some are generalists, while others specialize in areas such as estate planning, investments, tax planning, or insurance. Choose a planner whose background and practice fit your needs.

Myth: Financial planning is an unregulated profession.

Reality: Many financial planners are licensed and regulated as accountants, insurance agents, stockbrokers, or lawyers. They are subject to sanctions if they violate the standards of professional conduct governing those fields.

Myth: A financial plan will identify the best possible solution for your future needs.

Reality: There isn't necessarily a "best" answer in financial planning. In most situations, different approaches can produce satisfactory results. Financial planning is as much a method of avoiding bad strategies as one of trying to pinpoint the single best strategy.

What You Should Expect from the Planning Process

Financial planning, as we saw in Chapter 1, is the process of managing money trade-offs throughout your life. It enables you to achieve a balance between current spending needs and future spending needs. That balance is known as financial equilibrium, and it offers substantial benefits to those who can achieve it. Among those benefits are greater peace of mind, more control over your own future, and the good feeling that comes from knowing you are using your financial resources in a way that is consistent with your goals and values. What else should you expect from the financial planning process? Let's look at the steps involved.

Step 1: Committing to the Task

The benefits of financial planning don't come for free. You can expect to spend time and effort in the financial planning process. You'll need to spend money, too, if you seek the help of a professional financial planner.

STEPS INVOLVED IN THE FINANCIAL PLANNING PROCESS

Step 1:   Committing to the task
Step 2:   Developing your goals and setting priorities
Step 3:   Assessing your resources
Step 4:   Determining what is needed to reach your goals
Step 5:   Developing a strategy for each goal
Step 6:   Refining your goals
Step 7:   Incorporating your strategies into an overall plan
Step 8:   Listing and scheduling action steps to implement your plan
Step 9:   Putting your plan into effect
Step 10:   Monitoring and evaluating the results

It may take hours, for example, to organize your financial records and tabulate a personal cash flow statement to see how you are currently using your financial resources. Even with a financial planner or a financial planning computer program to help, you will need to spend additional hours refining your goals until you feel comfortable about being able to achieve them. Your time and money may be wasted if you don't commit upfront to seeing yourself through the development of a financial plan and then following it.

Along the way, you can expect to encounter personal or emotional roadblocks. Financial planning makes some people uncomfortable, so they are reluctant to do it. For example, you may feel uneasy about setting your life's goals down on paper and then dealing with them in dollars and cents. You may find that the financial planning process, because it looks at the future in terms of your life span, is an unwelcome reminder of your own mortality. Or you and your spouse or partner may disagree about important goals. Sometimes such differences can be stark and hard to reconcile. For example,

The benefits of financial planning don't come for free.

you may view retirement as a liberating event that will offer opportunity for travel and self-fulfillment. Your spouse, on the other hand, may see retirement as a period of enforced idleness that is best avoided for as long as possible. Your view implies a great need to reduce current spending and save to finance a retirement that begins at the earliest feasible date. Your spouse's view speaks for much less emphasis on retirement funding, with perhaps more money spent on current consumption. An experienced financial planner can help you and your spouse or partner work through personal or emotional roadblocks like this and keep the financial planning process on track.

Step 2: Developing Your Goals and Setting Priorities

Goals are your financial objectives or targets. Each goal will have its own time horizon—the period over which you will accumulate money for that goal and the period over which it will be spent. You can start developing your goals simply by making a list, then revising and refining it as you go. The first time, describe your goals in qualitative terms only, then begin to revise them. The revisions should make your goals increasingly specific and measurable. You should be able to revise each goal two or three times without stating it in terms of a particular dollar amount. Instead, express your goal as a percentage of your current income or current living expenses. Or state it in relation to the current cost of some category of goods or services, such as the average cost of a year at a private college. Thinking of your goal in terms of today's dollars makes it easy to compare it to your present level of income and investments.

Your goals will fall into one of two categories: accumulation goals and income replacement goals. With an accumulation goal you are targeting an amount of money that will be needed on a certain date. For example, if you want to buy a larger house, you may plan to accumulate the money over five years and spend it when you make the down payment on your new house. College funding is another type of accumulation goal. You plan to save the money over a certain period and spend it when tuition bills come due.

An income replacement goal, on the other hand, aims to generate a stream of income starting at some point and continuing into the future. As a result, the time horizon of an income replacement goal has two parts: an initial period when you build up the required amount of money and a subsequent period when the money is spent. Examples of income replacement goals include planning for retirement; planning for your survivors, where you are estimating the amount of money required to provide an income for your family in case of your death; and planning for possible disability.

Of these, planning for retirement represents the biggest challenge because your retirement time horizon extends decades into the future, creating many uncertainties. The length of that time horizon is unknown because you can't predict your retirement date with certainty and you don't know your life expectancy. The extended time horizon makes forecasts less reliable. As a result, your retirement goal and the strategies you develop to reach that goal are a "first shot" that will have to be revised many times as the future unfolds.

As financial planners, we have found that our time commitment with clients is roughly as follows:

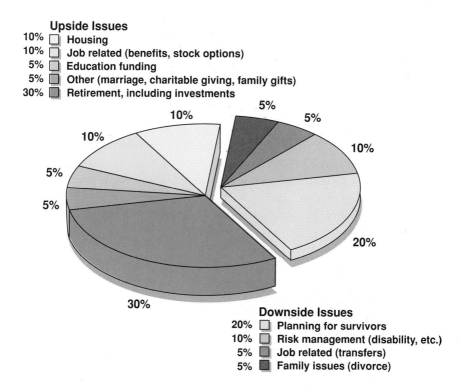

Upside Issues
- 10% ☐ Housing
- 10% ☐ Job related (benefits, stock options)
- 5% ☐ Education funding
- 5% ☐ Other (marriage, charitable giving, family gifts)
- 30% ☐ Retirement, including investments

Downside Issues
- 20% ☐ Planning for survivors
- 10% ☐ Risk management (disability, etc.)
- 5% ☐ Job related (transfers)
- 5% ☐ Family issues (divorce)

In developing your goals, you may identify with some of these issues.

As you review your list of goals, try to decide which ones are more important and which have a lower priority. At first thought, for example, you may list your children's education as your top priority if tuition bills will arrive relatively soon. But for parents of young children, maintaining an adequate amount of life insurance coverage is much more crucial than building a college fund. If you die prematurely, the insurance proceeds will be needed to pay for basic living expenses and support your children until they reach adulthood. (There should be enough insurance coverage to meet your college education goals, too. See Chapter 10.)

Also at first thought, retirement may seem to warrant a relatively low priority because you have more time and more leeway in planning for it. But be sure to weigh your priorities carefully. As we shall see in Chapter 4, the best time to save for retirement is when you're younger. For example, for every dollar you don't save for retirement by age 35, you'll need to put aside almost $4 at age 55, assuming a 7 percent rate of return on your investments. Later in the planning process you will see how to apportion your resources to each goal according to its relative priority. For now, if you can't decide which of two goals is more important to you, list them in the order in which the money will be needed.

> **Your retirement goal and the strategies you develop to reach that goal are a "first shot" that will have to be revised many times as the future unfolds.**

Here is a look at how the goal-setting process might begin.

List of Goals—Original

- Pay for the kids' college educations.
- Build a "rainy day" fund for emergencies.
- Make sure my spouse and children have enough money if I die.
- Retire with enough money to live comfortably.
- Buy a much bigger house.

List of Goals—Revision 1

- Pay for four years of college for our two children, ages 6 and 9, starting when each child is 18.
- Build a "rainy day" emergency fund large enough to cover six months of living expenses.

- In case of my death, replace 100 percent of my income until our younger child reaches age 21 and thereafter replace 50 percent of my income until my spouse reaches age 65.
- Accumulate enough money for the down payment on a house costing twice as much as our current house.
- Retire at age 65 with enough income to maintain our current lifestyle in a less-expensive community, and be prepared to retire earlier if necessary.

List of Goals—Revision 2

- In case of my death, replace 100 percent of my income in today's dollars until our younger child reaches age 21 and thereafter replace 50 percent of my income in today's dollars until my spouse reaches age 65.
- Build a "rainy day" emergency fund to cover six months of living expenses. Accumulate one-third of the required amount over each of the next three years.
- Accumulate enough money in five years for the down payment on a house costing twice as much as our current house.
- Pay for four years of tuition and expenses for our two children at an average-priced private college. Plan to accumulate 70 percent of the cost by the time the older child starts college and pay for the rest from current cash flow.
- Retire at age 65 with 80 percent of our current income in today's dollars for 25 years. Be prepared to retire at age 60 with 70 percent of our income in today's dollars for 30 years.

Focus on...

TODAY'S DOLLARS VS. FUTURE DOLLARS

One way to keep things simpler is to plan in terms of today's dollars, or what something is worth this year, not what it might cost after 10 or 20 years of inflation. The cost in today's dollars is easy to relate to your present level of income and savings. Future living expenses will climb higher over the years in all likelihood, but so will your income and your capacity to save. By stripping inflation out of the planning equation and concentrating on purchasing power, you will have a more understandable gauge of the real resources needed to meet your goals.

Step 3: Assessing Your Resources

In developing your goals, you are asking and answering the question, "What do I want?" The next step is to estimate the amount of financial resources that will be available to accomplish those goals. Here the question is, "What do I have?" or more precisely, "What will I have by the time I need to spend it to accomplish my goal(s)?" Here is the list of your resources:

1. What you have now, or your assets today.
2. What you will get, or the money you will save from future income.
3. Future earnings on your investment assets.
4. Expected future benefits from such sources as an employer pension or Social Security.

The best way to start assessing your resources is to prepare a personal financial summary. It should have two parts, a balance sheet and a cash flow statement. The balance sheet is a snapshot of your financial condition as of a single date, such as the last day of the year. It lists (1) the value of your assets, such as investments, your home, and your car; (2) the amount of your liabilities such as mortgage loans and credit card balances; and (3) your net worth, which is the difference between your assets and your liabilities. The cash flow statement, on the other hand, measures your cash inflows (income) and your cash outflows (expenses) over a period of time, usually a year. The difference between your income and your expenses represents savings.

Your personal financial summary will show the resources you have now. You will also use it as the basis for projecting both the money you will save from future income and the future earnings on your investment assets. To complete the assessment of your resources, ask the Social Security Administration for statements projecting your retirement benefits. (For more details, see Chapter 3.)

Step 4: Determining What Is Needed to Reach Your Goals

With a list of your goals and an accurate picture of your resources, you are ready for what some financial planners would call a sufficiency analysis, or gap analysis. We prefer to think of it as a reality check. The idea is to determine whether your resources will be sufficient to finance your goals and, if the answer is no, to measure the shortfall between them. Any shortfall will need to be made up either by increasing future savings or scaling down your goals. To start, you must make some assumptions. The assumptions involve important variables that will have a big impact on the outcome of your plans. They include:

- The inflation rate.
- The rate of return on your investments.
- Your life expectancy.
- Your tax bracket.

Why are they important? Let's take the inflation rate as an example. Over long time periods, seemingly small differences in inflation can add up to big differences in the amount of money you will need to maintain a particular standard of living. Let's say your current living costs are $40,000 a year and you want to maintain that standard of living for the next 30 years. That

With a list of your goals and an accurate picture of your resources, you are ready for a reality check.

means the $40,000 you spend today will have to increase each year by the rate of inflation. If you assume inflation will be 3 percent a year, you will need income of $97,000 in 30 years to equal today's $40,000. If you assume 4 percent inflation, you will need $130,000. The difference between 4 percent and 3 percent seems small. After all, it's only a single percentage point. But in fact 4 percent is a third greater than 3 percent. Thus, you need one-third more money to stay even with 4 percent inflation than you need to keep up with 3 percent inflation.

Your assumptions about the other variables can make big differences as well. A 40-year-old who expects to retire at 65 would need to save 28 percent more each month based on an assumed life expectancy of 90 years than would have to be set aside if the assumption were 80 years. That example also assumes a 7 percent investment return. What happens if we hold the life expectancy constant at 90 and increase the assumed investment return from 7 to 9 percent? Result: our 40-year-old could reduce monthly retirement savings by 59 percent.

The more conservative your assumptions, the more money you must save to close the gap between your goals and your resources. Conversely,

MAKING ASSUMPTIONS ABOUT THE FUTURE

More Conservative Assumptions

> **Higher inflation rate**
> **Lower investment return**
> **Longer life expectancy**
> **Higher tax bracket**

Less Conservative Assumptions

> **Lower inflation rate**
> **Higher investment return**
> **Shorter life expectancy**
> **Lower tax bracket**

Price Waterhouse Suggestions

Inflation rate	**4%**
Investment return	**7–9% pretax**
Life expectancy	**90 years**
Tax bracket	**Your current one**

the less conservative your assumptions, the easier it is to eliminate that gap because less is needed in the way of savings. But the point here is not simply to adjust your assumptions to close the gap on paper. You want to use reasonable assumptions that will make it highly likely you will achieve your goals. For example, it's not reasonable to assume a 15 percent annual rate of return on your investments. Sure, some types of investments occasionally generate returns of that magnitude but not over long periods and not without increased risk.

How do you determine what is needed to reach a particular goal? Let's take a fairly simple example from the list of goals developed in Step 2. Say you want to accumulate enough money in five years for the down payment on a house costing twice as much as your current house. To make the down payment and qualify for the larger mortgage on your new house, you expect to need $50,000 in addition to the net proceeds from the sale of your current house. Let's say you already have accumulated $23,000 of that amount, so we can revise your goal one more time and then analyze it.

Goal: Accumulate $50,000 in five years for the down payment on a house costing twice as much as our current house.

Assumption: Current resources ($23,000) will be invested for five years with an after-tax investment return of 5 percent (equals a pretax return of about 7 percent).

Result: You will have accumulated $29,000 at the end of five years.

Shortfall: $50,000 less $29,000, or $21,000.

Step 5: Developing a Strategy for Each Goal

How do you develop a strategy to meet each of your goals? The answer is to find a way to finance the shortfall through additional savings over the time horizon involved. Let's continue with the example above.

Assumption: Additional annual savings will be invested at an after-tax investment return of 5 percent.

Question: How much do you need to save each year for the next five years?

Strategy: Save $3,600 each year. Invested at a 5 percent after-tax return, this will provide an additional $21,000 at the end of five years, enabling you to meet the goal of $50,000.

Why did we assume a 5 percent after-tax investment return? A higher return would make the goal easier to reach. For example, with a 9 percent after-tax return you could accumulate the $50,000 total at the end of five years by saving just $2,300 annually. (Remember, you already have $23,000.) But seeking a 9 percent after-tax investment return means you would be taking on greater risk. Your returns over the five years would be more likely to vary, and the certainty of being able to reach your goal would be less than it would be if you sought a lower rate of return. By investing at a 4 percent after-tax rate of return, for example, you could be highly certain of having the full $50,000 on hand in five years. For the greater certainty and peace of mind offered by a 4 percent return, you would need to save $4,000 a year instead of $3,600 to reach your goal in five years. Thus, seeking a 5 percent after-tax return amounts to choosing a middle ground. You are taking on some risk that the outcome may not be exactly as you expect in exchange for an opportunity to reach your goal by using less in the way of current resources. With a different goal— say paying a college tuition bill due in two years—you may not want to take on the level of risk represented by a 5 percent after-tax return because the money absolutely must be there. We will look more closely at investment return and risk in Chapter 5.

Step 6: Refining Your Goals

You have now set a strategy to reach your goal of accumulating a down payment for a bigger house in five years. Let's assume you have gone through a similar process for each of the goals listed in Step 2. (See Chapters 7 through 10 for guidance on developing goals and strategies to achieve them.) Here are your goals and strategies:

Goal 1: In the event of my death, replace 100 percent of my income in today's dollars until our younger child reaches age 21 and thereafter replace 50 percent of my income in today's dollars until my spouse reaches age 65.

Strategy: Pay $2,800 a year for a 15-year level term life insurance policy to supplement the group life insurance available through my employer. The policy will be dropped in 15 years at our younger child's 21st birthday.

Goal 2: Build a "rainy day" emergency fund to cover six months of living expenses. Accumulate one-third of the required amount over each of the next three years.

Strategy: Save $5,000 a year and invest the money in a bank certificate of deposit.

Goal 3: Accumulate $50,000 in five years for the down payment on a house.

Strategy: Save $3,600 each year and initially invest the money in stock mutual funds.

Goal 4: Pay for four years of tuition and expenses for our two children at an average-priced private college.

Strategy: Save $4,200 a year (in addition to funds already accumulated toward this goal) and invest the money in a balanced portfolio of mutual funds.

Goal 5: Retire at age 65 with 80 percent of current income in today's dollars and be prepared to retire at age 60 with 70 percent of income in today's dollars.

Strategy: Save $2,500 a year initially (in addition to funds already accumulated toward this goal) and increase annual retirement savings as other goals are achieved. Invest the money in a balanced portfolio of mutual funds.

Let's also assume the cash flow statement you completed in Step 3 shows that you have about $9,600 in net cash flow available each year to apply toward these goals. Here is how things add up:

Putting It All Together—Strategies for Year 1

Strategy for Goal 1	$2,800
Strategy for Goal 2	5,000
Strategy for Goal 3	3,600
Strategy for Goal 4	4,200
Strategy for Goal 5	2,500
Annual cash flow required	$18,100
Annual cash flow available	− 9,600
Annual cash flow shortfall	$ 8,500

Now it's time to begin making trade-offs and refining your goals to bring them into line with your resources. Start each round of refinements by asking these questions:

- Can you reduce current consumption to increase savings?
- Are there any goals you are willing to scale back?
- Are there any goals for which you can postpone some or all the required funding, perhaps until after other goals have been accomplished and more cash flow is available?
- Are there any goals you are willing to eliminate?

First, let's assume you can increase savings by squeezing $2,000 from vacation and recreation spending. Next, a look at your list of goals shows some opportunities for refinements. Goal 1 should not be changed because your survivors need to be assured of replacement income in the event of your death. However, Goal 2 can be funded later. A "rainy day" account to cover emergency expenses is an important financial goal. But for the next five years, the assets you are accumulating for a down payment on a larger house (Goal 3) can serve to cover you. In the event of an emergency, you can scrap plans for the new house and use the down payment fund to cover emergency expenses. Taking these changes into account, here is how things add up after your first revision:

Putting It All Together—Revision 1
Strategies for Year 1

Strategy for Goal 1	$2,800
Strategy for Goal 2	—
Strategy for Goal 3	3,600
Strategy for Goal 4	4,200
Strategy for Goal 5	2,500
Annual cash flow required	$13,100
Annual cash flow available	−11,600
Annual cash flow shortfall	$ 1,500

The remaining shortfall of $1,500 can be made up by reducing funding for education (Goal 4) by $1,200 and reducing the initial amount invested for retirement (Goal 5) by $300.

Putting It All Together—Revision 2 Strategies for Year 1

Strategy for Goal 1	$2,800
Strategy for Goal 2	—
Strategy for Goal 3	3,600
Strategy for Goal 4	3,000
Strategy for Goal 5	2,200
Annual cash flow required	$11,600
Annual cash flow available	−11,600
Annual cash flow shortfall	$ 0

Step 7: Incorporating Your Strategies into an Overall Plan

The process of refining goals and making trade-offs in Step 6 prompted you to delay investments starting a rainy day fund and to trim allocations toward education funding and retirement. If you do not want to scale back those goals, however, you will have to plan to allocate sufficient extra funds toward meeting them in future years. As you plan your cash flow and savings allocations year by year, you can expect to eliminate certain allocations as goals are met, freeing up increased savings for those goals that remain. For example, in year 6 of your planning horizon, savings for a down payment are no longer needed. In addition, the cost in today's dollars of the fixed premium for your insurance policy will have dropped to $2,300 from $2,800. These two changes will free $4,100 in cash flow that can be reallocated. Also, your cash flow will be greater by $1,900 in today's dollars because of an increase in your real (after-inflation) earnings. Here is a look at year 6:

Strategies for Year 6 (Amounts in today's dollars)

Strategy for Goal 1	$2,300
Strategy for Goal 2	3,000
Strategy for Goal 3	—
Strategy for Goal 4	5,700
Strategy for Goal 5	2,500
Annual cash flow required	$13,500
Annual cash flow available	−13,500
Annual cash flow shortfall	$ 0

In year 16 of your planning horizon, your younger child will have reached age 21 and be finishing the final year of college that you have planned to finance. In addition, your need for a separate rainy day fund will have passed because you will have sufficient retirement assets available to draw on in case of an emergency financial need. By year 17, your cash flow will have increased to $18,600 in today's dollars because of continuing increases in your real earnings and reductions in your spending on current consumption. And you will be able to allocate the entire amount toward Goal 5, your retirement. Here is a look at year 17:

Strategies for Year 17 (Amounts in today's dollars)

Strategy for Goal 1	—
Strategy for Goal 2	—
Strategy for Goal 3	—
Strategy for Goal 4	—
Strategy for Goal 5	$18,600
Annual cash flow required	$18,600
Annual cash flow available	−18,600
Annual cash flow shortfall	$ 0

Step 8: Listing and Scheduling Action Steps to Implement Your Plan

Once you have your strategies mapped out for each year of your planning horizon, you can prepare a schedule for implementing your plan. The schedule should list each required step and a deadline for accomplishing it. Some steps, such as preparing and executing a will, can be done within days or weeks. Others, such as realigning your investment portfolio, are best accomplished gradually over several months to reduce your exposure to fluctuations in stock or bond prices.

Action Step	Deadline
1. Prepare and execute a will	Date
2. Prepare and execute a durable power of attorney for health care	Date
3. Evaluate insurance policies	Date
4. Develop asset allocation guidelines for each goal	Date
5. Prepare an investment plan	Date
6. Purchase a life insurance policy	Date
7. Implement the investment plan	Date to Date
Etc.	

Step 9: Putting Your Plan into Effect

One of the advantages of hiring a professional financial planner is that he or she will assist you by coordinating the tasks needed to implement your plan. Your planner can also help in selecting the other professionals who may be needed to carry out your plan. For example, you will need a lawyer to handle such matters as drawing up your will and preparing a living will and durable power of attorney for health care. You may require the assistance of an insurance professional to recommend specific insurance products to meet your income replacement and estate liquidity needs. If your financial planner is not an investment adviser, you may also need help in selecting and managing investments from a stockbroker, money manager, or bank.

Step 10: Monitoring and Evaluating the Results

After your plan has been implemented, the results need to be monitored. At least once each year, perhaps in January or February after you receive year-end statements from your investment accounts, you should expect to sit down either on your own or with your financial planner and do the following:

- Update your personal financial summary, including balance sheet and statement of cash flows.
- Evaluate your investment performance for the year.
- Rebalance your investment portfolios if necessary to maintain the mix of investments you want.
- Ask "How am I doing?" to determine if you are staying on track toward meeting your goals.
- Ask "What has changed?" to see if any new developments in your life should prompt you to revise your goals.

Choosing a Financial Planner

In some ways, choosing a financial planner is no different from choosing any other professional who provides you with advice and services. The best means of locating candidates is through professional referrals from people such as your lawyer, accountant, banker, or business associates.

You want a planner who is experienced, established in the profession, and highly knowledgeable about the issues and technicalities of personal finance. You also want someone with whom you can feel comfortable, someone who has a good "bedside manner," in the parlance of the medical profession.

In other ways, however, choosing a financial planner poses more of a challenge than picking a doctor, lawyer, or accountant. Unlike those other fields, financial planning is a still-emerging profession. Financial planning practitioners are not uniformly trained, licensed, or regulated as are other types of professionals. In most states, for example, you can set up shop as a financial planner without obtaining a license or meeting any particular professional requirements.

That's not to say that financial planners as a group are not well trained, or that they operate without any regulation. Many financial planners are licensed accountants, insurance agents, stockbrokers, or lawyers and must follow the regulations that apply to those professions. The absence of uniform professional training and regulations, however, means you must take particular care in evaluating the credentials of a planner that you hire.

There is also a lack of uniformity in the way planners are compensated. Some charge fees for their services and others earn their money solely through commissions on the sales of financial products such as life insurance or investments. Still others charge a combination of fees and commissions. Following are the three principal categories of planners:

1. **Fee-Only Planners.** These are compensated solely by the client. Neither the planner nor any related party receives compensation that is contingent on the purchase or sale of any financial product.

2. **Commission-Only Planners.** These are compensated from commissions on the sale of financial products such as insurance or investments to the client.

3. **Fee-Based Planners.** These are compensated from fees paid by the client or commissions on the sale of products. Typically, commissions are offset against the fees charged for planning. If the commissions are not large enough to cover the planner's services, the client pays for the difference in the form of a fee.

The important thing is the quality of the service the planner provides, not the form of compensation. But we must make our own bias clear. Price Waterhouse offers financial planning services on a fee-only basis and we believe clients are best served by the 100 percent objectivity that comes from fee-only compensation. Fee-only planners have no financial incentive to recommend a certain type of product or to favor one financial provider's product over another's.

The clear trend in the financial services field has been away from commission-based compensation and toward compensation through fees. A major reason is that consumers increasingly are demanding objective advice and information. They want to be fully informed and to shop and compare before committing their money. They also understand the conflict of interest inherent when a planner is being paid by a third party to sell them a product.

The accompanying illustration, based on the ideas of Harold W. Gourgues, Jr., and Jeffrey R. Lauterbach from their book *Revolution in Financial Services* (Washington, DC: Bureau of National Affairs, 1987) shows how the traditional approach to providing financial product "manufacturing," marketing, and advice through one organization is evolving to the point where each of these functions is being performed by different organizations. We believe fee-only financial planners hold an important place in this evolving landscape because of the independent, objective advice they provide.

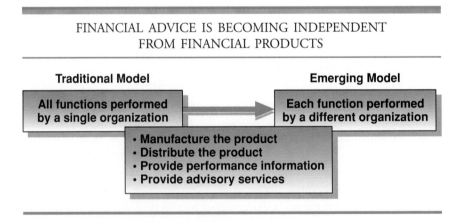

FINANCIAL ADVICE IS BECOMING INDEPENDENT
FROM FINANCIAL PRODUCTS

Traditional Model   **Emerging Model**

All functions performed   Each function performed
by a single organization   by a different organization

• Manufacture the product
• Distribute the product
• Provide performance information
• Provide advisory services

Now that our bias has been stated, let us also recognize these facts: (1) there are competent commission-based financial planners who serve their clients well; and (2) commission-based planning may be the only way some clients can afford a financial planner.

Before choosing a planner, try to define the scope of your needs. Here are your primary options:

- A comprehensive financial plan addressing all your financial goals.
- A single-purpose plan, such as a retirement plan or estate plan.
- Coaching/review of a financial plan you develop on your own.
- Investment advice or money management services.

Next, prepare a list of questions to ask the planners you interview. Here are some suggestions:

Question   How much experience do you have as a planner, and what is your professional training, including credentials? Comment: The education and professional backgrounds of financial planners vary widely. Some are highly trained in areas such as investment management, estate planning, accounting, insurance, or estate planning and have earned professional credentials in their fields. Others are essentially sales representatives who are paid to sell you investments or insurance. Experience and credentials are evidence that you are dealing with a professional adviser, not a salesperson.

Question   What is the scope of the services you provide, and do you specialize in a particular area of financial planning? Comment: Financial planning has become increasingly specialized. Some planners handle only retirement planning while others may specialize in estate planning or investments. You want to make sure that the planner offers the type of services you need. For a comprehensive plan, you should look for a generalist instead of a planner who focuses on a particular specialty. Ideally, the generalist planner will have specialist colleagues within his or her firm available to help as needed.

Question   Describe your average client in terms of age, income, net worth, the services you provide, and the fee you charge. Comment: You want a planner who is accustomed to dealing with clients like you, those in about the same circumstances in terms of age, income, net worth, and range of goals.

Question   Will you show me a copy of a comprehensive plan you recently prepared, with the client's name and any other identifying information blanked out? Comment: A recently prepared comprehensive plan

Focus on...

GUIDE TO FINANCIAL PLANNER CREDENTIALS

Designation:	CFP—certified financial planner.
Organization:	Certified Financial Planner Board of Standards.
Requirements:	Must pass a two-day comprehensive financial planning examination and meet educational/professional experience requirements. Requires 30 hours of continuing education every two years.
For information:	Certified Financial Planner Board of Standards, 1660 Lincoln St., Suite 3050, Denver, CO 80264 (303-830-7543). Institute of Certified Financial Planners, 7600 E. Eastman Ave., Suite 301, Denver, CO 80231 (800-282-7526).

Designation:	CFA—chartered financial analyst.
Organization:	Association for Investment Management and Research.
Requirements:	Must pass three six-hour exams related to financial analysis and investments. Requires three years of experience as a financial analyst.
For information:	Association for Investment Management and Research, 5 Boar's Head Lane., P.O. Box 3668, Charlottesville, VA 22903 (804-980-3668).

Designation:	ChFC—chartered financial consultant.
Organization:	The American College in Bryn Mawr, Pennsylvania.
Requirements:	Pass 10 two-hour financial planning exams. Requires three years of professional experience and 60 hours of continuing education every two years.
For information:	The American College, 270 South Bryn Mawr Ave., Bryn Mawr, PA 19010 (215-526-1000). American Society of CLUs and ChFCs (800-392-6900).

can serve as a useful gauge of the planner's thoroughness, attention to detail, and professional standards.

Question How are you compensated, and how will I pay you? Comment: Ask for full disclosure about fees and means of compensation. If your planner will receive ongoing compensation through "trailing" com-

Focus on...

concluded

Designation: PFS—personal financial specialist.
Organization: American Institute of Certified Public Accountants.
Requirements: Must be a certified public accountant and pass compre-
                    hensive six-hour financial planning examination. Requires
                    minimum of three years of professional experience pro-
                    viding financial planning services. Continuing education
                    and reaccreditation required every three years.
For information: American Institute of Certified Public Accountants, Per-
                    sonal Financial Planning Division, Harborside Financial
                    Center, 201 Plaza III, Jersey City, NJ 07311 (800-862-
                    4272).

Designation: RIA—registered investment adviser.
Organization: U.S. Securities and Exchange Commission.
Requirements: Complete registration form and pay $150 fee.
For information: SEC (202-942-8088).

missions or investment management fees, ask what ongoing services you
will receive.

Question   How much will you charge for the particular services I
want? If you will be referring me to other professionals for additional services, can you estimate how much they will charge? Comment: Fees will
vary, so it pays to ask. Many planners will have minimum fees.

Question   Are you a registered investment adviser? If so, please show me
parts I and II of your Form ADV filed with the Securities and Exchange
Commission. Comment: SEC registration is generally required for anyone
who is paid to offer investment advice or manage money. Registrants must
provide a copy of Part II of Form ADV to new clients. It contains important information about the adviser's services, fees, client reports, and business affiliations. You can request to see Part I, which lists any disciplinary
actions taken against the registrant by state or federal agencies.

Question   What will you expect from me as your client if I hire you to prepare a financial plan for me? Comment: A successful financial plan will require a considerable amount of effort on *your* part, as well as on the part of your planner. You want a planner who expects you to contribute to the process and will be able to ask questions, get you to examine your own goals and priorities, and help you to articulate your own needs and desires.

Question   What will you do to help me implement my financial plan? Comment: Expect your planner to spell out for you how the plan will be implemented.

GETTING STARTED

This chapter focuses on the information needed to prepare a financial plan. It will describe the data-gathering process and show what inputs are needed to develop your plan. It will also explain how to prepare a personal financial summary, including a cash flow statement and balance sheet. Gathering and organizing this data has the beneficial side effect of requiring you to get your house in order where your records are concerned.

Myth vs. Reality

Myth: Financial plans are nothing more than a bunch of charts, spreadsheets, and columns of figures on paper.

Reality: Numbers are important, but only one part of the financial planning process. Done right, a financial plan will embody your own values and personal aspirations. It will help you live your life the way you want to live it.

Myth: Financial planning can't be done piecemeal. Only a comprehensive plan, covering all the financial issues you face—retirement, estate planning, college funding, and so forth—will be effective in meeting your needs.

Reality: A plan that focuses on a single goal such as retirement is far better than no plan at all. In fact, digging into one area will undoubtedly lead you to others.

Myth: My financial plan is complete and the planner is handling all the details.

Reality: It's your financial plan, not the planner's. You're the one most concerned about your finances and your family's future well being. And you're the one who will live with the consequences if your plan is not implemented properly. That means you need to take "ownership" of your plan to reach your goals.

Assessing Resources: Where Am I Financially?

Assessing your resources is a crucial step in developing a financial plan. You need to know your financial position before you can determine what steps will be required to reach your goals. Let's take retirement, for example. It may turn out that based on your financial resources—employer pension, your investments, your own continued savings, and Social Security—you will have no trouble reaching your retirement goals. You are on target.

But that may not be the case for your other goals. For example, the resources available for your survivors in the event of your death—investments, life insurance coverage and perhaps Social Security—might leave them far short of their income replacement needs. To provide for your survivors, you will have to devote more of your resources to buying life insurance, perhaps diverting some money from the amount you are currently saving. These kinds of insights about the trade-offs you face are among the greatest benefits you will derive from the financial planning process, but to gain them you must first take stock of your current financial position.

> **Assessing your resources is a crucial step in developing a financial plan.**

In Chapter 2, we phrased the question as, "What do I have?" or, more particularly, "What will I have by the time I need to spend it to accomplish my goals?" To assess what you have, you need to look at these three areas:

- **Your Own Financial Resources.** These include assets such as your home, cars, and personal property as well as the money you have in the bank and the value of your investments. They also include protection you have purchased in the form of life insurance or disability insurance policies. And perhaps more importantly, your financial resources include your earning power over the years ahead.

- **Employer-Paid Benefits.** These may include a monthly pension benefit at retirement, benefits paid to your survivors in the event of your death, and disability benefits that will typically replace a portion of your monthly salary if you are disabled and cannot work. You may also be entitled to a pension or other benefits earned while working for a previous employer.

- **Social Security Benefits.** You can expect a retirement benefit from Social Security that will replace a portion of your preretirement earnings (see Chapter 8). Social Security also provides disability benefits if you are totally disabled and survivor benefits if you die with children at home up to high school age (see Chapter 10).

Let's take a look at these three in reverse order.

Estimating Your Social Security Benefits

You can obtain an estimate of your Social Security retirement, disability, and survivor benefits by filling out, signing, and returning Form SSA-7004 (Request for Earnings and Benefit Estimate Statement) to the Social Security Administration. Forms can be obtained by calling 1-800-772-1213.

The earnings portion of the statement will show a year-by-year record, going back to the start of your career, listing your annual earnings up to the maximum taxable amount for Social Security ($61,200 in 1995). The statement may not include some or all of your earnings from the most recent year if the Social Security Administration has yet not had time to add them.

The benefit portion of the statement will give you an estimate of your future retirement, disability, and survivor benefits. Actual benefit amounts will depend on your age, your earnings history, and your expected future earnings. For more information on Social Security benefits see Chapters 8 (retirement), 9 (disability), and 10 (planning for your survivors).

The Social Security Administration has begun a multiyear program to send Earnings and Benefit Estimate Statements to everyone covered by Social Security. Anyone age 60 and older, for example, was expected to automatically receive a statement in 1995. You should submit a new Form SSA-7004 every three years to check the accuracy of Social Security records regarding your employment. Check the figures carefully to see that you have been credited properly for each year you have worked. If an error has been made, it will be much easier to correct if you file Form SSA-7004 periodically during your working years rather than waiting until you are ready to retire before checking your records.

Estimating Your Employer-Paid Benefits

Your employer may distribute a comprehensive benefits statement each year to all employees. If so, it should contain most of the information you need. If not, you may have to seek additional information from your employer's human resources or benefits department. Here is what you want to determine:

- **The Death Benefit Paid to Your Survivors in the Event of Your Death.** Typically, an employer's group life insurance plan provides a death benefit equal to some multiple of your annual earnings, say two or two-and-a-half times your salary. You should maintain a copy of the insurance certificate or some other evidence of the coverage and amount of benefit to which you are entitled. If, as is likely, your employer's death benefit is provided as part of a group insurance policy, you can probably obtain a certificate of insurance or other information containing the name of the insurer and the group policy number.

- **Disability Income Benefits.** Many employer plans provide different *short*-term and *long*-term disability benefits. A typical plan might offer a short-term benefit equal to 50 percent of your salary for the first three months of your disability. After that, if your disability continues, your employer's long-term plan—when added to any Social Security disability benefits you receive—might replace 50 or 60 percent of your salary. You will need to know the amounts of the short- and long-term benefits, how soon each begins after you are disabled, and how long each lasts.

- **Pension Benefit.** If your employer offers a traditional defined-benefit pension, your benefit probably will be figured as a percentage of your average salary during your final work years multiplied times your number of years of service. With other types of retirement plans, your employer may commit to contributing an amount equal to a certain percentage of your salary to the plan each year on your behalf or may offer to match a portion of the contributions you make. Some plans are integrated with Social Security. Integrated plans typically replace a targeted percentage of your salary using a combination of Social Security and pension benefits. Your Social Security is considered first, then enough pension benefit is added to bring the total to the targeted replacement percentage.

  Your employer should be able to provide you with an estimate of your future pension (and any pension benefit for your surviving spouse) in the form of an individual benefit statement, based on assumptions about your retirement age and future salary increases. If an estimate is not available, the statement should at least list the total of your accrued pension benefits and identify how much of that amount is vested and how much is not.

Focus on...

PENSION PLAN INFORMATION

You can obtain the following information about your pension plan from the person designated by your employer as plan administrator:

Summary Plan Description. Explains plan operations, eligibility requirements, vesting schedule, retirement rules, benefit calculations, and claim-filing procedures. You must receive a copy within 90 days of enrollment and be given copies of updated versions in the future.

Summary Annual Report. Discusses the plan's financial condition and re-

sults for the past year. Must be provided to you annually.

Survivor Coverage Explanation. Describes any pension benefits available to surviving spouses of plan participants.

Individual Benefit Statement. Lists years of service and dollar amount of benefits you have earned, and may estimate your retirement benefit based on assumption about retirement age and salary increases. Can be requested in writing once a year.

When you have obtained details about your employer-paid benefits, use the information to begin filling out these three forms:

- Life insurance coverage record.
- Disability income coverage record.
- Pension/savings plan record.

The remaining information required to complete these forms will come from your own individual insurance policies and other personal records.

Estimating Your Resources with a Personal Financial Summary

The best way to measure your own financial resources is to prepare a personal financial summary. It should have two parts, a balance sheet and a cash flow statement. The balance sheet is a snapshot of your financial condition as of a single date, such as the last day of the year. It lists (1) the

PENSION CHECKLIST

- My pension plan is a defined benefit _____ defined contribution _____ plan.
- The name of my plan administrator is _____ . I can contact him/her at address _____ . Phone number _____ .
- I have _____ have not _____ received my Summary Plan Description, Summary of the Annual Report, and Survivor Coverage Data.
- I am now vested _____ or will be in _____ years.
- I have earned _____ years of service toward my pension.
- Under my plan, I can take early retirement, with reduced benefits, at age _____ .
- I can retire with full benefits at age _____ .
- I will receive my benefits in a lump sum _____ or in monthly installments for life _____ .
- My Social Security benefit will _____ will not _____ be deducted from my pension benefit.
- My spouse and I have _____ have not _____ declined in writing the joint and survivor option. (This step is required within 90 days before retirement.)
- My benefits are _____ are not _____ insured by the Pension Benefit Guaranty Corp.

Source: Pension Benefit Guaranty Corp.

LIFE INSURANCE COVERAGE RECORD

	Employer Plan Death Benefit	Policy 1	Policy 2
Insurance company			
Policy number			
Company/address/ phone			
Insurance agent Firm/address/phone	XXXXX		
Type of policy			
Death benefit			
Beneficiaries			
Annual premium cost to you			

DISABILITY INCOME COVERAGE RECORD

| | Employer Benefits | | |
	Short-Term	Long-Term	Individual Policy
Monthly benefit			
Benefit begins			
Benefit ends			
Insurance company			
Policy number			
Annual premium			
Company/address/ phone			
Insurance agent Firm/address/phone	XXXXX	XXXXX	

value of your assets, such as your home and the investments you own; (2) the amount of your liabilities such as mortgage loans and credit card balances; and (3) your net worth, which is the difference between your assets and your liabilities. The cash flow statement measures your cash inflows (income) and your cash outflows (expenses) over a period of time, usually a year. A positive difference between your income and your expenses represents savings. A negative differ-

> **Your personal financial summary will forcefully demonstrate why you can't reach your financial goals—no matter how high your income—unless you take in more than you spend.**

ence means your household operates like the federal government—you have borrowed money to make ends meet.

Your personal financial summary will show the resources you have now. You will also use it as the basis for projecting both the money you will save from future income and the future earnings on your investment

PENSION/SAVINGS PLAN RECORD

1. Employer
   Name:_____
   Address: _____
   Phone: _____
2. Plan administrator
   Name:_____
   Address: _____
   Phone: _____
3. Employment and compensation data
   Starting date:_____
   Date you became plan participant:_____
   Termination date: _____
   Compensation for each year you were a participant:

   Year 1 _____   Year 2 _____   Year 3 _____
   Year 4 _____   Year 5 _____   Year 6 _____
   Year 7 _____   Year 8 _____   Year 9 _____ etc.
4. Benefit information
   Total accrued benefits: _____
   Vested portion of accrued benefits: _____
   Nonvested portion of accrued benefits:_____
   Expected monthly pension benefit: _____
   Expected monthly survivor benefit:_____

Note: Keep this record with the copies of pension plan documents and benefit statements related to previous employer pension or benefit plans in which you have vested rights.

assets. And it will forcefully demonstrate why you can't reach your financial goals—no matter how high your income—unless you take in more than you spend.

Preparing a personal financial summary serves other purposes as well. It shows you how you have used your resources, for better or worse. You may be "house poor," for example. In that case, monthly mortgage payments will take a disproportionate share of your cash flow, and the value of your residence (as well as the mortgage debt related to it) will loom large on your personal balance sheet. Or you may have allocated your investments too conservatively, placing the bulk of your investable assets in bank savings accounts or CDs. This overcautious approach will mean

PERSONAL FINANCIAL SUMMARY—PART 1, CASH FLOW STATEMENT

Income (Annual)

Income Source 1	_____	$ _____
Income Source 2	_____	_____
Income Source 3	_____	_____
Income Source 4	_____	_____
Income Source 5	_____	_____
Income Source 6	_____	_____
Total income		$ _____

Expenses (Annual)

		% of Total Income
Fixed expenses		
Housing (mortgage, property taxes)	_____	____
Utilities	_____	____
Insurance (auto/property/liability)	_____	____
Insurance (life/disability)	_____	____
Car loan/lease payments	_____	____
Other fixed expenses	_____	____
Variable expenses		
Food and dining out	_____	____
Transportation and car maintenance	_____	____
Entertainment and recreation	_____	____
Medical expenses	_____	____
Home maintenance, furnishings, and supplies	_____	____
Clothing	_____	____
Travel and vacations	_____	____
Gifts and charity	_____	____
Other variable expenses	_____	____
Income taxes	_____	
Total expenses	_____	100%
(Income − Expenses) = Savings	_____	____

a lower long-term return on your assets and may prevent you from reaching your financial goals.

For some people, assessing personal resources may lead to a rude awakening or perhaps even distress. Few of us have the financial wherewithal we would like to have. In particular, it is often frustrating to

PERSONAL FINANCIAL SUMMARY—PART 2, BALANCE SHEET

Investment Assets

Category	Amount	Cash	Bonds	Stock	Hard Assets
Checking account	————	————	————	————	————
Savings/money market	————	————	————	————	————
Taxable investments					
Account 1	————	————	————	————	————
Account 2	————	————	————	————	————
Account 3	————	————	————	————	————
Account 4	————	————	————	————	————
Account 5	————	————	————	————	————
Account 6	————	————	————	————	————
Tax-deferred investments					
401(k) plan	————	————	————	————	————
401(k) plan	————	————	————	————	————
IRA/Keogh plan	————	————	————	————	————
IRA/Keogh plan	————	————	————	————	————
Annuity	————	————	————	————	————
Total	————	————	————	————	————
Percentage of investment assets	100%	___%	___%	___%	___%

Other Assets

Residence	————————
Car(s)	————————
Furniture	————————
Jewelry	————————
Recreational/electronic equipment	————————
Other personal assets	————————
Total other assets	————————
Total assets	————————

Liabilities

Short-term liabilities	
Bills currently due	————————
Credit card balances	————————
Balance on car loan/lease	————————
Payments due within next year on long-term liabilities	————————

Long-term liabilities
  (Less payments due in next year)   _____
  Balance on mortgage loan   _____
  Balance on home equity loan/2nd mort.   _____
    Total liabilities   _____

Net Worth

(Assets − Liabilities) = Net Worth   _____

PROFESSIONALS/ADVISERS RECORD

1. Physician
    Name: _____
    Firm/Address: _____
    Phone: _____
2. Attorney
    Name: _____
    Firm/Address: _____
    Phone: _____
3. Accountant
    Name: _____
    Firm/Address: _____
    Phone: _____
4. Financial planner or consultant
    Name: _____
    Firm/Address: _____
    Phone: _____
5. Life insurance agent
    Name: _____
    Firm/Address: _____
    Phone: _____
6. Property/casualty insurance agent
    Name: _____
    Firm/Address: _____
    Phone: _____

compare how much you earn with how much you manage to save at the end of the year. Seeing just where the money is going doesn't necessarily make the task of increasing savings any easier.

On the other hand, you may be pleased upon examination to learn your resources are greater than you might have expected. Adding up all your bank and investment accounts—IRAs, savings, 401(k)s, money market funds, college accounts, life insurance cash value—probably isn't something you normally do.

> ## The whole idea of financial planning is to go from where you are now to where you want to be.

The size of the total may be a pleasant surprise. Likewise, you may be encouraged to learn just how much is available from your employer's benefit package and from Social Security.

One way or another, assessing your personal resources serves as a starting point. The whole idea of financial planning is to go from where you are now to where you want to be. We'll return to that process in Chapter 7, after looking at the basics of money, investments, and mutual funds in the next three chapters.

SAVING AND
INVESTING

BEGINNING
THE
PROCESS

LIFE
EVENT
PLANNING

INTEGRATING
YOUR
PLANS

SAVING AND INVESTING

LEARNING
MONEY
BASICS

This begins a three-chapter exploration of some basic money concepts. You need an understanding of the basics if you are going to be a knowledgeable participant in the financial planning process. Among the topics explored in this chapter will be the time value of money and the effects of inflation. We will discuss investment return and follow that with a look at the many facets of risk.

Myth vs. Reality

Myth: Federally insured savings accounts are risk free.

Reality: Bank accounts up to the $100,000 FDIC insurance limit are free of one type of risk—the risk of loss of principal and interest. But they're vulnerable to purchasing-power risk, or the chance that money invested in them will have less purchasing power in the future than it does today.

Myth: I'm not saving enough for retirement, but I can catch up in my late 40s and 50s because my income will keep going up and my expenses will level off or even fall.

Reality: Good luck. For every dollar you didn't save for retirement by age 35, you'll need to put aside $3.90 at age 55, assuming a 7 percent rate of return on your investments.

Myth: The impact of inflation on retirees is overstated because most of them own their homes, so they aren't affected by increased housing costs.

Reality: True in many cases. On the other hand, inflation's impact may be understated for retirees in other categories. Take medical care. Retirees are disproportionately heavy consumers of medical services and drugs. Over the past two decades, inflation in medical care costs has far outpaced price increases for other categories of goods and services.

Myth: The more different types of investments you have, the more risk you are taking on.

Reality: An investment that might be considered risky if owned in isolation can actually reduce the overall risk of your portfolio if its returns are not closely correlated with those of your other investments. Two examples are adding stocks to a bond portfolio and adding foreign stocks to a U.S. stock portfolio. In each case, you can increase return while reducing overall portfolio risk.

Myth: "Risky" investments are fine if you have a high degree of risk tolerance and can handle the prospect of losing some of your money. Otherwise, play it safe.

Reality: Any investment purchased solely because of its level of risk—low or high—is likely to prove unsatisfactory. Similarly, any investment bought because of its level of return is also likely to be unsatisfactory. When selecting investments, look at both expected return and expected risk, then strike the appropriate balance for you.

What You Should Know about the Time Value of Money

Financial planning, as we have seen, is a process of setting goals, determining your financial resources, and then taking the steps needed to reach those goals. A key element in that process is time. Understanding the relationship between time and money will help you develop the appropriate strategy for your financial future. And once you have put that strategy in place, time will be your most powerful ally in making it a success. The more years that time can be allowed to work for you, the more likely you will be able to reach your goals. That's because where money is concerned, time makes all the difference.

Time works its effect on money through a phenomenon known as compound interest. The compounding of interest is sometimes described as a miracle, and it's easy to see why. Interest compounds as earnings from your principal are reinvested and then generate earnings on their own. Seemingly by magic, money begets more money, doubling, tripling, quadrupling, and so forth as the years roll by. Albert Einstein, whose theories helped unlock the secrets of the universe, considered compound interest such a wonder that he called it the greatest mathematical discovery of

Understanding the relationship between time and money will help you develop the appropriate strategy for your future . . . once you have put that strategy in place, time will be your most powerful ally in making it a success.

all time. Certainly, its power is impressive. Even a small sum can reach colossal size, given enough time. For instance, consider the $24 paid by the Dutch for the island of Manhattan in 1626. That amount, if it had been invested at 7 percent, would have grown by now to $1.7 trillion.

Granted, this example may be farfetched. No one has three or four centuries to wait while money grows. But even during much shorter periods, compound interest packs plenty of power. For instance, let's say you're just starting out in your career at age 21 and want to retire with a $1 million nest egg at age 65. How much do you have to invest each year? The answer: just $1,185, assuming a return on your money equal to the 10.2 percent average annual return delivered by common stocks since 1926. (This also assumes no current tax on your earnings. Current tax would not be due, for example, if you invested the money in an individual retirement account (IRA) or 401(k) company savings plan. As we will see later in this chapter, paying income tax each year on investment earnings erodes the long-term benefits of compounding.)

What if you could afford to set aside $2,200 a year, instead of $1,185, at 10.2 percent, beginning at age 21? If so, you could simply stop investing after 10 years and let the earnings accumulate from that point. Even without further saving, you would achieve your goal of amassing $1 million for retirement by age 65—all with a total investment of just $22,000. Of course, as we shall see, $1 million built up by compounding over a 45-year period, while still a substantial sum, will be worth much less than today's $1 million because of the way inflation

BUILDING A $1 MILLION RETIREMENT NEST EGG—THE EASY WAY

A 21-Year-Old Invests $2,200 for 10 Years
(Assuming a 10.2% Return)

If You Invest $2,200 a Year for 10 Years Then Stop . . .

Age	Annual Amount	Total Value
21	$2,200	$2,400
22	2,200	5,100
23	2,200	8,100
24	2,200	11,300
25	2,200	14,900
26	2,200	18,800
27	2,200	23,100
28	2,200	27,300
29	2,200	33,200
30	2,200	39,000
Amount Invested	$22,000	

. . . Total Value Will Be This Much at Age

Age	Total Value
40	$ 103,000
50	272,200
60	718,800
65	$1,000,000

erodes the purchasing power of money. How much less? Assuming a 4 percent inflation rate, $1 million in 45 years will be worth just $171,000 in today's dollars.

You can explore the interplay of time and return with the "Rule of 72." When money doubles over a certain time, the product of the number of compounding periods and the rate of return per period will equal roughly 72. Therefore, if you pick an annual rate of return and divide it into 72, the answer will be a close approximation of the number of years required for your money to double. At a 7 percent return, for example, your money doubles in roughly 10 years (72 divided by 7). At 9 percent, it takes about eight years (72 divided by 9) for money to double. How many years will it take to quadruple? Multiply the years required to double times two. At 8 percent, for example, your money will double in nine years and quadruple in 18. The Rule of 72 works the other way as well. Pick the number of years in which you want your money to double and divide that number into 72. The answer will be your required rate of return. If six years is your target to double your money, for example, then you will need a rate of return of about 12 percent.

A dollar received today is worth more than a dollar received in the future. Why? Today's dollar can be invested and earn a return. For example, a dollar in your possession today will be worth $1.23 three years

THE RULE OF 72

Figuring What It Takes for Your Money to Double

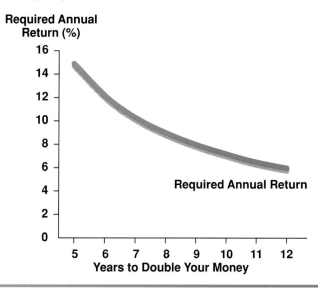

from now, assuming a 7 percent annual investment return and no taxes or inflation. Conversely, a dollar to be received three years from now is worth less than a dollar today. Using the same assumptions, a dollar received in three years has a present value of 82 cents. Putting it another way, the 82 cents if invested today would grow to $1 in three years.

In this fashion, the mathematics of compound interest enables you to project the impact of time on money, such as the money you expect to save and spend in the years ahead. If you are planning for retirement, for example, you can use the mathematics of compound interest to estimate your living costs over the period of years when you expect to be retired. Likewise, you can use it to figure how much to save each year to build a certain nest egg by retirement and to estimate how long that money will last.

To be sure, no projection made years into the future can be anything other than an approximation. The cost of living 40 years from now may turn out to be half as much, or twice as much, as the figure you project today. Likewise, money invested now for the next 40 years could grow at the exceptionally high rates that prevailed in the 1980s, when stocks delivered an average annual return of 17.6 percent. Or it could perform disappointingly, as stocks did when they returned an average 5.9 percent annually during the 1970s. We can't know the future, so we can't predict those outcomes with any degree of certainty. Yet sensible assumptions can be made about the long-term performance of investments and the future level of inflation. For example, pretax returns on large-company common stocks have averaged 10.2 percent a year since 1926, while government bonds have returned an average 5.0 percent over the same period. So if your planning horizon is a long one, say 20 years or more, and you expect to invest in a mix of stocks and bonds, it would be reasonable to assume you could achieve returns between 7 and 8 percent.

How to Make the Power of Compounding Work for You

You can harness the power of compounding and use it to help achieve your financial goals. The most important step in making compounding work for you is to give it plenty of time by investing early and letting your money grow for the long term. Let's look at these steps and see how important they can be to a successful investment strategy.

Invest Early

Saving $2,000 each year for retirement can leave you with a substantial nest egg at age 65, or just a modest amount, depending on when you get started. The sooner you begin saving, the bigger the long-term boost you will get from the power of compounding. If you start setting aside $2,000 a year at age 30, for example, your money will grow to $296,000 by age 65, assuming a 7 percent return and no current taxes. Begin saving at 25 and you will accumulate more than twice as much by retirement as you would have if you started at 35 ($427,000 vs. $202,000). Manage to start at age 21 instead of 25 and you will reap a huge bonus by the time you reach age 65. The

> **The most important step in making compounding work for you is to give it plenty of time by investing early and letting your money grow for the long term.**

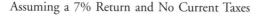

HOW A $2,000 ANNUAL INVESTMENT GROWS

Assuming a 7% Return and No Current Taxes

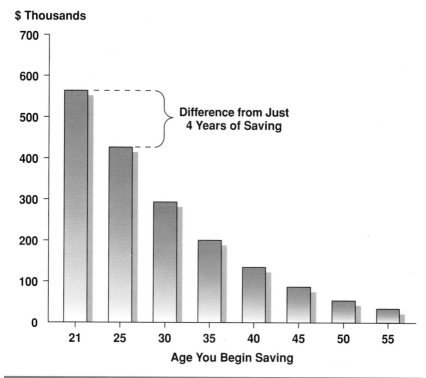

$8,000 you invest from age 21 through 24 (4 × $2,000) adds $142,000 ($569,000 – $427,000) to your retirement nest egg.

The importance of investing early doesn't just apply to the age when you start putting money aside. Over the long term, it also makes a difference how early in the year you actually make your investments. Investing at the start of each year gives your money a full 12 months to grow. Invest several months later and there will be less time for compounding to work in your favor. Year in and year out, that can have a big impact.

Let's compare two investors who contribute $2,000 a year to their individual retirement accounts. One invests on January 1, the earliest day an IRA contribution can be made for a given tax year. The other investor waits until the last day an IRA contribution can be made, which by law

WHAT YOU LOSE BY WAITING UNTIL NEXT APRIL 15

Investing $2,000 in an Individual Retirement Account Each Year on January 1 vs. Waiting Until the Next April 15 (Assuming a 7% Return)

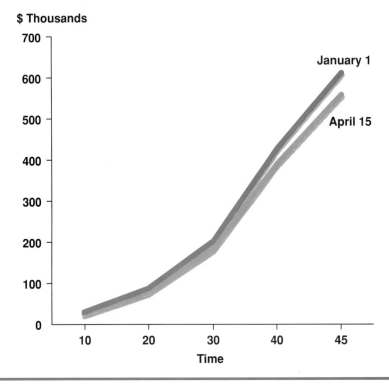

is April 15 of the following year. The result: the first investor's IRA contribution each year has 15½ more months to grow. After 40 years, the first investor's balance is $427,000 while the second investor accumulates $390,000. The difference of $37,000 is attributable to the difference in timing of their annual IRA contributions.

Save Regularly

Whatever amount of money you can set aside will grow over time through compounding. But reaching your goals will be possible only if you become committed to making investments in regular amounts every year, quarter, or month, instead of the occasional contribution. Developing a financial plan will enable you to determine the amount that ought to be set aside regularly. But you must make the commitment to save and put the money to work on schedule if you are to reach your goals.

Many things can interfere. You may face emergency expenses and be short of cash. Or you may have second thoughts about the near-term prospects for investments and become reluctant to commit more money to stocks or bonds. Whatever the cause, getting off a regular saving schedule will cost you money over the long run in lost earnings because you will be missing the full benefit of compounding on the investments you delayed or skipped.

One technique you can use to build long-term wealth from regular investing is known as dollar-cost averaging. The term may sound complicated but the benefits of dollar-cost averaging are straightforward. To use this technique, you simply invest a regular amount of money on an ongoing basis, say monthly or quarterly, in stocks or mutual funds. And you stick with it for the long term.

With dollar-cost averaging there is no reason to hesitate before you invest because you don't know where prices are heading. Or to second-guess yourself after each decision. There will always be people who say the stock market is headed down. Periodically, they will be right and prices will drop before returning to their long-term upward trend. (See Chapter 5 about the hazards of trying to time the investment markets.) With dollar-cost averaging, you decide on a regular investment and simply keep making it, without concern for the ups and downs of your investment's current price.

Along the way, dollar-cost averaging lets market fluctuations work for you, not against you. Here's why: When prices are low, you are buying more shares or units each time with your regular investment. When they rise, you automatically are buying fewer. For example, say you invest $2,000 each quarter in a mutual fund offered as part of your company savings plan. If your fund is selling at $15 a share, your $2,000 will buy 133.33 shares. But if the price rises to $18 a share, the same $2,000 will buy only 111.11 shares. Because you buy more shares when prices are lower, the average cost of your shares will be less than the average prevailing market price over the period when you accumulate them.

Let's look at the accompanying table to see how dollar-cost averaging works. Assume you make a regular quarterly investment of $2,000 in a mutual fund over a three-year period and the price of your fund fluctuates from a low of $10.46 to a high of $40.17. At the end of the three years, the average cost of the shares you purchased would be less than the average

REGULAR INVESTING THROUGH DOLLAR-COST AVERAGING

Quarterly Investment	Average Price per Share	Number of Shares Purchased
	Year 1	
$2,000	13.00	153.85
2,000	11.85	168.78
2,000	10.46	191.20
2,000	13.35	149.81
	Year 2	
$2,000	17.87	111.92
2,000	18.10	110.50
2,000	20.33	98.38
2,000	16.06	124.53
	Year 3	
$2,000	23.61	84.71
2,000	33.79	59.19
2,000	36.30	55.10
2,000	40.17	49.79

Total Investment	Average Price per Share Over 3 Years*	Average Cost for All Shares Purchased†
$24,000	$21.24	$17.68

* Add the 12 quarterly prices and divide by 12.

† Divide your total investment by the total number of shares purchased.

prevailing price of the shares over the period, in this example $17.68 vs. $21.24. Why? Because your regular $2,000 investment bought more shares when the price was low and fewer shares when the price was high, keeping your cost below the average price.

Could you have done better? Possibly. If you had the entire $24,000 in hand at the beginning of the three-year period, you could have bought the shares all at once for $13 apiece; or you could have waited until later that year and started buying shares when the price reached its low for the period. For those with a big lump sum to invest or an unfailing ability to buy at the lowest price, dollar-cost averaging may not be the best strategy. For the rest of us, however, it provides a disciplined approach to avoiding the two psychological pitfalls that trip up many investors: jumping in and out of the market as prices rise and fall, and sitting on the sidelines because you don't know if it's the right time to invest. If you make the commitment to investing regularly, dollar-cost averaging will help you achieve your long-term financial goals.

Take Advantage of Tax Deferral

Taxes work as a drag on the power of compounding by substantially reducing your effective rate of return. If you are in the 28 percent tax bracket, you keep 72 percent of dividend or interest earnings exposed to

---

Focus on...

SAVING VS. INVESTING

Many of us would consider saving and investing to be the same thing. We may not see any difference, for instance, between saving for retirement and investing for retirement. Both words cover the process of putting away money for the future. Yet it can be helpful to distinguish between saving and investing. Try thinking about it this way: Saving money means not spending it. Investing money, on the other hand, means taking money you have saved and doing something with it to earn a return.

Separating the two notions can do a world of good. Saving money becomes easier when the choice not to spend is separated from the choice about where to invest. That's because saving is a simple, onetime decision (though not necessarily an easy or painless one). After the decision is made, savings can be put on automatic pilot through a payroll deduction plan and accomplished in small amounts that fit easily into your budget. If you are not ready to decide on an investment, you can leave the money temporarily in the bank.

Investing, on the other hand, is *not* a simple, one-shot decision. It takes time, and possibly help from a professional adviser, to research and select individual investments. Whereas it's perfectly OK to rush out and start a savings program as soon as possible, investing should be done deliberately. By separating saving from investing, you can help make sure (1) you are setting money aside in a disciplined, regular way, and (2) your investments are chosen carefully and with due consideration for your overall financial goals.

---

tax. In the 36 percent bracket, you retain only 64 percent of pretax earnings, and in the 39.6 percent bracket, just 60.4 percent.

As a result of taxes, you require significantly greater investment returns to reach a particular goal. If you are in the 31 percent tax bracket, for example, you will need a pretax return of 10.1 percent to attain an after-tax return of 7 percent. In the 36 percent tax bracket, you need a 10.9 percent pretax return to be able to keep 7 percent after taxes. The chart on the following page shows after-tax returns in various income tax brackets for pretax returns of 5, 6, 7, and 8 percent.

The best outcome where taxes are concerned, of course, is not to have to pay them. And that's a major reason many investors favor municipal bonds. Interest on municipal bonds is not generally subject to federal

HOW TAXES BITE INTO INVESTMENT RETURNS

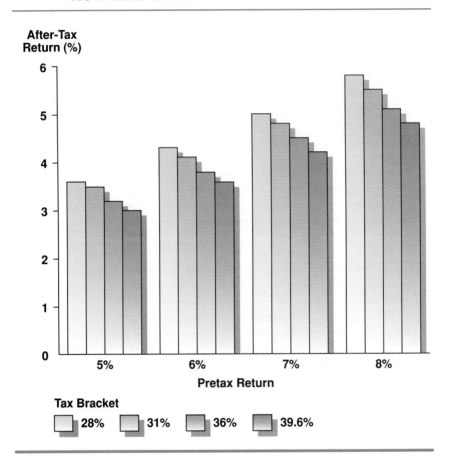

After-Tax Return (%)

Pretax Return

Tax Bracket
28%   31%   36%   39.6%

income taxes, although state or local income taxes may be due if you own municipal bonds issued outside your home state. (Capital gains on municipal bond investments are subject to federal capital gains tax.) But municipal bonds may not be suitable for your investment strategy. For example, you may need the long-term growth offered by common stocks. Unfortunately, all earnings from common stocks are taxable. Which brings us to the next-best outcome where taxes are concerned, and that is to delay or defer them as long as possible. The longer you can keep your money from being taxed, and leave all your earnings free to compound, the easier it will be for you to reach your goals.

MAXIMUM FEDERAL INCOME TAX RATES FOR INDIVIDUALS

After Decades of Decline, the Trend Is Up

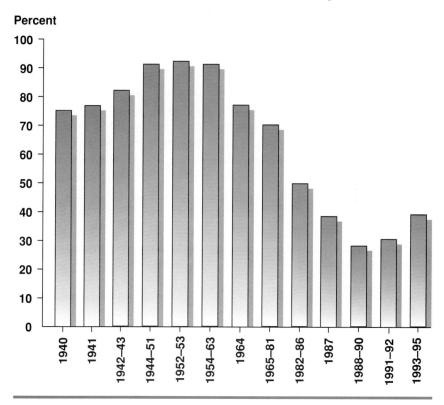

The case for taking advantage of tax deferral when it is available to you is quite compelling. After a downward trend lasting from the 1960s to the mid-1980s, tax rates on savings and investments have been heading up. For many taxpayers, the tax rates understate the actual impact of income taxes because deductions and exemptions are now phased out as income rises above certain levels. For example, those families in the highest income bracket now face an effective top tax rate of about 44 percent, even higher for larger families, although the maximum tax bracket is 39.6 percent. Investments not protected in tax-deferred accounts are fully exposed to the eroding effects that rising tax rates have on long-term compounding. As a result, it almost always makes sense to direct as much savings as allowed to retirement accounts that offer shelter for pretax contributions, such as 401(k)s or the 403(b) plans sponsored by nonprofit employers.

Other savings vehicles such as annuities, where you can obtain tax deferral on earnings but no upfront tax deduction on your contributions, may also make sense for you, depending on your circumstances. Keep in mind, however, that higher costs and certain restrictions typically associated with annuities may offset some of the benefits of tax deferral.

If you can put off paying taxes on investment earnings through tax deferral, your money will grow much faster. Let's look at some examples. Say you are 40 years old and your salary puts you in the 31 percent tax bracket. You have $10,000 to invest for retirement and expect an average annual return of 8 percent. If you invest on a fully taxable basis, your balance will be $38,300 when you reach age 65. With the same return but tax deferral on your earnings, the balance will be a substantially higher $68,500.

When a tax deduction is also available for the amount you invest, in addition to deferral of tax on earnings, the advantage is even more compelling. Let's say you can afford a cash outlay of $2,000 a year after taxes to save for retirement. On a fully taxable basis, if you save that much each year for 25 years you will accumulate $108,000, assuming the same 8 percent return and 31 percent tax bracket. Now let's say you

> **If you can put off paying taxes on investment earnings through tax deferral, your money will grow much faster.**

participate in your employer's 401(k) savings plan and can deduct your annual contribution from taxable income. That means you could increase the amount you save each year to $2,900 and still only pay $2,000 out of pocket. How? The extra $900 will come off your tax bill. In effect, it will be a loan from the government, to be repaid when you withdraw the money from the savings plan. After 25 years of $2,900 tax-deductible contributions, your plan balance would total $230,000.

Of course, once you start taking money out of a tax-deferred account, taxes are due on your withdrawals. But remember, the purpose of investing long term is to generate income for your retirement. If tax deferral will enable you to accumulate a substantially larger amount of capital for retirement, as compared to what you could accumulate on a

Focus on...

INVESTING TO MINIMIZE TAXES

Minimizing or deferring taxes on your investments doesn't necessarily require a tax-advantaged vehicle such as a 401(k) employee savings plan or an individual retirement account. You can also defer taxes by choosing investments whose expected returns will consist largely or entirely of capital gains. Capital gains are a form of income that results from an increase in the value of an investment over time and the realization of that increase through the sale of the investment. For example, if you purchased an investment for $3,000 and later sold it for $5,000, the difference of $2,000 would represent capital gain income.

This type of income offers two important tax advantages over current income from such sources as interest or dividends. One is deferral. Increases in value remain untaxed until the investment is sold and the gain is realized. The IRS doesn't get to take a bite out of *unrealized* capital gains every year, as it does from current income. The other advantage is a lower tax rate. If you own the investment for a year or more before selling, the income qualifies as a long-term capital gain and is subject to a maximum tax rate of 28 percent, compared to the statutory 39.6 percent top rate on other income. Note, however, that while the tax rate is lower on long-term returns, the investment risk is greater. (See Chapter 5, page 76.)

fully taxable basis, you will be better off. You'll pay taxes on your income stream either way, whether it comes from a tax-deferred or fully taxable account. With the tax-deferred account, the income stream will likely be greater.

Considering that your savings are most likely to be consumed in the latter stages of your retirement, the tax-deferred money you invest may be sheltered from Uncle Sam for 50 years or more, free to compound without an annual tax bite. That means tax deferral is usually too good a gift to pass up.

Inflation's Long-Term Threat

No discussion of time, money, and compounding would be complete without a look at inflation. Just as investment returns compound over the years and cause your savings to grow, inflation also compounds and

HOW COMPOUNDING INFLATION BOOSTS CONSUMER PRICES

Index of Prices (1964 = $100)

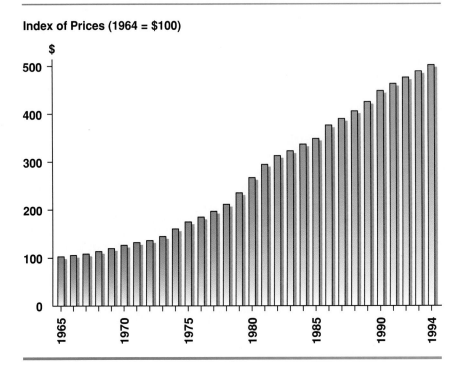

causes the level of prices to grow. As prices rise, the purchasing power of your investments declines. So in that sense, inflation is also like a tax. The 2.7 percent increase in the consumer price level during 1994, for example, was equivalent to a 2.7 percent tax on savings and investments. Since 1964, the price level has increased fivefold.

During your working years, you can cope with inflation by angling for a pay raise, seeking a higher-salaried job, working extra hours, and so on. Retirees, however, have stopped getting paychecks and salary increases. That makes them vulnerable to the relentless effects of rising prices on their standards of living. Their pensions tend to be fixed. And their investments must be largely directed toward safely generating income, not aggressively seeking growth to do better over the long run in keeping up with inflation.

A LOOK AT THE IMPACT OF A 3 PERCENT INFLATION RATE

How It Erodes the Purchasing Power of a $40,000 Income		How $40,000 Income Would Have to Increase to Keep Up with 3% Inflation	
By Year	Purchasing Power Has Dropped to	Year	From $40,000 in Year 1 to
5	$34,500	5	$46,400
10	29,800	10	53,800
15	25,700	15	62,300
20	22,100	20	72,200

Recently, inflation at around 3 percent seems mild in comparison to the double-digit increases during the late 1970s and early 1980s. Yet over time, 3 percent inflation can still do considerable damage to the purchasing power of your savings and investments.

Today's Dollars vs. Future Dollars

Since inflation behaves like a tax on savings and investments, you must incorporate it into your financial plan. Rising prices (and your rising income) will impact both your future spending needs and future financial resources, so failure to consider inflation might well leave you wide of the mark in reaching your financial goals. Yet thinking in terms of inflated dollars many years in the future can lead to a form of "sticker shock."

Consider what has happened to the price of a candy bar in your lifetime. If a candy bar costs 55 cents today (up from 10 cents 30 years ago) and inflation averages 4 percent in the future, that same candy bar will sport a price tag of $1.78 in another 30 years. On a larger scale, if your annual retirement spending goal is $50,000 in today's dollars (91,000 candy bars) and you plan to retire in 30 years, you will need $162,000 (still 91,000 candy bars) the first year of retirement, assuming a 4 percent inflation rate, and 4 percent more each year thereafter. The bigger your spending goal, the steeper your inflation assumption, and the more years until retirement, the uglier it gets.

HOW TO GAUGE INFLATION'S FUTURE IMPACT

Inflation Multipliers

| Years | *Inflation Rate* | | |
	3%	4%	5%
5	1.16	1.22	1.28
10	1.34	1.48	1.63
15	1.56	1.80	2.08
20	1.81	2.19	2.65
25	2.09	2.67	3.39
30	2.43	3.24	4.32

You can use the inflation multipliers in this table to figure how your future expenses will grow at different rates of inflation. Let's say you assume a future inflation rate of 4 percent and your living costs now total $50,000 a year. After 20 years those costs would grow to about $109,500 ($50,000 × 2.19).

Too often, the prospect of facing inflated costs denominated in future dollars can cause you to throw up your hands and want to forgo the whole idea of financial planning. Don't despair. You'll be more comfortable planning in terms of today's dollars. That way you can strip inflation out of the picture and think about money in terms of its purchasing power today. Using the example above, you would base your retirement planning on an annual income goal of $50,000.

Recall earlier in this chapter when we described how a 21-year-old could save $2,200 a year for 10 years, then stop saving and still accumulate $1 million by age 65, assuming an investment return of 10.2 percent. The good news was a $1 million retirement nest egg. The bad news was that $1 million in 45 years has a spending power in today's dollars of just $171,000. To accumulate $1 million worth of purchasing in today's dollars, our 21-year-old would have to save $2,200 in today's dollars for 56 years. That means the $2,200 contribution would have to rise each year by the amount of inflation, which is assumed in this example to be 4 percent a year.

To plan effectively to maintain your future purchasing power, you should target a level of "real" return, that is, after-inflation return, instead of "nominal" return, or return before considering inflation. For example, if your nominal investment return is 7 percent interest and the level of inflation is 3 percent, your real return is 4 percent. The levels of real returns available from different types of investments vary over time depending on the relationship between inflation and nominal investment returns. Stocks in recent years have usually generated substantial real returns. In contrast, real returns for money market funds and bank certificates of deposit are generally lower. There was a time in the early 1990s when short-term interest rates were so low that they provided virtually no margin over the rate of inflation. As a result, real returns on investments such as bank savings accounts and money market mutual funds approached zero; when taxes were considered, the real returns in some cases were negative.

The Relationship between Risk and Return

We saw earlier how the Rule of 72 illustrates the trade-off between time and return. Given more time, you can accept a lower investment return while still reaching your financial goal. With less time, however, you may find yourself pressed to seek a higher return to attain your goal. Implicit in that trade-off is the notion of risk. With a higher expected return comes a greater level of risk. But just what constitutes risk? How is it measured? And more importantly, how does an investor determine whether the terms of a particular trade-off between return and risk is (a) worthwhile or (b) foolish?

Most of us have a good idea of what is meant by return. It's the gain you make on an investment, your earnings, how much you are ahead. With a bank savings account, your return is the amount of interest you collect. The principal is guaranteed not to vary, so there is no gain or loss in value to add into the return equation. Buy a corporate bond, however, and the price may rise or fall before you sell the bond. In that case, your return would have two elements: the amount of interest you receive plus or minus any gain or loss on the bond's price if sold before maturity. Likewise with stocks. Their return is made up of dividend income plus or minus any gain or loss in price. The total of those two elements constitutes your total return.

Risk, on the other hand, is a more difficult concept to define. Some would say that where investments are concerned, risk is simply the likelihood of losing money. If the price can go down, the investment is risky. A more generally accepted notion equates risk with price fluctuations, or more accurately the volatility of total return. Slight changes in return up and down each year denote lower risk, while wider swings constitute higher risk. One common measure of that volatility is called standard deviation. It's a statistic that measures the degree to which a series of annual returns varies above and below its average. The more volatile the investment, the larger the standard deviation.

Over time, investors have been rewarded for taking on the risk posed by more volatile returns. Between 1926 and 1994, for example, large-company stocks posed more than twice the risk of U.S. government

RISK VS. RETURN

How Asset Categories Performed, 1926–1994

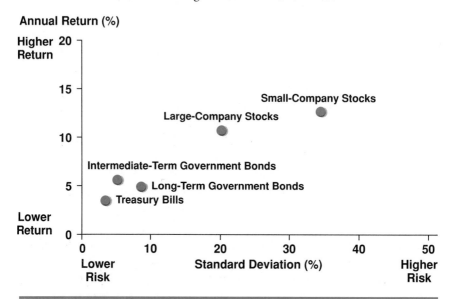

bonds, as measured by the standard deviations of their returns. But the returns of large-company stocks were also more than twice as large as those of government bonds. Even more volatile, and more rewarding, were small-company stocks.

A World of Risk

From the perspective of financial planning, the most serious risks are the ones that can prevent you from achieving your goals. The biggest of those by far is purchasing-power risk, or the risk that your money will not keep pace with inflation. It represents a substantial long-term hazard; the greater your time horizon, the greater the risk that is posed by inflation. To mitigate purchasing-power risk, you should invest for the long

HOW A LONGER HOLDING PERIOD
SMOOTHES OUT VOLATILITY RISK

Best and Worst Average Annual Returns for Large-Company Common Stocks over Holding Periods of Various Lengths between 1926 and 1994

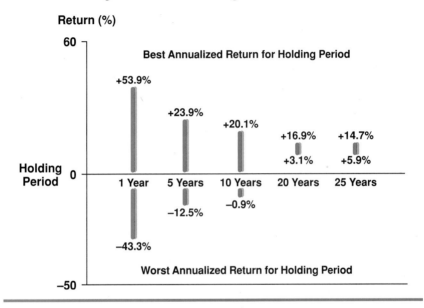

term in assets whose returns have traditionally outpaced inflation, such as common stocks. Paradoxically, such investments are usually seen as more risky because of their higher volatility, while those seen as safest carry the greatest degree of purchasing-power risk.

Treasury bills and federally insured bank accounts are good examples. Your principal and interest will be guaranteed by the government (up to insurance limits), but your returns may not keep pace with inflation. Between 1926 and 1994, for instance, Treasury bills returned an average 3.7 percent annually, barely beating the 3.1 percent inflation rate and losing on an after-tax basis. Long-term U.S. government bonds didn't do much better, topping inflation by less than two percentage points a year.

Only stocks returned a comfortable margin above inflation. Large-company stocks beat the price index by more than seven percentage points, enough to pay taxes and still stay well ahead of rising prices. And small-company stocks, considered among the riskiest of investments, beat inflation by more than nine percentage points.

Another major hazard, as noted above, is volatility. You can protect yourself from volatility by investing for the long term. In the short run, for example, common stocks can be quite volatile. Stock prices fell 22 percent on a single day in 1987. They rose 54 percent in one year (1933) after dropping 43 percent two years earlier (1931). The bear market of 1974–75 ground 37 percent out of the value of stocks over a two-year period, while stocks almost doubled during the booming four years of 1988–1991. Over longer periods, however, the stock market's ups and downs have been much more moderate. For example, the best annualized return for any of the 10-year holding periods between 1926 and 1994 was 20.1 percent. The worst was a loss of just 0.9 percent. For the 25-year holding periods between 1926 and 1994, the best average return was 14.7 percent while the worst was a positive 5.9 percent a year.

We have looked at the two biggest risks, inflation and volatility. Over the long term, inflation is the chief investment risk; over the short term, volatility is the chief threat. Here is a look at other categories of investment risk.

Business Risk

When you buy a stock or bond issued by a corporation, you face the risk that the corporation's business prospects may deteriorate and your investment will decline in value. The prices of a corporation's outstanding stock or bonds will fall if investors decide the company's future profits or financial strength have suffered an unexpected weakening. If you invest your entire portfolio in a single stock or handful of stocks, you have taken on a significant degree of business risk. Your investment value can potentially go to zero (a 100 percent loss). Fortunately, business risk (called default risk when referring to bonds) is one of several types of risk that can either be eliminated or substantially reduced through diversification of your investments.

Market Risk

This type of risk, on the other hand, is hard to diversify away. If you own stocks, or stock mutual funds, and the stock market drops significantly, you will most likely suffer a loss regardless of which individual stocks or mutual funds (or how many) are in your portfolio. You can moderate your exposure to market risk, however, by investing in different categories of assets in different markets. When U.S. stocks perform badly, for example, foreign stocks and bonds may do well. Likewise with U.S. real estate, where returns are not closely correlated with those of the stock market. To the extent that your portfolio contains only one or two asset categories, it is probably too concentrated and thus subject to market risk.

Marketability Risk

Marketability risk is the chance that there will be no ready market for your investment when you want to sell it. An owner of real estate may have to cut the asking price significantly to sell during a slump. Some investment securities carry varying degrees of marketability risk as well. There may be no ready buyers for the stock of a particular small company, for example.

Accepting a degree of marketability risk is the price of seeking out the higher long-term returns offered by such investments as real estate and small-company stocks. You can reduce marketability risk by investing in mutual funds, which will buy back their shares on request, or in actively traded securities, such as those listed on major stock exchanges or over-the-counter markets. Remember, however, that just because an investment is marketable and can be quickly sold does not mean you will recoup your purchase price or make a profit when you sell.

Interest Rate Risk

Many investments are subject to interest rate risk. When rates change, their prices change as well, sometimes dramatically. Bond prices move up and down in the opposite direction of interest rates. When rates rise, bond prices fall, and vice versa. The longer the maturity of a particular bond, the more its price reacts to a swing in rates (see Chapter 5, page 81).

While rising interest rates hurt bond prices, falling rates pose a risk as well. Many corporate and municipal bonds can be redeemed, or called, by their issuers. When interest rates fall, issuers take advantage of that privilege and call in their bonds. So a high-interest bond may be redeemed for cash when investments available in the market yield much less. You can moderate the effect of interest rate risk by investing in bonds of various maturities, a technique known as "laddering" maturities.

HOW TO REDUCE RISKS

Type of Risk	Techniques to Reduce It
Inflation risk	Invest in stocks or hard assets.
Volatility risk	Hold investments for the long term.
Business risk	Diversify within an asset category.
Market risk	Diversify among asset categories.
Marketability risk	Choose investment according to time horizon.
Interest rate risk	"Ladder" portfolio with different maturities.
Currency risk	Diversify among countries or hedge.

Currency Risk

Investments denominated in foreign currencies are subject to currency translation risk. Take a U.S. investor who buys Swiss securities. If the value of the dollar falls in relation to the Swiss franc, Swiss securities will rise in value and the U.S. investor will have a gain, at least on paper. The reason? The higher-valued franc-denominated securities will buy more dollars than they did before. The converse is also true. A rising dollar value will hurt the value of investments denominated in foreign currencies.

Professional money managers sometimes take steps to hedge, or limit, the effect currency changes will have on the value of their portfolios. These steps involve such things as the use of currency options or futures contracts. As a U.S.-based investor, you can avoid currency risk only by choosing investments whose underlying assets are dollar denominated, or by using mutual funds that hedge the currency risk posed by their foreign securities. ⚖

INTRODUCTION TO INVESTMENTS

This chapter offers a discussion of the risk-return characteristics of the major classes of investment assets, with a review of historical return and volatility patterns. Among the subjects explored, for example, is the long-run importance of dividends on stock market total returns. International investing and small-company stocks will also be discussed, as will investment management styles. Finally, the chapter will return to the discussion of asset allocation begun in Chapter 4. The fundamental importance of asset allocation decisions on investment returns will be stressed. Asset allocation decisions will also be considered in terms of investment time horizon and portfolio risk.

Myth vs. Reality

Myth: The most important part of investing is picking specific stocks.

Reality: Ninety percent of investment results are attributable to asset category selections rather than picking specific securities or the timing of the purchase or sale of the securities.

Myth: If the stock market is headed down, you're better off selling and getting back in later.

Reality: Stock market movements are not predictable. You may be selling at a low point and have to pay dearly to get back in later. Market timing is a recipe for investor disappointment.

Myth: Stocks are too volatile.

Reality: Popular stock market indexes overstate actual price movements. An 80-point "plunge" in the Dow Jones Industrial Average, for example, represents a decline in stock prices of just 2 percent. The average daily movement of stock prices up or down is much less than 1 percent.

Myth: Real estate is a better investment than stocks or bonds because real estate prices are not so volatile.

Reality: Real estate can be an excellent investment, particularly as a way of diversifying your portfolio. Although real estate is arguably less volatile than stocks or bonds, it also offers less marketability. You can sell a stock or bond with a single call to your broker. Real estate, on the other hand, may require months or years to sell.

Myth: Government bonds are a safe investment.

Reality: You will get your principal back. However, returns on long-term government bonds failed to keep pace with inflation for the four decades beginning with the 1940s and ending with the 1970s.

An Introduction to Investments

Our approach to investing will focus on the major asset categories: cash equivalents, bonds, stocks, and hard assets such as gold and real estate. Every investment represents an exchange of cash flows separated by time. The investor pays out cash now in return for cash to be received at some future date. That future cash comes back in two forms: (1) periodic interest or dividend payments and (2) the return of principal, which may have grown or shrunk in the meantime, resulting in a capital gain or loss. With some investments—Treasury bills are a good example—the investor's cash returns quickly and reliably. That cash comes back either in the form of a government check issued in a few months at maturity or through selling the Treasury bills before maturity in the highly liquid secondary market for government debt. Because of this liquidity, such investments are known as cash equivalents.

Bonds offer ownership of future cash flows over much longer time periods, making them riskier than cash equivalents. The purchaser of a newly issued long-term bond, for example, can expect to receive a stream of semiannual interest payments plus a final payment of principal when the bond matures or is redeemed by the issuer in 10 to 30 years. The uncertainty about future inflation and the bond issuer's creditworthiness in the years ahead make the future cash flows from bonds much more risky than those from cash equivalents. The corporation issuing the bond could become bankrupt. And even if every coupon payment is made as promised, there is uncertainty about the value of those future cash flows because of inflation.

These higher risks mean that investors will demand greater returns from bonds than from cash equivalents.

> **Every investment represents an exchange of cash flows separated by time. The investor pays out cash now in return for cash to be received at some future date.**

Investors anticipate that stocks will generate cash flows from future corporate dividend payments. Because stocks don't mature and dividends tend to be raised over time, owning stock in a successful company represents a claim on an open-ended series of growing cash flows. The rewards for long-term investors in such companies tend to be very high. They have to be, because substantial risks are posed by common stock investing. Many corporations fail before ever paying a dividend. And as the last decade has shown, even mighty companies can be humbled by business setbacks, causing losses for their shareholders as stock prices plummet.

The fourth category, hard assets, includes a variety of investment types, such as gold, real estate, and commodities. Their cash flows, liquidity, and risk characteristics vary quite a bit. Raw land and gold bullion, for example, generate no cash flow. An apartment building, in contrast, can provide a steady stream of rental income as well as tax benefits. But the asset group has one quality in common: It tends to perform better in the face of rising inflation than do the other asset categories.

As inflation heats up, investors turn to hard assets such as gold and real estate as a source of future cash flows that will maintain their "real" or after-inflation values. You can invest in hard assets directly; an example would be purchasing land, a building, or gold bullion. Alternatively, you can purchase shares in companies or mutual funds whose returns are tied to the prices of hard assets, such as a mutual fund that owns stocks of mining companies. A note of caution: Don't assume that different

INVESTMENT VEHICLES

Risk Increases When Return Is Deferred

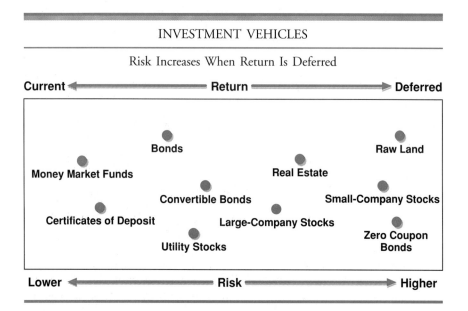

Current ◀══════════════ **Return** ══════════════▶ Deferred

Bonds   **Raw Land**

Money Market Funds   **Real Estate**

                        Convertible Bonds   **Small-Company Stocks**

Certificates of Deposit   **Large-Company Stocks**

                                                                        Zero Coupon
            Utility Stocks   **Bonds**

Lower ◀══════════════ **Risk** ══════════════▶ Higher

types of hard assets are interchangeable. Investment returns will vary among categories of hard assets, as will their responses to changes in inflation.

Let's look at the return characteristics of different types of investments. The accompanying chart presents a spectrum of investments arranged in terms of the components of their return. At the left end of the spectrum are investments whose return consists solely of current income with no potential for price appreciation and capital gains. Examples are money market funds and certificates of deposit. At the right end are investments that offer no current income, only the potential for price appreciation, such as raw land. Between are alternatives providing a mix of current income and potential for gain. Returns from utility stocks, for example, consist mostly of current income from quarterly dividends, with some potential for price gains. Real estate investments generally provide less current income than utility stocks but more capital gains income.

The lesson of this chart? Investments that provide a greater portion of their return *currently* are less risky. Those that provide a greater portion of the return on a deferred basis, in the *future,* are more risky

RETURNS BY DECADE FOR MAJOR ASSET CLASSES

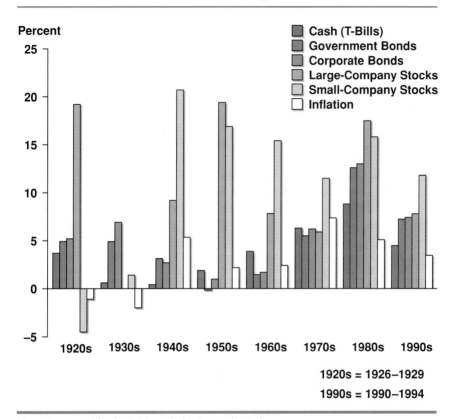

Note: As measured by the Goldman Sachs Commodity Index.

Source: © *Stocks, Bonds, Bills, and Inflation 1995 Yearbook™*, Ibbotson Associates, Chicago (annually updates work by Roger G. Ibbotson and Rex A. Sinquefield). Used with permission. All rights reserved.

because of the greater uncertainty about the stream of cash flows they will generate.

Investments ought to fit your time horizon. If you need the money in a year, stick with low-risk investments providing current return and no principal fluctuation, such as money market funds or certificates of deposit. On the other hand, if you have 25 years until your investment goal, stocks and real estate will provide you with higher levels of return, yet still pose reasonable levels of risk because of your long time horizon.

A Look at Cash Equivalents

Cash equivalents provide a reliable home for money that might be needed within a relatively short time. While liquid and relatively safe, cash equivalents have not historically provided much in the way of investment returns. Over most periods, their returns have generally been about the same as the rate of inflation. For example, $1 invested in U.S. Treasury bills at the end of 1925 would have grown to $12.19 by the end of 1994. That compares to $8.35 for $1 invested over that period at the rate of inflation.

SNAPSHOT OF INVESTMENT PERFORMANCE BY CASH EQUIVALENTS

U.S. Treasury Bills

	1920s	1930s	1940s	1950s	1960s	1970s	1980s	1990s
Annual returns	3.7%	0.6%	0.4%	1.9%	3.9%	6.3%	8.9%	4.7%

Value (as of 12/31/94) of $1 invested 1/1/26: $12.19
                                After inflation: $ 1.46

Value (as of 12/31/94) of $1 invested 1/1/69: $ 5.80
                                After inflation: $ 1.38

Note: 1920s = 1926–1929; 1990s = 1990–1994.

Source: © *Stocks, Bonds, Bills, and Inflation 1995 Yearbook*™, Ibbotson Associates, Chicago (annually updates work by Roger G. Ibbotson and Rex A. Sinquefield). Used with permission. All rights reserved.

Cash equivalents are short-term debt obligations such as U.S. Treasury bills, bank certificates of deposit, and commercial paper. They offer the advantages of liquidity and stability of principal because of their high credit quality and short maturities. Treasury bills, for example, are offered at maturities of one year or less. Commercial paper, a debt obligation issued by top-rated companies, typically has a maturity of 90 days or less. The financial strength of most borrowers in the market for cash equivalents, such as government agencies, large corporations, and banks, combined with the short maturity of cash reserve instruments means cash equivalents are essentially immune from significant market risk and interest rate risk.

CASH EQUIVALENTS GROWTH BY DECADE

$1 Invested at Start of 10-Year Period

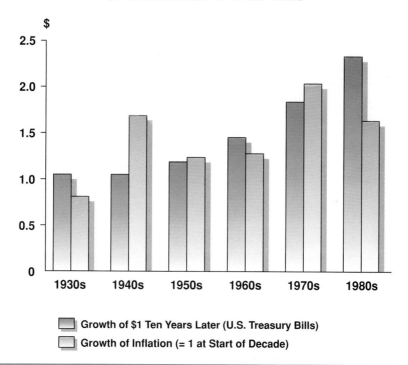

Growth of $1 Ten Years Later (U.S. Treasury Bills)

Growth of Inflation (= 1 at Start of Decade)

Source: © *Stocks, Bonds, Bills, and Inflation 1995 Yearbook*™, Ibbotson Associates, Chicago (annually updates work by Roger G. Ibbotson and Rex A. Sinquefield). Used with permission. All rights reserved.

A Look at Bonds

Bonds are called fixed-income securities because the interest they pay, known as the coupon, is typically a fixed amount. A $1,000 bond issued with a 7 percent coupon would pay a fixed $70 in interest each year. While the coupon amount may be fixed, the price of a bond is not. As interest rates rise, bond prices will drop, while falling rates cause bond prices to move upward. Investors will bid up or push down a bond's price until its yield to maturity is in line with market interest rates. For example, if interest rates rose suddenly from 7 percent to 8 percent, a $1,000 bond with a 7 percent coupon and a 20-year maturity would

Focus on...

YIELD VS. YIELD TO MATURITY

Yield is the income you earn from an investment, expressed as a percentage of the investment's price. For example, a $1,000 bond providing coupon interest of $65 a year has a current yield of 6.5 percent. You can calculate the current yield by dividing the amount of income by the investment's price, then multiplying the result by 100 to convert it into a percentage.

Yield is a useful measure of return for income investments that will not change in value, such as bank certificates of deposit. The difference in returns between two bank CDs during a particular period will result entirely from the difference in their yields.

However, bond prices move up and down with interest rates. If you buy a bond at a price above or below its par value, your return will consist of two elements, the current yield derived from coupon interest payments and the capital loss or gain you would experience if you held the bond until redemption at maturity.

To account for both elements, bond investors use a measure known as *yield to maturity*. It reflects the present value of future coupon payments and the present value of the principal to be returned at maturity adjusted for any capital loss or gain. Thus, the yield to maturity of a bond selling for more than its par value will be less than its current yield to account for the capital loss at maturity. Conversely, the yield to maturity of a bond priced below par value will exceed its current yield because of the expected capital gain at maturity.

drop in price to about $900, the point where its yield to maturity would equal the current market rate of interest.

Bonds are loans in the form of a publicly traded security. An investor who buys a bond is making a loan for a certain number of years to the government agency, corporation, or other entity that issues the bond. Bonds are attractive to investors for several reasons. First, they provide higher income than cash equivalents such as Treasury bills or money market funds. Accordingly, many investors, such as retired individuals who require current income to meet their living expenses, allocate the bulk of their investment portfolios to bonds.

Second, bond income is also highly predictable. If you purchase a government bond, you are assured of receiving payments of interest and principal when they come due. Thus, bonds can be used to fund future

HOW CHANGES IN INTEREST RATES AFFECT BOND PRICES

Here is what happens to the price of a $1,000 bond paying 7% coupon interest and trading at par when market interest rates rise (top half) and fall (bottom half).

	If Rates Rise above 7% by							
	1/2%	1%	1.5%	2%	2.5%	3%	3.5%	4%
Maturity	*Price of $1,000 Bond Falls to*							
2 year	$991	$982	$973	$964	$956	$947	$938	$930
5 year	980	960	940	921	902	884	867	849
20 year	949	901	857	816	778	743	710	679
30 year	941	887	838	794	753	716	682	651
	If Rates Fall below 7% by							
	1/2%	1%	1.5%	2%	2.5%	3%	3.5%	4%
Maturity	*Price of $1,000 Bond Rises to*							
2 year	$1,009	$1,019	$1,028	$1,038	$1,047	$1,057	$1,067	$1,077
5 year	1,021	1,043	1,065	1,088	1,111	1,135	1,159	1,184
20 year	1,056	1,116	1,181	1,251	1,327	1,410	1,500	1,598
30 year	1,066	1,138	1,219	1,309	1,409	1,521	1,647	1,788

obligations. For instance, if you know you will need $20,000 in three years to pay college tuition bills, you can purchase a government bond today that will mature in three years and return $20,000 in principal at that time. You would not invest in stocks, for example, because of their volatility. You would not know whether at the end of three years you would have the $20,000. And because it is steady and predictable, bond income can be reinvested and grow over time through the power of compounding.

Finally, bonds provide portfolio diversification, which can help dampen the effects of swings in stock prices. This is because bond prices, in general, do not correlate to the movement of stock prices. They are less volatile than stocks.

Returns from bonds derive from the coupon payments and the compounding that results from reinvestment of those payments. Over the long run, bonds as a class of assets do not offer returns from capital appreciation, although there are often lengthy periods of falling interest rates where bond investors can enjoy handsome capital gains. The most notable of such periods recently was the 1980s, when the annualized return for long-term government bonds reached 12.6 percent. In one year, 1984, bonds returned an unprecedented 40.4 percent. Outsize returns were also posted in 1985 (31.0 percent) and 1986 (24.5 percent). A major component of those returns was capital appreciation as bond prices rose in a declining interest rate environment.

Large as those capital gains were, however, they failed to make up for previous decades of capital losses suffered by long-term bonds when inflation and interest rates were on the climb. In fact, from 1926 to 1993, long-term government bonds have posted capital losses. Reflecting those capital losses, $1 invested in long-term bonds in 1926 would have declined to 73 cents in 1994 if compound interest from coupon earnings is ignored. Include that compounded coupon interest and total return from the $1 investment over the 1926–1994 period would have been $25.86.

Though bonds are considered to be conservative, low-risk investments, their prices can be volatile when interest rates change. The longer a bond's maturity, the more its price is affected by a dip or a rise in rates. That's because the present values of the cash flows to be derived in the later years from a long-dated bond swing much more widely with interest rate changes than do the values of those cash flows that will be paid within the next few years. For example, a $1,000 bond with a 7 percent coupon and a maturity of five years would fall in price to about $960 if market interest rates rose from 7 percent to 8 percent. If the bond's maturity were 20 years, as noted above, the fall in price would be approximately to $900.

Should you be concerned about fluctuations in bond prices? Not if you intend to hold bond investments until they mature. Unlike stocks, bonds have a maturity date at which point the bond issuer will return the principal at par value. In the meantime, swings in interest rates may cause your bond's price to rise above or fall below par, but you don't need to worry. You can be assured of getting your money back as long as the bond issuer is creditworthy. (This applies to individual bonds but not to bond mutual funds because the funds do not have a particular maturity date when principal is returned. For more on the subject of bond funds, see Chapter 6.) One way to reduce the impact of interest rate changes on the value of a portfolio of individual bonds is to "ladder" maturities, or hold a mix of short-, intermediate-, and long-term bonds.

SNAPSHOT OF INVESTMENT PERFORMANCE
BY LONG-TERM GOVERNMENT BONDS

	1920s	1930s	1940s	1950s	1960s	1970s	1980s	1990s
Annual returns	5.0%	4.9%	3.2%	−0.1%	1.4%	5.5%	12.6%	8.3%

Value (as of 12/31/94) of $1 invested 1/1/26: $25.86
After inflation: $ 3.10

Value (as of 12/31/94) of $1 invested 1/1/69: $ 7.95
After inflation: $ 1.89

Note: 1920s = 1926–1929; 1990s = 1990–1994.

Source: © *Stocks, Bonds, Bills, and Inflation 1995 Yearbook™*, Ibbotson Associates, Chicago (annually updates work by Roger G. Ibbotson and Rex A. Sinquefield). Used with permission. All rights reserved.

LONG-TERM GOVERNMENT BONDS GROWTH BY DECADE

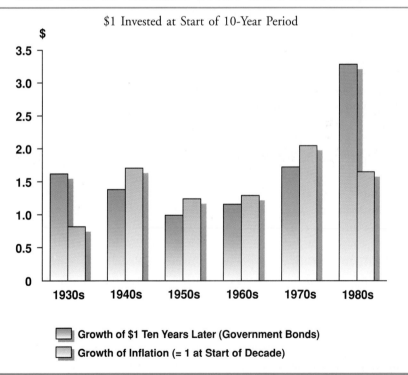

$1 Invested at Start of 10-Year Period

■ Growth of $1 Ten Years Later (Government Bonds)
□ Growth of Inflation (= 1 at Start of Decade)

Source: © *Stocks, Bonds, Bills, and Inflation 1995 Yearbook™*, Ibbotson Associates, Chicago (annually updates work by Roger G. Ibbotson and Rex A. Sinquefield). Used with permission. All rights reserved.

Inflation and rising interest rates have proved costly for investors in bonds. As the table on the previous page shows, bond returns lost out to inflation in each of the four decades preceding the 1980s. Only in the last decade did bonds provide "real" returns topping inflation.

Bonds fall into the following subcategories by type of issuer:

U.S. Treasury Bonds

Most of the federal government's debt is financed by issuing Treasury bonds with maturities of 10 to 30 years or notes with maturities of 1 to 10 years. Treasury securities are considered the most creditworthy of all debt instruments because they are backed by the "full faith and credit" of the government.

U.S. Government Agency Bonds

A number of federal government agencies or federally chartered organizations, such as the Federal National Mortgage Association, issue their own bonds. Some of their bonds are explicitly guaranteed by the government. Others are not, but garner top credit ratings anyway because their government sponsorship is considered valuable.

The largest category of agency bonds is a type of security backed by pools of individual home mortgages. Though mortgage-backed securities typically come with designated maturities of 30 years, their effective maturities are much shorter, often in the range of 10 to 12 years, because principal is returned throughout the life of these securities. Because homeowners can pay off their mortgages at any time, mortgage-backed securities can suddenly take on even shorter maturities. When homeowners refinance their mortgages, the entire principal is repaid and passed through to investors, sharply reducing both effective maturities and the returns provided by mortgage-backed securities. This characteristic, known as prepayment risk, explains why prices of mortgage-backed securities do not necessarily behave like prices of other types of bonds and rise automatically when interest rates fall.

Corporate Bonds

Corporations issue bonds in various maturities, including short-term (1–3 year maturity), intermediate-term (3–10 year maturity), and long-term (over 10 years). A subcategory is a type of security known as high-yield or junk bonds, because of their low credit ratings. Corporate (and municipal) bonds receive credit evaluations from agencies such as Moody's Investors Service or Standard & Poor's Corp. The lower the credit rating, the higher the yield an issuer must offer to attract investors to its bonds. Investment-grade corporate bonds offer somewhat higher yield than government bonds, while high-yield

SNAPSHOT OF INVESTMENT PERFORMANCE
BY LONG-TERM CORPORATE BONDS

	1920s	1930s	1940s	1950s	1960s	1970s	1980s	1990s
Annual returns	5.2%	6.9%	2.7%	1.0%	1.7%	6.2%	13.0%	8.4%

Value (as of 12/31/94) of $1 invested 1/1/26: $38.01
After inflation: $ 4.55

Value (as of 12/31/94) of $1 invested 1/1/69: $ 8.55
After inflation: $ 2.03

Note: 1920s = 1926–1929; 1990s = 1990–1994.

Source: © *Stocks, Bonds, Bills, and Inflation 1995 Yearbook™*, Ibbotson Associates, Chicago (annually updates work by Roger G. Ibbotson and Rex A. Sinquefield). Used with permission. All rights reserved.

CORPORATE BONDS GROWTH BY DECADE

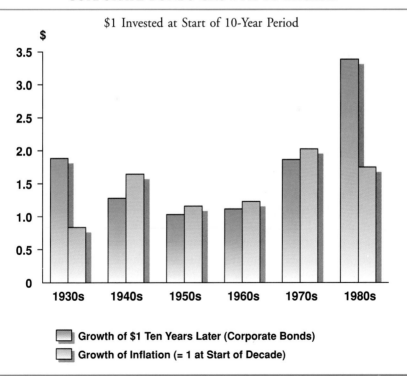

$1 Invested at Start of 10-Year Period

Growth of $1 Ten Years Later (Corporate Bonds)
Growth of Inflation (= 1 at Start of Decade)

Source: © *Stocks, Bonds, Bills, and Inflation 1995 Yearbook™*, Ibbotson Associates, Chicago (annually updates work by Roger G. Ibbotson and Rex A. Sinquefield). Used with permission. All rights reserved.

corporate bonds provide both the greatest level of income and the greatest potential for default.

Municipal Bonds   State and local governments issue bonds to finance their operations or invest in new facilities, such as school buildings and sewage plants. The interest on municipal bonds is exempt from federal income tax and may be exempt from state and local taxes as well. Municipal bonds come in two subgroups. General obligation bonds are usually backed by the full taxing power of the issuing agency, while revenue bonds are backed by the income from a particular public project, such as a turnpike or bridge authority.

Beyond those categorizations by issuer, there are many different types and structures of bonds. Some bonds, the zero coupon variety, pay no interest. Instead they are issued at a deep discount and gradually increase in value until they reach par, or face value, at maturity. Other bonds may be convertible at the investor's option into the common stock of corporations issuing them. Thus they offer both current income and the potential for price appreciation. Corporate and municipal bonds frequently have call provisions. They can be redeemed, or called, by their issuers under certain circumstances. When interest rates fall, issuers take advantage of that privilege and call in their bonds. So an investor who is happily holding a high-interest bond may find it redeemed for cash when investments available in the market yield much less.

A Look at Common Stocks

Common stocks represent a share of ownership in a business. You can become part-owner of a public corporation simply by purchasing shares of its common stock. Your investment will provide current income if the company pays a dividend, and you can also expect the value of your stock to grow as the company's revenues and profits rise over time. But there are no guarantees. Your stock's price will move up and down due to the same forces that sway stock prices in general.

The stock market reflects the outlook of investors for the economy and future corporate profits and dividends. Sometimes those movements also reflect waves of optimism or pessimism that sweep over investors. If a bear market develops, your stock is likely to be hurt, even if its prospects for future profits seem as bright as ever. Your stock's price will also be driven by economic forces impacting all the companies in its

SNAPSHOT OF INVESTMENT PERFORMANCE
BY LARGE-COMPANY STOCKS

	1920s	1930s	1940s	1950s	1960s	1970s	1980s	1990s
Annual returns	19.2%	0.0%	9.2%	19.4%	7.8%	5.9%	17.5%	8.7%

Value (as of 12/31/94) of $1 invested 1/1/26: $811
After inflation: $ 97

Value (as of 12/31/94) of $1 invested 1/1/69: $ 12
After inflation: $ 3

Note: 1920s = 1926–1929; 1990s = 1990–1994.

Source: © *Stocks, Bonds, Bills, and Inflation 1995 Yearbook™*, Ibbotson Associates, Chicago (annually updates work by Roger G. Ibbotson and Rex A. Sinquefield). Used with permission. All rights reserved.

industry. When oil prices rise, for example, airline company stocks generally suffer. An expected decline in mortgage interest rates, on the other hand, will lift the stocks of home builders because investors foresee increased sales and profits.

At the individual company level, other factors come to bear on the prospects for your stock. Profits may be hurt by an aggressive competitor, poor company management, or a big lawsuit, causing the stock price to decline.

For stocks, both risks and potential rewards loom large. Over the long haul and for the stock market as a whole, basic economics dictates that equity returns must exceed interest rate returns, that is, return on capital investment must exceed the cost of borrowing.

As the accompanying table demonstrates, the rewards have dominated over the years as common stocks far outperformed other asset classes. They have also done the best job at keeping ahead of inflation. One dollar invested in large-company stocks in 1926 would have grown to $811 by the end of 1994. Long-term investors in small company stocks have done even better. One dollar invested in this asset category in 1926 would have grown to $2,843 over the same period. The real return for $1 over that period, after adjustment for inflation, was $97 for large-company stocks and $340 for small-company stocks.

While the performance of stocks has been impressive, it has also been highly uneven. As we saw in Chapter 4, returns from 1926 to 1994 have ranged from a one-year gain of 53.9 percent (1933) to a one-year loss of

COMMON STOCKS GROWTH BY DECADE

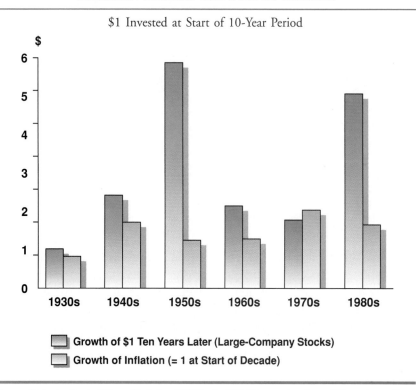

$1 Invested at Start of 10-Year Period

■ Growth of $1 Ten Years Later (Large-Company Stocks)
□ Growth of Inflation (= 1 at Start of Decade)

43.3 percent (1931). Investors who stay put, as we noted, have not received that kind of buffeting over multiyear periods. The longer the holding period, the less the variation in stock returns. For five-year periods between 1926 and 1994, for example, the largest annualized gain was 23.9 percent, while the largest loss was 12.5 percent.

But even over periods as long as a decade, the market's returns, while not highly volatile, nonetheless have been erratic. Stocks generated nothing for investors in the 1930s, for example, ending the decade with no return. While positive, returns in the 1960s and 1970s were also meager. Clearly, much of the overall return from stocks in the 1926–1994 period is attributable to two decades: the 1950s and the 1980s. These results demonstrate the importance to investors of owning stocks for long periods so they benefit from such periods of extraordinarily high returns.

Focus on...

WHY DIVIDENDS ARE IMPORTANT

It may come as a surprise to learn that most of the return from large-company common stocks derives from reinvested dividends, not price appreciation. Stocks are considered a growth investment, but the real engine of growth behind their returns is the long-term compounding of increasing dividends. For example, $1 invested in large-company stocks over the 1969–1993 period grew to $12. Of that gain, $4.50 came from capital appreciation and the other $7.50 resulted from reinvested dividends. Those dividends boost returns in years when the stock market is rising, and they help make up for losses in the down years. For example, $1 invested in the stock market in 1966 was worth 98 cents at the end of 1975 counting price changes alone. Without dividends that would have meant a loss of 2 percent. With reinvested dividends, however, the value rose to $1.38, for a gain of 38 percent.

Over the long term, dividends from stocks have shown substantial growth, although year-to-year changes are uneven. Dividend increases reflect the economic health and confidence of corporations. When they are optimistic, companies raise their dividend payouts. For example, during the decade ending in 1994, dividends per share paid by the 30 stocks in the Dow Jones Industrial Average rose in eight years and declined in only two. Over the period, per-share dividends for this bellwether group of stocks rose a total of 70 percent.

Not all stocks have the same pattern of returns over time. Stock performance can be classified in these categories: growth and income, growth, and aggressive growth. The growth and income category represents stocks of large, well-established companies, with returns coming from both capital appreciation and dividend income. The growth category includes faster-growing companies that pay little or no dividends, while aggressive growth is characteristic of small companies whose stocks are highly volatile. In addition to those categories, there are two groups of stocks that offer different, and highly attractive, performance characteristics—small-company stocks and stocks of non-U.S. companies.

Small-Company Stocks

The returns of small-company stocks historically have been much higher than the returns of the stock market as a whole—and more volatile. The

SNAPSHOT OF INVESTMENT PERFORMANCE
BY SMALL-COMPANY STOCKS

	1920s	1930s	1940s	1950s	1960s	1970s	1980s	1990s
Annual returns	−4.5%	1.4%	20.7%	16.9%	15.5%	11.5%	15.8%	11.8%

Value (as of 12/31/94) of $1 invested 1/1/26: $2,843
After inflation: $ 340

Value (as of 12/31/94) of $1 invested 1/1/69: $ 17
After inflation: $ 4

Note: 1920s = 1926–1929; 1990s = 1990–1994.

Source: © *Stocks, Bonds, Bills, and Inflation 1995 Yearbook™*, Ibbotson Associates, Chicago (annually updates work by Roger G. Ibbotson and Rex A. Sinquefield). Used with permission. All rights reserved.

difference in annual return between small- and large-company stocks averages more than two percentage points over time. In shorter periods, usually multiyear cycles that can last up to a decade, small-company stocks have alternatively outperformed, then underperformed large-company stocks. From 1974 to 1983, for example, small-company stocks dominated. One dollar invested in the group at the start of 1974 would have returned $12.18 at the end of 1983, compared to a return of just $2.74 during the same period for $1 invested in large-company stocks. In 1984, their fortunes turned. From that year through 1990, large-company stocks took the lead. One dollar invested in large-company stocks returned $2.60, vs. just $1.20 for a dollar invested in small stocks. It now appears that the cycle turned once again starting in 1991. For the years 1991–1993, small stocks offered a cumulative return of 116 percent, compared to 55 percent for large-company stocks.

We saw in the case of large-company stocks that the bulk of investment return is derived from compounding of dividends. In contrast, small-company stocks generally do not pay dividends, so their return is the result of capital appreciation. This absence of dividends contributes to their volatility. Dividends provide a cushion that keeps a stock more attractive to investors during market swings. With no dividends, small stocks are more likely to be dumped if their prices fall. Also a factor in their volatility is the heavy selling of small-company stocks toward the end of the year by individual investors who want to realize capital losses for tax purposes. When these investors return to the market as buyers in the first few days of the new year, small-company stocks tend to jump in price in a pattern that has been documented as the "January effect."

International Stocks

A generation ago, U.S. stocks represented two-thirds of the value of all stocks outstanding worldwide. Now, it's the other way around: Two-thirds of all stock value lies in foreign markets. Currently, opportunities for investors are growing much faster overseas. Foreign stocks tend to offer higher returns than domestic U.S. issues, as well as greater volatility. Economic growth overseas, in the Pacific Rim, Latin America, and other emerging markets, has recently outpaced growth rates in the United States, providing for rapid expansion of sales and profits by corporations in those countries.

> **Stocks are considered a growth investment, but the real engine of growth behind their returns is the long-term compounding of increasing dividends.**

Just as importantly, stock markets around the world don't move in synch with the U.S. market. Returns from Asian stock markets, for example, have tended to be down when U.S. returns are up, and vice versa. That means investing overseas could add an important measure of diversification to a portfolio of U.S.-based stocks.

Of course, investing outside of the United States carries risks, including political risk. The trend since World War II has been to open national borders to flows of outside capital and investment. But at some point, the world is likely once again to see trade disputes, political unrest, and wars that will disrupt international markets and imperil the value of overseas investments.

Another pitfall facing international investors is currency risk. Let's say you buy a non-U.S. stock and the dollar subsequently rises 10 percent against the value of that stock's home-country currency. Even if the stock's price hasn't changed, the value of your investment in dollars has declined by 10 percent. Currency risk can result in quick and painful losses for investors who must sell after a major currency realignment. For long-term investors, however, the currency risk posed by international stocks is of less concern. The variations in return related to currency fluctuations will enhance the diversification effects provided by investing in international stocks. And if future economic growth proves to be much greater overseas,

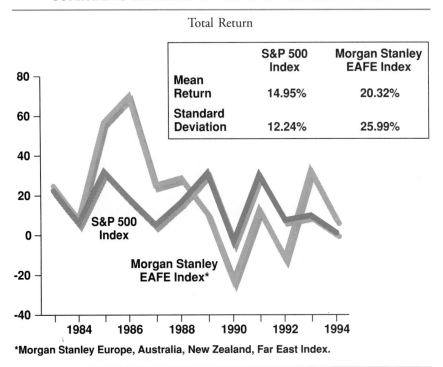

COMPARING RETURNS OF U.S. AND FOREIGN STOCKS

Total Return

	S&P 500 Index	Morgan Stanley EAFE Index
Mean Return	14.95%	20.32%
Standard Deviation	12.24%	25.99%

S&P 500 Index

Morgan Stanley EAFE Index*

*Morgan Stanley Europe, Australia, New Zealand, Far East Index.

foreign currencies will tend to strengthen vs. the U.S. dollar over time. Such a trend would be favorable for U.S. investors holding international stocks because the value of those stocks would rise in dollar terms.

How to Invest Internationally

Several alternatives are available for individuals who want to invest in the growth of foreign economies. You can choose from these.

- **Stock in U.S.-Based Companies with Extensive Overseas Operations.** Some examples include Caterpillar Tractor, Coca-Cola, Citicorp, Exxon, and Gillette. These stocks benefit from international growth. And unlike the other alternatives listed below, they do not pose currency risk for U.S. investors. However, the stock prices of U.S. corporations tend to move with the U.S. equity markets, even for those companies whose predominant business is outside the United States.

- **Stocks Listed on Foreign Exchanges.** They can be purchased through major U.S. stock brokerages and international banks. Ownership of foreign stocks entails marketability risk and currency risk. Stockholders may also encounter problems with documentation and timely receipt of dividend payments.
- **American Depository Receipts.** ADRs are listed on U.S. stock exchanges. They certify ownership of a particular number of shares of a foreign company on deposit at a foreign branch of an American bank. They avoid problems with documentation and dividend payments that can be involved with direct ownership of foreign stocks. There are disadvantages. First, the ADR market is thin and liquidity can be an issue. Second, you are subject to currency fluctuation. The price of your ADRs will rise and fall with the exchange rate even when the underlying stock price is stable.
- **International Mutual Funds.** Some funds take a global approach, buying both foreign and U.S. stocks, while others limit themselves to non-U.S. investments. More specialized funds invest in a single region, such as Europe, the Pacific, or emerging markets. In addition, there are several dozen funds specializing in single countries, such as Italy, Spain, India, Korea, and Mexico.

A Look at Hard Assets

The final category of investments is known as hard assets, so called to distinguish them from paper assets such as bonds and stocks. Their common characteristic and the basis of their attractiveness is as an inflation hedge. Hard assets include commodities, real estate, precious metals, timber rights, oil and gas leases—any of a wide variety of natural resources whose values tend to rise along with the overall level of consumer prices. Some, such as commercial real estate or oil and gas properties, can offer current income as well the opportunity for price appreciation. Others, such as gold bullion and raw land, provide no current income and may even carry expenses, such as real estate taxes, that give them a negative cash flow. We will look here at two principal categories of hard assets, real estate and precious metals.

Real Estate

Unlike such investments as stocks and bonds, each parcel of real estate is a singular asset. Its individual characteristics, including location, type of building, improvements, amenities, and lease arrangements, make it unique. There is no standard price per square foot for a given type of building, even within a local geographic market. Instead, each real estate investment needs to be valued individually. Real estate may also offer limited marketability. Once acquired, a property may take months or years to sell.

These factors mean that direct investments in real estate can be risky, even for professional investors with detailed information about a particular market. On the other hand, direct investments in real estate often prove to be enormously profitable. Leverage in the form of mortgage financing is available to enable an investor to acquire property with a relatively small equity investment, boosting the potential for profit. For instance, if you buy a parcel of real estate with a 10 percent down payment and then sell after just a 10 percent appreciation in price, you have doubled your money. It's no wonder that many of the country's largest fortunes have been based on real estate investments.

Investors who want exposure to real estate without buying property directly often turn to real estate investment trusts, or REITs. REITs are structured much like closed-end mutual funds and offer diversification, liquidity, and the opportunity to make a small initial investment. They pool cash from investors and issue shares, which subsequently can be bought or sold on a stock exchange or in the over-the-counter market. Like mutual funds, REITs also don't pay taxes. Instead, they pass through to shareholders the income from rents, interest, and gains from property sales.

Investment strategies of REITs fall into two broad categories. Equity REITs purchase interests in real estate developments and may specialize in a certain category of property, such as apartment buildings or shopping centers. Mortgage REITs, on the other hand, make mortgage and construction loans. As a result, their performance tends to be similar to fixed-income investments such as bonds.

Real estate limited partnerships and REITs were poor performers over the last decade. The Tax Reform Act of 1986 took away many of the tax advantages of real estate ownership in general and clamped down in particular on tax-shelter-oriented real estate partnerships. The 1980s also saw a series of severe regional slumps in real estate and the collapse of the savings and loan industry. These events combined to hurt property values in many markets and cause losses for real estate investors. However, as real estate markets have recovered recently, the investment performance of REITs as a group has improved.

Focus on...

WHEN IS YOUR HOME AN INVESTMENT?

You probably already have a significant portion of your net worth in real estate—your home. But generally your principal residence should not be considered part of your investable assets, and its value should not be counted in determining your asset allocation mix. The reason? You have to live somewhere. If you sold the house, you would have to reinvest in another house or set aside funds to generate enough income to pay rent. The exception: If the value of your house is significantly in excess of your present or near-future requirements, the excess value may be considered as an investable asset allocated to real estate. For example, if you are within a few years of retirement and plan to move to a less expensive house, you may not need to allocate any additional funds toward investment in hard assets. (A reminder: your home does not represent a diversified investment like a REIT, and therefore you have a higher degree of risk associated with the investment portion.)

Gold and Precious Metals

Gold and other precious metals traditionally have been considered a hedge against the possibility of economic turmoil caused by war, hyperinflation, or other catastrophic events. However, this most stable of metals is a highly unstable investment whose returns show no consistent correlation with the direction of U.S. inflation. For example, while inflation held steady in the 3 to 4 percent range during the mid-1980s, gold returns careened between +20 percent and –20 percent. Precious metals mutual funds gyrated even more wildly, losing or gaining more than 20 percentage points in annual return during 7 of the 10 years from 1981 to 1990.

There are numerous ways to invest in gold. You can purchase bullion or gold coins or establish a gold deposit account similar to a savings account with a bank or dealer. Bullion offers no income and may entail expenses such as safekeeping or account maintenance fees. For this reason, many investors turn to precious metals mutual funds, which own stocks of gold mining companies. The returns of funds within this category vary significantly depending on their investment strategies. All are

VOLATILE INVESTMENT RETURNS
OF PRECIOUS METALS FUNDS

	Precious Metals Funds
1981	−25.18%
1982	47.89
1983	2.53
1984	−29.18
1985	−9.35
1986	34.06
1987	36.79
1988	−17.73
1989	25.65
1990	−23.78
1991	−3.88
1992	−15.15
1993	84.97
1994	−11.67

Source: *Morningstar Principia for Mutual Funds,*
Morningstar, Inc., Chicago, IL.

affected by changes in the price of gold, but some limit their price swings compared to gold while others magnify the metal's volatility. Returns also vary geographically. Funds that invest heavily in South African mining companies, for example, have moved up and down based on the political outlook in that country.

Lastly, gold is attractive as a way to add diversification to your investment portfolio. Gold returns tend to move in the opposite direction from the returns of other types of investments such as stocks and bonds. When stocks and bonds do well, gold often performs badly, with the reverse also being true. Thus, gold becomes more than just a hedge against the possibility of an outbreak of severe inflation. It is also an effective way to add balance to your investment portfolio.

Allocating Investment Assets

Let's summarize some important inferences to be made from our survey of the major asset categories:

- Stock returns are a powerful long-term creator of wealth. Historically, stocks are the only asset category whose returns have far-outpaced inflation.
- Subcategories of stocks offer markedly different patterns of return. Allocating a portion of your portfolio to each subcategory can enhance return and reduce risk through diversification.
- Bonds provide predictable income for compounding and a cushion against the effects of stock price volatility on portfolio value. A "laddered" portfolio (with various maturities) can mitigate against sudden changes in interest rates and inflation.

Focus on...

THE PITFALLS OF MARKET TIMING

What's the secret to successful investing? Some people would say timing is everything. Particularly common among amateur investors is the concept of avoiding stocks when the market is "too high." In their view, the winning investors are the ones who know how to invest at the troughs and avoid the peaks.

Does timing make a difference? Not much, in the long run, even assuming you were 100 percent correct in calling the market's highs and lows. A recent study by Sanford C. Bernstein & Co., Inc., an investment firm headquartered in New York City, illustrates our point effectively.

Bernstein tracked the returns from two sets of five hypothetical $100,000 investments made in a Bernstein equity account between 1974 and 1994. The first group was made at the five market peaks during that period; the second group at the five market troughs. What was the difference in outcomes?

In each case, the total of $500,000 invested increased more than sixfold over the 21-year period—to $4.2 million under the worst conditions (investing at the peaks) and $4.7 million under the best conditions (investing at the troughs). While the $500,000 difference is not small change, the ending values are in fact similar.

The moral: stock investing is for the long term. While you may find it frustrating that you can't call the market peaks and valleys, your capital committed to stocks, regardless of when invested, would have grown substantially over time.

WORST-CASE SCENARIO			BEST-CASE SCENARIO		
$100,000 Invested at Each Market Peak			$100,000 Invested at Each Market Trough		
Date	Account Value	Amount Added	Date	Account Value	Amount Added
Jan. 1974	$ 100,000	$100,000	Oct. 1974	$ 100,000	$100,000
Jan. 1977	149,000	100,000	Apr. 1978	197,000	100,000
Dec. 1980	424,000	100,000	Dec. 1980	538,000	100,000
Sept. 1987	2,359,000	100,000	Sept. 1987	1,904,000	100,000
Jan. 1990	2,594,000	100,000	Jan. 1990	2,102,000	100,000
Dec. 1994	$4,218,000		Dec. 1994	$4,719,000	

Source: Analysis by Sanford C. Bernstein & Co., Inc.

- As with stocks, subcategories of bonds exhibit different patterns of return. Allocating a portion of your portfolio to each subcategory may enhance return and reduce risk through diversification.
- Cash equivalents preserve capital but offer little or no real return.
- Hard assets are an appropriate investment even though they may be illiquid (real estate) or volatile (gold). They provide portfolio diversification because of their lack of correlation with the price movements of stocks and bonds.

Selecting the Right Investment Mix

Clearly, it makes sense to diversify your investments across the major categories of assets. But how do you select the right mix? This brings us to the concept of asset allocation. Asset allocation refers to the mix of broad categories of investments in your portfolio. A portfolio allocation may consist of one-third stocks, one-third bonds, and one-third cash equivalents. Or it may be 70 percent stocks, 20 percent bonds, and 10 percent cash equivalents. The notion of asset allocation sounds simple. But it is the most important task in investing and will have far greater impact on your investment return than the subsequent decisions about which particular stock, bond, or cash securities to select. Many studies have shown this

Portfolios invested for long time horizons can afford to accept the greater short-term price volatility that comes with a more significant allocation to stocks. Shorter time horizons call for less volatile mixes.

to be true. One oft-cited example concluded that 91.5 percent of the investment return among a sample of pension funds was determined simply by the portfolio mix of asset classes. Only 4.6 percent came from actually picking the investments themselves.

What's the best asset mix? Most portfolios should be sufficiently diversified so that all major asset categories are represented. Beyond that, allocation decisions depend largely on your investment time horizon. Portfolios invested for long time horizons can afford to accept the greater short-term price volatility that comes with a more significant allocation to stocks. Shorter time horizons call for less volatile mixes.

WHAT DETERMINES INVESTMENT RETURNS?

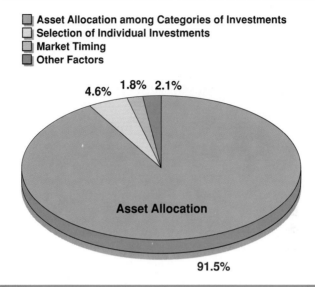

- Asset Allocation among Categories of Investments
- Selection of Individual Investments
- Market Timing
- Other Factors

Source: Brinson, Singer, Beebower, "Determinants of Portfolio Performance II: An Update," *Financial Analysts Journal,* May–June 1991.

The following tables cover performance of portfolios constructed from the three major asset categories and reflect their actual performance from 1969 to 1994. We have altered the asset mix and this results in substantial differences among the portfolios in both returns and volatility (as measured by the extent of losses and gains over one-year and five-year periods). A mix of 100 percent stocks offered the best overall gains in the period 1969 through 1994, but it also suffered the biggest losses in bad stock market years. On the other hand, the worst year for an all-cash portfolio was much better than the worst year for other mixes, but over the entire 26-year period the cash portfolio badly trailed all others and barely stayed ahead of inflation. A portfolio of one-third stocks, one-third bonds, and one-third cash showed significantly dampened risk compared to the all-stock portfolio, never losing more than 5 percent of its value in a year. Yet it delivered a much higher return than the all-cash portfolio.

ASSET ALLOCATION AMONG STOCKS, BONDS, AND CASH

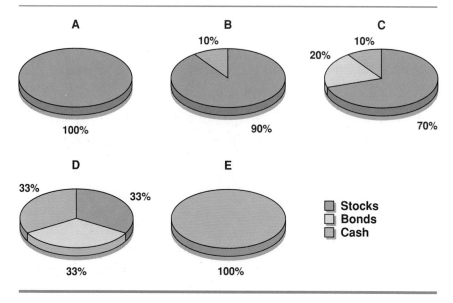

What is the right asset allocation strategy to meet your goal? It will vary depending on (1) whether you are investing for an accumulation goal or an income replacement goal such as retirement and (2) your investment time horizon. Let's say the planning horizon for your goal is 10 years from now when the money you are investing will be spent. Examples would include money you have invested for a specific goal such as purchasing a vacation home or for your child's freshman year in college. With a 10-year time frame, your assets should split fairly evenly between bonds (40 percent) and stocks (50 percent), with hard assets making up the remaining 10 percent of your portfolio. As you approach the year when the money will be needed, you should gradually reduce the amount committed to stocks and increase the portion of your investments allocated to cash and bonds. With a year to go, the money should be 100 percent in cash equivalents.

In a similar fashion, you should allocate your investments within the larger categories of stocks and bonds. The subcategories we recommend for bonds are short-term (1- to 3-year maturity) and intermediate-term (3- to 10-year maturity). We do not suggest long-term bonds for individual

GROWTH OF $10,000 INVESTMENT

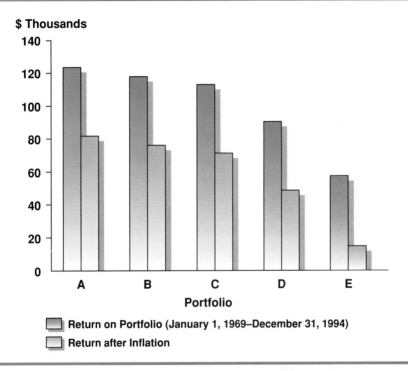

$ Thousands

Portfolio

■ **Return on Portfolio (January 1, 1969–December 31, 1994)**
□ **Return after Inflation**

PORTFOLIO RETURNS FOR 5-YEAR PERIODS ENDING 1973–1994

Growth of $10,000 Invested Five Years Ago

Portfolio	*Best Five-Year Performance* Period Ending	Return	*Worst Five-Year Performance* Period Ending	Return	Average Performance of Five-Year Periods
A	1989	$25,300	1974	$ 8,900	$17,700
B	1989	$23,900	1974	$ 9,300	$17,300
C	1986	$24,300	1974	$10,400	$17,100
D	1986	$21,900	1974	$12,300	$16,000
E	1983	$16,900	1994	$12,600	$14,300

PORTFOLIO LOSS OR GAIN IN STOCK MARKET 1969–1994

Six Loss Years

	Portfolio A	Portfolio B	Portfolio C	Portfolio D	Portfolio E
Stocks	100%	90%	70%	33%	0%
Bonds	0	0	20	33	0
Cash	0	10	10	33	100
1974	−26%	−23%	−17%	− 5%	+ 8%
1973	−15	−13	− 9	− 2	+ 7
1969	− 9	− 7	− 7	− 3	+ 7
1977	− 7	− 6	− 4	No change	+ 5
1981	− 5	− 3	− 2	+ 3	+15
1990	− 3	− 2	No change	+ 4	+ 8

Six Best Years

	Portfolio A	Portfolio B	Portfolio C	Portfolio D	Portfolio E
Stocks	100%	90%	70%	33%	0%
Bonds	0	0	20	33	0
Cash	0	10	10	33	100
1975	+37%	+34%	+30%	+19%	+ 6%
1980	+32	+30	+23	+14	+11
1985	+32	+30	+29	+23	+ 8
1989	+31	+29	+26	+19	+ 8
1991	+31	+28	+26	+18	+ 6
1976	+24	+22	+21	+16	+ 5

Source: © *Stocks, Bonds, Bills, and Inflation 1995 Yearbook*™, Ibbotson Associates, Chicago (annually updates work by Roger G. Ibbotson and Rex A. Sinquefield). Used with permission. All rights reserved.

investors because they have twice the volatility of intermediate-term bonds with little or no increase in return. Stock investments should be split among domestic and international stocks. We suggest three types of mutual funds to use for your suballocations to domestic stocks:

- **Growth and Income**—for capital growth and dividend income. These funds invest primarily in stocks of large companies with solid history of performance. Moderate risk.
- **Growth**—for capital growth with little or no dividend income. This group invests in faster-growing companies with some history. Moderate to higher risk.

ASSET ALLOCATION

Investing for a Specific Goal: Subcategory Allocations

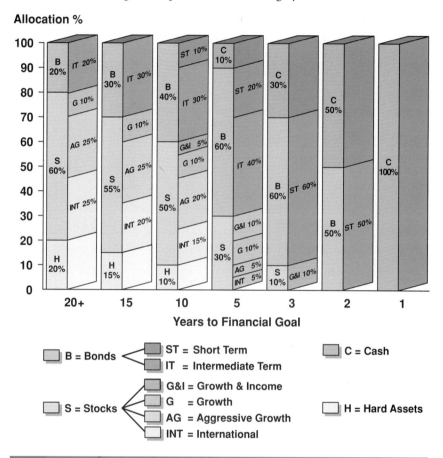

Allocation %

Years to Financial Goal

B = Bonds — ST = Short Term / IT = Intermediate Term
C = Cash
S = Stocks — G&I = Growth & Income / G = Growth / AG = Aggressive Growth / INT = International
H = Hard Assets

- **Aggressive Growth**—for long-term capital growth, no dividends. These funds invest in small companies with highly volatile returns. High risk.

(For more information on mutual fund investments, see Chapter 6.)

As an example of subcategory allocation, let's look at your 10-year accumulation goal, where you initially invest 50 percent of your assets in stocks. The subcategory stock allocations should be 5 percent to growth

ASSET ALLOCATION

Investing for Retirement: Subcategory Allocations

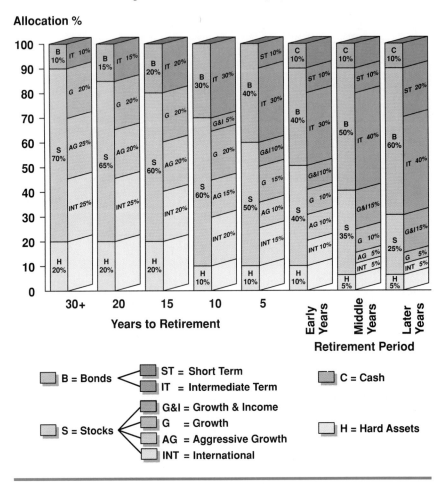

and income, 10 percent to growth, 20 percent to aggressive growth, and 15 percent to international stocks. As you approach the year when the money will be needed, the assets you have invested in stocks should be allocated increasingly toward less-risky bonds. Over the 10-year time frame, you would start with most of your bond allocation in intermediate-term issues, then move gradually toward short-term bonds and cash.

Focus on...

HOW TO TREAT A SUBSTANTIAL INVESTMENT IN EMPLOYER STOCK

Ownership of stock in your employer's company potentially can leave your asset allocation out of balance. For example, let's say you own employer stock that represents 50 percent of the value of your total investments. And let's say the appropriate asset allocation for your portfolio is 50 percent stocks, 40 percent bonds, and 10 percent hard assets. Does that preclude you from any further investment in stocks?

Our advice in general is to ignore the value of the employer stock for asset allocation purposes. Otherwise you may find yourself dangerously underdiversified. In this example, you would apportion the half of your portfolio that is not employer stock according to the 50–40–10 allocation of stocks, bonds, and hard assets to allow for sufficient diversity in your stock investments.

If you are investing for retirement your time horizon depends on your present age and your life expectancy. If you are currently 35 years old, for example, you will not likely tap into your retirement account for at least 30 years. And even if you are within a few years of retirement, you will most likely spend your dollars gradually over the remainder of your life, which would be another 25 years or more after retirement. In the case of retirement, because it is an income replacement goal, there will be no single point when you plan to expend all of your funds, as was the case with buying a vacation home or sending a child to college. And because of the longer time horizon involved, you will want to give relatively more weight to hard assets to protect against long-term harm from inflation. Someone with 30 years until retirement, for example, would want 70 percent of his or her investment assets in stocks, 20 percent in hard assets, and 10 percent in bonds. During retirement, your asset allocation should vary depending on whether you are in the early years (65 to 75), the middle years (75 to 85), or the later years (85 and older).

We will return to the subject of asset allocation as it pertains to the investment strategies to achieve your goals in the areas of college funding, retirement planning, and planning for your survivors in Section 3, Life Event Planning, of this book.

MUTUAL FUNDS

This chapter focuses on mutual funds and describes the ways they can be used to carry out the investment strategies covered in Chapter 5. Among the attractions of mutual funds are their broad diversification, professional management, daily liquidity, audited performance statistics, and automatic investment/reinvestment programs. We look at the major categories of mutual funds, with an explanation of the investment objective and performance characteristics of each. We also examine the variety of commission and fee structures used by mutual funds and describe the importance of mutual fund costs in determining long-term investment returns. We show you how to read a prospectus and give you advice on the value, and limitations, of mutual fund rankings and ratings.

Myth vs. Reality

Myth: Mutual funds should be chosen on the basis of past performance.

Reality: Numerous studies have concluded that recent past performance by itself is not a good predictor of how well a fund will do in the future. In choosing mutual funds, be sure to consider other factors as well, such as consistency of performance over the long term, the tenure of the fund manager, and the level of fees and expenses.

Myth: Never purchase a load fund.

Reality: There is no evidence that load funds perform any better or worse than no-load funds, apart from the effect of the load itself. You may need the expertise and assistance of a full-service broker in selecting a fund that meets your needs. If so, the load is one way of compensating the broker for providing that valuable service.

Myth: You can't lose money in a government bond fund.

Reality: Share prices of government bond funds fluctuate as interest rates rise and fall. When you sell your shares, they may be worth more or less than when you purchased them.

Myth: Small mutual funds offer better performance than big funds.

Reality: Not necessarily. In some categories, such as growth and income funds, the largest funds often do better than their average small competitor. Big funds can spread their costs over a larger base of assets, making per share expenses lower.

Myth: Municipal bond funds are tax free.

Reality: Dividends from municipal bond funds may be subject to state or local income taxes. In addition, you must pay tax on any capital gain income distributed by your municipal bond fund or any capital gain (or ordinary income) realized when you sell your shares.

Myth: You can tell how well your fund is doing by watching its net asset value in the mutual fund tables in your newspaper.

Reality: Yes, but watch carefully. When the fund distributes income from dividends or capital gains, its net asset value per share will drop by the amount of the distribution. That doesn't mean the fund lost money.

Myth: The best-performing mutual funds charge higher fees and commissions. You pay more for good performance.

Reality: Sometimes yes, sometimes no. The simple fact is that a fund's performance does not necessarily relate to its level of fees and commissions.

What Are Mutual Funds?

Mutual funds are open-end investment companies (see page 136 for description of closed-end funds) that pool money from individuals and invest it in securities such as stocks or bonds. They must distribute earnings from the securities in their portfolios, both dividends and realized capital gains, to their shareholders every year. Mutual funds fall into four broad categories based on the types of investments they make: stock funds, bond funds, money market funds, and "other," a catch-all fourth category for funds that don't fit exactly within the first three. This group would include hybrids that invest in both stocks and bonds as well as specialized funds that concentrate on real estate or precious metals.

Within those broad categories, mutual funds are grouped by their investment objectives. Recall from Chapter 4 that there are two fundamental types of investment return, current income and capital appreciation. Every investment offers the expectation of either income, capital appreciation, or some combination of the two. That's true of mutual funds as well. Every fund intends to provide either income, capital appreciation, or some blend of the two forms of return, as set out in its investment objective. For example, a growth fund may simply state that its objective is to seek long-term capital appreciation. Or it may elaborate by adding that current income is a secondary objective or, alternatively, say that current income is not a consideration.

Likewise, every fund has some strategy for achieving that goal by investing in a particular class or classes of assets and by using a certain set of techniques and approaches known as investment style. The growth fund we just mentioned, for example, may attempt to reach its objective by investing in stocks of large companies, and it may employ a "value" style (approach), looking for stocks whose prices appear low relative to their underlying value. (See the discussion on investment styles on page 117.)

> **Standard deviation is a statistic that measures the degree to which a series of annual returns varies above and below the group's average return. The greater the standard deviation, the greater the volatility of a particular fund category.**

The investment objective guides the fund manager in selecting securities. Aggressive growth funds, for example, aim for capital gains by purchasing stocks in fast-growing companies; however, they offer little or no current income. In contrast, corporate bond funds seek current income by investing in debt securities issued by large companies.

The return and risk characteristics of different funds vary according to their investment objectives. The accompanying chart ranks major fund categories by return and risk. Standard deviation, as we saw in Chapter 4, is a common benchmark of risk. It's a statistic that measures the degree to which a series of annual returns varies above and below the group's average return. The greater the standard deviation, the greater the volatility of a particular fund category.

SOME TOP PERFORMING MUTUAL FUND OBJECTIVES

10-Year Average*

	Total Return	Standard Deviation
Major Stock Fund Categories		
International—foreign stock	14.71%	16.49%
Aggressive growth	13.37	21.56
Small company	13.29	19.05
Growth	12.75	16.20
Growth and income	11.77	13.93
Equity income	11.59	12.30
Balanced	11.53	10.71
Asset allocation	10.13	11.55
S&P 500 Index	14.38	12.92†
Major Income Fund Categories		
High-yield bond	9.92%	7.08%
Corporate bond—general	9.46	5.34
Municipal bond—national	8.43	5.57
U.S. government bond—general	8.29	4.49
U.S. government bond—mortgage	8.33	4.45
Lehman Aggreg. Bond Index	9.94	7.18†

*As of December 31, 1994.
†Standard deviations calculated by Price Waterhouse.
Source: *Morningstar Mutual Funds OnDisc,* Morningstar, Inc., Chicago, IL.

Mutual funds are known formally as open-end investment companies because they continuously issue new shares and must always be willing to repurchase, or redeem, outstanding shares at a price based on the current market value of their investments. Share prices of mutual funds—other than money market funds—fluctuate with changes in the value of their portfolios. At the end of every business day, each mutual fund calculates the value of its portfolio and divides that figure by the number of shares outstanding to determine its net asset value per share, or price.

While mutual funds are not insured or guaranteed by any government agency, their operations are closely regulated by the U.S. Securities and Exchange Commission and by state agencies. Fund sponsors must provide extensive disclosure about their investment activities, risks, fees, and sales commissions. The Investment Company Act of 1940, the principal federal law regulating mutual funds, also requires funds to operate in the interest of shareholders and to take steps to safeguard their assets.

From $100 billion in total assets in 1980, mutual funds have grown to become a $2 trillion-plus industry. Their popularity can be attributed in part to the benefits of strict government regulation and full disclosure. Industry growth was also fueled by the introduction of money market funds in the 1970s, then accelerated by the stock and bond market rallies of the 1980s, which drew millions of new investors to the attractive returns offered by mutual funds. In the 1990s, the investment markets have stopped booming, but

Even a small investment in mutual fund shares brings you immediate, broad diversification . . . the single most important step you can take to reduce investment risk.

mutual funds continue to grow, due in part to the increasing popularity of 401(k) company savings plans. Four out of 10 American households now use mutual funds to invest for retirement or to meet other financial goals. Let's take a look at some of the features that make mutual funds such a popular investment vehicle.

Why You Should Use Mutual Funds
Diversification

A typical mutual fund invests in dozens of different securities; large funds own hundreds. As a result, even a small investment in mutual fund shares brings you immediate, broad diversification. And as we have seen in Chapter 5, diversification among asset categories is the single most important step you can take to reduce investment risk. Mutual funds enable you to take a step further by diversifying *within* a particular asset category.

Say, for example, that you purchase $5,000 worth of shares in a growth fund and its portfolio is invested equally in stocks of 75 different large companies. If one company went bankrupt and its stock became worthless, your share of the loss as a mutual fund shareholder would be less than a penny and a half on the dollar. To purchase stocks on your own, and achieve comparable diversification, you would need to invest in a substantial number of individual issues.

Market Participation

You can use a mutual fund to *buy* an entire market or category of investments. For example, index funds are available that seek the same return as the Standard & Poor's 500, an index of large-company stocks widely viewed as a proxy for the U.S. stock market. Other funds aim to mirror the returns of market indexes for global bonds, small-company stocks, or regional groupings of foreign stock markets. If your strategy is to allocate a portion of your assets across the entire U.S. stock market, an index fund will reliably deliver for you the same performance as that market, year in and year out. That kind of predictability is not available from other types of investments.

Professional Management

Many investors don't have the time or expertise to manage investments effectively. Mutual fund shareholders get the full-time services of a professional money manager. The manager takes responsibility for following the financial markets, monitoring securities in the fund's portfolio, and keeping an eye out for new investment opportunities.

Good managers are consistent in their approach, year after year. They aren't swayed by the ups and downs of the stock market and don't let emotions affect their judgment. When you own mutual funds, you can let the pros make the decisions for you.

Marketability

Shares in a mutual fund can be sold quickly and conveniently. The fund is required to establish a daily price for its shares. You can redeem your shares at that price and have the money wired to your bank the next business day. Or you can transfer the sale proceeds into a money market fund in the same fund family and write a check on it. This marketability allows for a ready sale of your investment, but has no effect on whether you will experience a gain or loss. Marketability means you can sell your investment with ease, either at a profit or a loss, depending on the net asset value at the time of the sale.

Low Cost

Mutual funds spread the costs associated with investing, such as administration, safekeeping, and management advisory fees, over a broad base of shareholders. Those costs, as a result, are less of a drag on the investment returns of individual shareholders. Brokerage charges and expenses for securities bought and sold by a mutual fund are also lower because funds can negotiate lower brokerage commissions. Caution: Costs and expenses vary widely among funds. (See page 123.)

Automatic Reinvestment Programs

Successful investing depends on the continuous long-term compounding of dividends and interest. If these earnings are not reinvested, or if they sit idle for days or weeks before you decide what to do with them, you are less likely to reach your investment goals. That's why the automatic reinvestment programs offered by mutual funds for dividend and capital gain distributions are so valuable. Once you elect to have dividends reinvested, everything is taken care of automatically and the power of compounding stays at work for you.

Variety of Investment Objectives

More than 5,000 mutual funds are currently available under dozens of different categories. That means you can meet just about any investment objective with a mutual fund.

Recordkeeping and Performance Monitoring

Mutual funds provide detailed statements and help you keep track of your original investment as well as any reinvested dividends and capital gains. You can easily monitor and evaluate your fund's performance through newspapers and mutual fund ratings services.

Administrative Ease

Fund families make it easy to invest in different kinds of funds and to switch money among funds with different objectives as the need arises. The fund family will also provide you with a consolidated account statement, showing the status of all the fund investments you maintain with that family. If you want to buy funds offered by several different families, consider using a discount brokerage service. They also offer ease of transfer among investments and the convenience of consolidated statements for all your funds.

Types of Mutual Fund Investments

Mutual funds come in many different varieties. Some types are well-diversified and therefore appropriate as "core" portfolio holdings. Others are highly specialized and volatile, suitable for no more than a small percentage of a typical investor's portfolio. Returns and risk vary, depending on investment objective. Here is a listing of the major categories of mutual funds.

Money Market Funds

Money market funds offer stability of principal with interest income that rises and falls with current market rates. Net asset value is held steady at $1 per share, so there is no gain or loss of principal.

Money market funds come in five varieties:

- General purpose—invest in obligations of large, highly rated corporations and banks, as well as federal government obligations.
- Treasury—invest in U.S. Treasury obligations.
- Government—invest in obligations of the U.S. Treasury and other U.S. government agencies.
- World—invest in dollar-denominated obligations of issuers inside and outside the United States.
- Tax-exempt—invest in obligations of state and local government agencies.

Money market funds make short-term, high-quality investments to limit risk. The average maturity of a money market fund portfolio cannot be more than 120 days. In addition to U.S. government obligations, they purchase commercial paper issued by corporations and banks that falls within the top two grades of debt as rated by a major credit rating agency such as Moody's Investor Services or Standard & Poor's Corp. As a result of their short maturities and high credit quality, money market funds provide a stable, highly liquid investment. Whatever you do with the rest of your portfolio, you will probably want to keep some of your money in a money market fund.

Bond Funds

Bond funds provide current income and can add diversification to a portfolio that includes stocks. Return is derived from dividend yield plus or minus share price changes. Bond fund returns will rise and fall depending on market conditions and characteristics of the bonds in the fund's portfolio. Following are the major types of bond funds.

U.S. Treasury or U.S. Government

Government funds invest in a variety of securities issued by the federal government. Because they are obligations of the government, these securities are considered to have the highest credit rating. Government securities, however, are subject to interest rate risk and prices of these funds will fluctuate. Some government funds invest exclusively in U.S. Treasury obligations, known as Treasury notes (2- to 10-year maturities) and Treasury bonds (10- to 30-year maturities). Others will invest in securities issued by federal agencies or those carrying federal government guarantees. Some government funds may invest in government securities of any maturity, depending on the manager's outlook for changes in bond prices. Others confine themselves to a particular range of maturities, such as short-, intermediate-, or long-term funds.

Mortgage

These funds, often known as Ginnie Mae funds, invest in securities guaranteed by a U.S. government agency such as the Government National Mortgage Association (Ginnie Mae). Income to pay the principal and interest on government mortgage bonds comes from pools of home mortgage loans. As with other fixed income funds, government mortgage funds are subject to interest rate risk. Their prices will fall when interest rates rise. Falling rates can also hurt government mortgage funds. When interest rates decline, many homeowners refinance at lower rates and pay off their old mortgages. This results in a return of principal to the government mortgage fund, which reinvests the money at the lower prevailing interest rate.

Corporate (Investment Grade)

Corporate bonds offer higher yields than government bonds because of their credit risk. Corporate borrowers range from big companies to small start-ups and financially troubled companies with speculative-grade ratings. Investment-grade corporate bond funds stick to issues rated BBB or higher by Moody's Investor Services and Standard & Poor's Corp., two of the leading credit rating agencies.

Corporate Bond (High Yield)

High-yield bonds, known as junk bonds, are debt securities issued by corporations that carry credit ratings below investment grade. Many high-yield securities were issued in connection with corporate mergers, restructurings, or recapitalizations during the 1980s. These bonds are considered speculative, are relatively risky, and therefore command higher yields.

Municipal   Municipal bond funds invest in obligations of state and local government agencies. The interest from municipal bonds is not generally subject to federal income taxes, so current income from a municipal bond fund is tax free. Bonds issued in the state where you live are usually free of state and local taxes as well. However, capital gains on municipal bond investments are subject to tax, as are market discounts resulting from purchasing bonds at less than face value. Some municipal funds concentrate on intermediate or long maturities. Others invest largely in high-yield or junk municipal bonds.

International Bond   International bond funds invest in securities of foreign issuers, often foreign governments or agencies with government backing. Those that invest in both U.S. and non-U.S. securities are known as global or world bond funds. International bond funds are popular because interest rates overseas may be much higher than those available in the United States. However, international bond funds are subject to currency risk. Their prices will fall if the dollar gains against other currencies, and they will rise if the dollar declines.

Hybrid Funds

Balanced funds seek both growth and income, usually investing in a relatively stable mix of about 50 percent of their assets in stocks, 30 percent to 40 percent in bonds, and the remainder in cash. A balanced fund can be an excellent core investment in your retirement portfolio.

Asset allocation funds also invest in stocks, bonds, and cash but will vary the mix depending on the portfolio manager's outlook for the investment markets. This kind of market timing carries the risk that the manager's view may be incorrect. For example, the fund could be concentrated in bonds and miss out on a stock market rally.

Stock Funds

Stock funds aim for growth in capital. Dividend income may be equally important as capital appreciation or less so, depending on the type of fund. Here are the major types of stock funds:

Equity Income

Equity income funds seek a high level of current income by investing in stocks of companies with high dividend yields such as utilities. Equity income funds will also purchase corporate bonds, preferred stocks, and convertible bonds. Growth is not a primary objective, although equity income funds will benefit when stock prices rise.

Growth and Income

Growth and income funds attempt to combine long-term capital growth with the compounding of dividend income. They are less volatile than growth funds but somewhat more volatile than equity income funds.

Growth

The primary objective of these funds is to provide capital appreciation. They typically give little or no consideration to current income and therefore offer relatively low dividend yields. Growth funds in the aggregate have demonstrated a risk level that is at or just below that of the S&P 500 Index.

Aggressive Growth and Small Company

The most risky categories of general stock mutual funds, aggressive growth funds and small-company funds, are for long-term investors. These funds invest in stocks of untested, fast-growing companies, many of which may not be closely tracked by Wall Street analysts. As a result, they may offer undiscovered values to investors willing to take the risk of buying them. Prices of these funds are highly volatile.

Sector

Sector funds invest in stocks of companies in a single industry or market sector such as energy, financial services, health care, utilities, software, airlines, chemicals, bio-tech, or real estate. They are much more risky than owning a diversified portfolio of stocks from many industries.

International Stock

These funds invest in stocks of companies outside the United States. Those that buy only non-U.S. stocks are known as international or foreign funds, while those investing both in U.S. and non-U.S. companies are called global or world funds. Many international funds specialize either in developed countries or developing/emerging markets. Further subcategories include funds that concentrate on regions, such as Europe or the Pacific, or individual countries.

Why Investment Style Is Important

We saw in Chapter 5 how the pattern of investment returns varies over time among asset categories. Small-company stocks may outperform all others one year, corporate bonds may do best the next, and large-company stocks may come out on top the year after. Returns will vary *within* a category of assets as well, depending on the management approach, or style, being used. Though there are variations in the styles used by some bond managers, the issue of style comes into play most significantly where stocks are concerned. Before you purchase shares in a mutual fund, particularly a stock fund, it is important to understand not only the fund's investment objective, but also the style used by the manager to obtain that objective.

Perhaps the most fundamental difference is between active managers and passive managers. Active managers research industries and companies, then purchase securities based on their outlook for each particular stock or bond. Some may buy and sell frequently, looking for short-term gains. Others tend to hold investments for long periods. In any case, active managers try to "beat" the average return of the market over time by purchasing securities whose returns will outpace the overall market return.

Passive managers, in contrast, seek to equal the average market return over time through the use of index funds, which track the performance of a broad market index, most commonly the S&P 500. Index funds consistently outshined the average actively managed stock mutual fund during the 1980s because the large-company stocks in the S&P 500 outperformed other categories of assets, including small-company stocks. More recently, the performance has tended to even out. In 1994, for example, the S&P 500 Index, and the index funds that track it, posted a 1.31 percent gain, while the average domestic stock fund lost 1.73 percent.

Active Management—Growth and Value Styles

Value managers and growth managers differ markedly in their approaches. Value managers look for stocks priced below some yardstick of their true worth. In essence, they are bargain hunters. They like out-of-favor companies with depressed stock prices in relation to cash flow. Even better for a value manager is a corporate balance sheet full of goodies that other managers have ignored. A stock may be priced at less than book value per share, or less than the amount of cash per share on its balance sheet. Or there may be assets such as real estate listed on the balance sheet at

GROWTH VS. VALUE STYLES

How They Differ

Stock Characteristics

Growth	Value
• Rapid and increasing growth in sales and earnings	• Unglamorous or out-of-favor businesses
	• High cash flow
• High price-to-book value and price-to-earnings ratios	• Low price-to-book value and price-to-earnings ratios

Risk Characteristics

Growth	Value
• High volatility with changes in expectations or earnings performance	• Less volatility
	• May take considerable time for the market to recognize value
	• Upturns in performance may not occur

historical value that have appreciated and could bring stockholders a windfall if sold.

Value managers tend to hold stocks for long periods, which reduces transaction costs and helps boost returns. And because value stocks by definition have low valuations in terms of price-to-earnings or price-to-cash flow ratios, they offer less volatility and risk in the short term than growth stocks.

For their part, growth managers look for companies that will generate above-average increases in earnings and outperform the market in the long run. They want stocks whose rate of future earnings growth is not yet reflected in their stock prices. And they are often willing to pay high prices, relative to the current earnings of these stocks, because they expect continued gains in future earnings that will support even higher stock price levels in the future.

Some growth managers are known as momentum players. They identify stocks whose prices are trending up, regardless of the reason, and then buy in, hoping the trend will continue. When the momentum slows, and the stock moves below the average of its recent prices, they sell.

GROWTH VS. VALUE STYLES

Performance

	Winner
1975	Value
1976	Value
1977	Value
1978	Growth
1979	Value
1980	Growth
1981	Value
1982	Growth
1983	Value
1984	Value
1985	Growth
1986	Value
1987	Growth
1988	Value
1989	Growth
1990	Growth
1991	Growth
1992	Value
1993	Value
1994	Growth

Source: Standard & Poor's Corp.

Other growth managers take a top-down approach, first making judgments about the overall direction of the stock market, based on their outlook for economic growth, interest rates, and other broad trends. Then they focus on industry groups that are likely to do relatively well under the particular economic scenario that they envision. Only then do they select the individual stocks from within those industry groups that appear most attractive.

Finally, there are the bottom-up managers. They ignore economic and stock market trends. Instead, they look at individual companies one at a time, regardless of industry, in search of stocks that appear to be good buys.

A note of caution here: Terminology can be confusing. Where mutual funds are concerned, the word *growth* is used in two different ways—to describe the investment *objective* of a certain category of funds ("growth funds") and to describe the investment *approach* of certain fund managers ("growth style"). Thus, one growth fund might be run by a growth-style manager, while another growth fund is managed by a value-style manager. The overall objective of the two funds is the same—capital appreciation— but the two managers seek to accomplish that objective in much different fashions. As a result, the return characteristics of these funds over time can be expected to be different.

Growth investing and value investing have been around for years, but only recently have stock market analysts come to appreciate the importance of these styles. Analysts have discovered that these two approaches make for meaningful differences in investment returns over time. Diversifying between growth-style and value-style investing brings significant benefits in terms of enhanced return and lower risk. As a result, investment information services such as Morningstar Mutual Funds have begun to offer "Style Box" matrices illustrating the particular approach used by each stock fund manager.

Return figures show seesawing performance over the years between value-style and growth-style investing. In the 20 years from 1975 and 1994, for example, value investing came out on top 11 times, while growth investing was No. 1 9 times, according to indexes of each style's returns tracked by Standard & Poor's Corp. An investor whose portfolio was exposed to only one style over those years lost out almost half the time.

Passive Management—Index Funds

Instead of an active money manager researching and selecting individual stocks or bonds, index funds use a passive approach. An index fund is a mutual fund designed to track a market index, such as the Standard & Poor's 500 Index. It does so either by owning the stocks (or bonds) that make up the index or by holding a statistically representative sample of securities whose returns are expected to closely track the returns of the index.

The reasons for investing in an index fund are both theoretical and practical. The notion of index investing was introduced by economists who argued that stock and bond markets are highly efficient. Information on each security and its prospects is widely transmitted and instantly incorporated into market prices, the theory holds, so that stocks and bonds at all times are accurately valued. As a result, it is difficult for investors to find securities that are mispriced and consistently outperform the market by investing in them. The economists predicted that simply buying and holding all the securities in a broad market index would yield better results than active management over the long run, in large part because of the higher expenses associated with actively managed portfolios.

Passive investing gained wide acceptance in the 1970s among institutional investors such as pension funds, which now have more than $300 billion in index funds. Over the years, indexing has begun to catch on with individual investors as well. Although there are many types of index funds, by far the most popular variety tracks the S&P 500 Index, a group of large-company stocks that represents about 70 percent of the total value of all U.S. stocks. Other indexes used for index investing include the broader Wilshire 5000 Index, which tracks more than 6,000 U.S. stocks, and the Russell 2000 Index, an index of small-company stocks.

Index funds derive much of their long-term attractiveness from two practical advantages: predictability and low costs. Index investing is predictable in the sense that it can be relied on to deliver a market average return. By "owning the market," an index investor is buying the return of *all* the securities in a certain asset category, such as the S&P 500's large-company stocks. An investor in an actively managed fund, on the other hand, is buying the return of *some* securities, those chosen by the manager. Some managers will make better choices than others, so their individual performance relative to the market is not predictable.

The cost advantages of index funds are another important consideration. An index fund offers low costs because the manager's only job is to make sure the fund's portfolio closely tracks the composition of its target index. Index funds also trade securities less often than actively managed funds, saving money on brokerage commissions and dealer markups. For instance, portfolio turnover for the Vanguard Index Trust 500 Portfolio, an index fund that tracks the S&P 500, was 7 percent in 1994, compared to an average turnover of 74 percent for all stock funds, according to Morningstar.

Heavy trading and the higher advisory fees for active management can each add one percentage point or more in annual expenses, as compared to passive index management. That means an actively managed fund will probably have to exceed the gross return (before transaction costs and advisory fees) of an index by up to two percentage points to beat the net return of an index fund investing in the same asset class.

Index funds have another attraction as well. They are tax-efficient because low portfolio turnover results in fewer capital gains distributions. This can make a difference if you are investing on a fully taxable basis, in other words outside a tax-deferred account such as a 401(k) or IRA. As a result of their lower costs and tax efficiency, index funds over the long term are usually competitive with even the most successful active managers.

Active vs. Passive

Which is better, active management or indexing? The answer may depend the asset class you are considering. Economists can marshal substantial evidence to bolster their belief that indexing is hard to beat when investing in highly efficient markets, such as the market for large-company stocks. A study conducted in 1992 by Morningstar Mutual Funds, for example, compared the performance of 78 actively managed mutual funds that invested mostly in stocks from the S&P 500 with the performance of the

INDEXING PERFORMS WELL WITH LARGE-COMPANY STOCKS

		Index Fund*	Actively Managed Funds (78)
3-year	total return	15.0%	14.0%
5-year	total return	12.3	9.9
10-year	total return	16.0	14.3
3-year	risk rating	0.84	0.85
5-year	risk rating	0.87	0.89
10-year	risk rating	0.86	0.90

Note: 1.0 equals the average equity risk score.

*Vanguard Index Trust 500 Portfolio, tracking the S&P 500 Index.

Source: *Morningstar Mutual Funds,* January 10, 1992, Morningstar, Inc., Chicago, IL.

Vanguard Index Trust 500 Portfolio. Due to their higher fees, trading costs, portfolio holdings of some cash, and perhaps their lack of stock-picking success, the actively managed funds as a group consistently lagged the index over a 10-year period despite taking on more risk.

Indexing does not always come out on top, however. In less efficient markets, such as those for small- and medium-size company stocks, active management seems to do better. After testing large-company funds, Morningstar ran a similar study with small- and medium-size company funds to see whether active management or indexing would win. This time Morningstar's analysts looked at 95 actively managed funds owning stocks with market values of between $400 million and $2 billion. They compared the performance of the funds with that of the Vanguard Index Extended Market Portfolio, an index fund that tracks the Wilshire 4500 Index of small- and medium-size company stocks. The actively managed funds in the study owned stocks with the same range of market values as the stocks represented in the index. In this instance, the actively managed funds outperformed the index fund, although with a higher level of risk.

The two Morningstar studies have implications for investments in other asset classes. Few actively managed funds may be able to add enough value to make up for their added costs when investing in large, highly efficient markets. Besides large-company domestic stocks, such markets include government bonds and investment-grade corporate bonds. In these arenas, index funds merit careful consideration. On the other hand, funds in less efficient markets may thrive through astute

ACTIVE MANAGEMENT DOES BETTER
WITH SMALL-COMPANY STOCKS

		Index Fund*	Actively Managed Funds (95)
3-year	total return	12.8%	15.7%
5-year	total return	9.6	10.3
3-year	risk rating	0.98	1.12
5-year	(not available)		

Note: 1.0 equals the average equity risk score.
*Vanguard Index Extended Market Portfolio, tracking the Wilshire 4500 Index.
Source: *Morningstar Mutual Funds,* January 10, 1992, Morningstar, Inc., Chicago, IL.

management, offering their shareholders attractive returns and acceptable risks even if their expense levels are somewhat high. Among the categories of assets fitting in this category are stocks of small- and medium-size companies, foreign-company stocks, high-yield bonds, and convertible bonds.

Sorting Out Mutual Fund Fees and Expenses

At one time, mutual funds came in just two varieties, load and no-load. The differences between them were clear, and the two types of funds were easy to tell apart. Load funds, distributed through stockbrokers, carried a uniform front-end sales commission. With a front-end load, the commission is added to the net asset value to determine the fund's offering price.

No-load funds, on the other hand, were sold directly by mutual fund sponsors at net asset value per share, without a sales charge. If you needed help in selecting a fund and valued the advice offered by a broker, a load fund was the right choice for you. If you could select a fund on your own, there was no need to pay a sales commission, so a no-load fund made the most sense.

In recent years, the distinction between load and no-load funds has been blurred as mutual fund companies developed new ways to market and distribute their products. In addition to the two traditional varieties, load and no-load, funds can now be bought featuring low loads, back-end loads, or level loads. These changes have benefited mutual fund investors by providing them with more choices. But this new array of choices also makes it increasingly difficult to evaluate funds and select the one that is right for you. Which is better, a load fund or a no-load fund? A front-end load or a back-end load? Investors often focus too narrowly on questions like these when instead they should be looking at the entire range of fees charged by a particular fund.

The long-term impact of fees can be illustrated by looking at the returns of a familiar group of stocks, the Standard & Poor's 500. If you had invested $10,000 at the beginning of 1969 in the S&P 500, your money would have grown to $123,600 26 years later at the end of 1994, ignoring taxes. The investment, of course, is hypothetical because the S&P 500 is an index of stock values, not a mutual fund. And not being a mutual fund, it has no sales load or annual expenses acting as a drag on its returns.

Let's add a front-end load and see what would have happened. If you had paid a 5 percent sales commission in 1969, the effect on your return would have been small. Twenty-six years later, the value of your investment would have been $117,400, just 5 percent less than the $123,600 you accumulated without the load. Contrast that with the damage caused to your returns if the S&P 500 featured annual expenses of the same magnitude as those levied by many mutual funds over the 1969–1994 period. With an expense ratio of 1 percent (i.e., subtracting 1 percent from the S&P 500's total return every year), your investment would have grown to $97,200. Raise the expense ratio to 1.3 percent, roughly the average amount charged by stock mutual funds as a group, and your total would have dropped to $90,400. At an expense ratio of 2 percent, the total would have fallen to $76,300. Put another way, your investment return with a 1 percent expense ratio would have been 27 percent greater over 26 years than your return with a 2 percent expense ratio ($97,200 vs. $76,300).

The above example was hypothetical. Let's turn to a real one by looking at the category of foreign-stock funds. In 1993, the average expense ratio for funds in this category covered by Morningstar Mutual Funds was 1.63 percent. But the range of fees charged by individual funds was remarkably wide. The most costly fund reported an expense ratio of 2.94 percent, seven times the cheapest fund's 0.40 percent ratio. Did investors in the highest-expense fund get better performance? The answer is no. The most expensive and least expensive funds posted virtually identical 1993 returns—30.40 percent and 30.45 percent, respectively—after deducting expenses.

What about the long term? The cheapest foreign-stock fund's average annual return over the 10 years ending with 1993 was 16.16 percent. For the most costly fund, hurt by the long-term drag of high expenses, the average 10-year return was 11.42 percent. For every dollar earned over that period by shareholders of the lowest-cost fund, shareholders of the highest-cost fund earned just 70 cents. As these examples show, time and the effects of compounding greatly magnify the impact of annual expenses. The lesson for mutual fund investors? Know what you are buying when you invest in a mutual fund.

Fund costs fall into three basic categories: sales loads, annual operating expenses, and a fund's costs of buying and selling portfolio securities.

Sales Loads

If levied when you buy shares, these commissions are known as front-end loads. They typically range between 4 percent and 5.75 percent. Low-load refers to a front-end load of 3 percent or less. These commissions come right off the top, reducing the amount of your net investment. In that sense, front-end loads are understated because they customarily are expressed as a percentage of the gross amount you pay, rather than the amount that actually gets invested. For example, a 5 percent front-end load on a $10,000 investment equals $500. But since the broker keeps the $500, your actual investment totals $9,500 and $500 is 5.3 percent of that amount. It also turns out that 5.3 percent is the return you will need on the $9,500 over the first year to break even on your $10,000 total investment.

In addition, the investment performance of front-end load funds is typically overstated because independent rating services generally ignore the effect of the load in calculating returns. Using the above example of $10,000 used to buy a fund with a 5 percent front-end load, let's assume further that the fund reported an 8 percent total return over the next year. That 8 percent applies to the $9,500 you actually invested, so your return in dollar terms amounted to $760 ($9,500 × .08). But that represents only a 7.6 percent return on your full $10,000 ($760/$10,000).

As an alternative to front-end commissions, many load funds offer shares with back-end commissions, known as contingent deferred sales charges or redemption fees. These charges apply if you sell your shares within a certain time. They gradually decline, typically over three to seven years, and are then eliminated. Another alternative is the level load, where the front-end commission is replaced by a permanent fee. Back-end loads and level loads may sound like a better deal than front-end loads, but they invariably are accompanied by higher annual fees. And as we have seen above, high annual fees are much more costly in the long term than front-end loads.

Annual Operating Expenses

Fund expenses are expressed as a percentage of a fund's average assets for a particular year, a figure known as the expense ratio. They fall into four general headings—management fees, 12b-1 fees, service fees, and other expenses—each listed as a separate item in mutual fund fee tables.

The management fee compensates the fund's investment adviser. Management fees will vary depending on a fund's investment objective. Fees for managing specialized stock funds are relatively high, while those for bond and money market funds are low.

The 12b-1 fee is for distribution-related expenses such as advertising or brokerage commissions and can range up to 0.75 percent of assets each year. The service fee, limited to 0.25 percent of assets, is used to compensate brokers or others who service mutual fund shareholders. Many funds don't charge 12b-1 or service fees. Others collect both up to the combined 1 percent limit as a substitute for a traditional front-end load. In any case, these fees are not officially classified as sales charges.

Finally, the other-expense category covers miscellaneous costs including accounting, administration, recordkeeping, and legal fees.

Transaction Costs

The third category of expenses includes the commissions that mutual funds pay to brokers when they buy or sell securities. These costs effectively reduce investment returns. The greater the rate of portfolio trading, the greater the cost of brokerage commissions and markups. Mutual funds don't report these brokerage expenses, so they are not listed in the fee table or included in a fund's expense ratio. But you can get a relative gauge of trading activity at different funds by comparing their turnover rates. Funds with high turnover rates relative to their peers are paying higher transaction expenses.

Examining a Fee Table

To get a picture of a fund's fees and expenses, turn to the fee table at the front of every fund prospectus. The prospectus is a legal document describing the fund. By law it must be provided to you before you purchase shares. The fact that the fee table is at the front of this document serves as reminder of just how important fees and expenses will be in determining a fund's returns.

The accompanying table combines fee data from two different funds for comparison purposes. Fund No. 1 is a no-load fund. Fund No. 2 has three classes of shares. Class A shares feature a 4.5 percent front-end load. Class B shares have a 4 percent back-end load that is phased out over six years, plus a 0.75 percent 12b-1 fee that is also phased out after six years when B shares convert to A shares. Class C has a level load in the form of a permanent 12b-1 fee of 0.75 percent.

FEE TABLE INFORMATION

		Fund No. 2		
	Fund No. 1	Class A	Class B	Class C
Shareholder Transaction Expenses				
Maximum sales load on purchases	None	4.50%	None	None
Maximum deferred load on redemptions	None	None	4.00%	None
Annual Fund Operating Expenses				
Management fees	0.70%	0.75%	0.75%	0.75%
12b-1 fees	—	—	0.75	0.75
Service fees	0.00	0.25	0.25	0.25
Other expenses	0.31	0.74	0.74	0.74
Total operating expenses	1.01%	1.74%	2.49%	2.49%

The following example illustrates the fees and expenses that you would incur on a $1,000 investment in these funds over various time periods, assuming (1) a 5 percent annual rate of return, and (2) redemption at the end of each period. B shares have a contingent deferred sales charge of 4 percent in the first year declining to zero at the end of the sixth year. Then they are automatically converted to A shares.

	Fund No. 1	Class A	Class B	Fund No. 2 Class B†	Class C
1 year	$ 10	$ 62	$ 65	$ 25	$ 25
3 years	32	97	108	78	78
5 years	56	135	153	133	133
10 years*	124	241	247	247	292

*10-year figures assume conversion of Class B shares to Class A shares at the end of the sixth year following the date of purchase.

†Assumes no redemption of B shares.

Reading a Mutual Fund Prospectus

Here is a section-by-section checklist of issues to consider when reading a mutual fund prospectus. If you have questions about a fund, call the fund's customer service number and request additional information.

Costs   The fee table will offer a complete breakdown of costs and fees. Annual operating costs will also be shown in the financial tables at the front of the prospectus.

Investment Objective   The fund's objective should match your own. The prospectus will describe the fund's primary objective and may list a secondary objective as well. For example, a growth fund's prospectus might list capital appreciation as a primary objective, with dividend income as a secondary objective.

Management Policies   The prospectus will describe the types of securities the fund intends to purchase. It may list minimum or maximum percentage limitations for certain categories of investments. For example, the fund's policy may require the manager to invest at least 80 percent of the fund's assets in U.S. Treasury securities. Or it may limit holdings of foreign securities to 25 percent of assets.

Investment Techniques   If unusual or risky investment techniques are authorized, this section will describe them. Some funds, for example, are allowed to borrow as part of a strategy to increase their returns. Others may sell stocks short, a way to profit from stock price declines. Or

Focus on...

A GUIDE TO MUTUAL FUND LOADS AND FEES

Back-end load—A sales commission paid when you sell your shares. Also known as a contingent deferred sales charge, exit fee, or redemption fee. Back-end loads are normally phased out over three to seven years.

Break points—Dollar amounts at which the front-end load is discounted when you make a large mutual fund investment. For example, a fund with a front-end load of 5 percent may reduce the charge to 4 percent if you invest $50,000, to 3 percent if your investment totals $100,000, and so forth.

Expense ratio—Annual fund operating expenses expressed as a percent of assets. Operating expenses include management advisory fees, 12b-1 fees, servicing fees, and other expenses.

Fee table—A detailed breakdown of mutual fund fees and expenses appearing near the front of a mutual fund prospectus.

Front-end load—A sales commission of up to 8.5 percent collected when you purchase mutual fund shares.

Management advisory fees—The fee charged by the investment adviser for managing the fund's investment portfolio.

Multiple class shares—Mutual funds may offer several classes of shares (Class A, Class B, etc.) in the same fund, each with a different type of sales commission. The features of a particular class may vary among fund companies, but these categories are widely used:

- A shares carry front-end loads, ranging from 4 percent to 8.5 percent.
- B shares feature a back-end load, or contingent deferred sales charge. They also have greater annual expenses than A shares because they charge relatively high 12b-1 fees. In many cases, B shares convert to A shares at the end of the phaseout period for the deferred sales charge.
- C shares carry a level load, typically 3 percent of assets annually.

Level load—An ongoing sales commission based on the value of your mutual fund shares. You pay the fee as long as you own the shares.

Low load—A front-end load of 3 percent or less.

12b-1 fees—An annual fee of up to 0.75 percent of assets intended to pay for distribution-related expenses, such as advertising or brokerage commissions. If a fund has a 12b-1 fee, its front-end load cannot exceed 6.25 percent.

Service fees—An annual fee of up to 0.25 percent of assets to compensate brokers or others who service mutual fund shareholders.

Turnover rate—A measure of a mutual fund's trading activity in a given year. It is figured by taking the lesser of the fund's total purchases or total sales of securities (not counting securities with maturities under one year) and dividing by average monthly assets.

Other expenses—This category covers miscellaneous costs including accounting, recordkeeping, and legal fees.

they may purchase derivatives, which are esoteric securities that can be used either to hedge risks or to speculate.

Risks   This section describes the risks involved in the fund's investments. For example, funds that invest in foreign securities are exposed to currency risk. Other funds may hold low-quality debt securities posing substantial credit risk. Or they may attempt to enhance return through high-risk techniques involving the use of such financial instruments as futures or options. Read this section carefully. If you don't understand the risks being discussed, or feel uncomfortable about them, ask questions before investing in the fund.

Holdings   The prospectus may list all the fund's investments, or its 10 largest investments. If you do not get a clear picture of the fund's portfolio, ask for a copy of the most recent annual or semiannual report. On request, the mutual fund company will also provide you with a "Statement of Additional Information," also known as Part B of the prospectus, which lists portfolio investments.

Past Performance   This table should provide 1-, 5-, and 10-year performance figures, or figures from the fund's inception if it is less than 10 years old. It should also supply a benchmark such as the Standard & Poor's 500 Index, against which the performance figures can be compared. Stock funds will show performance in terms of total return, while bond funds will specify yield and total return. Money market funds will report average yield. In some cases, the prospectus will also show the fund's performance in comparison to the group of competitive funds with the same investment objective.

Manager   You should know the name, qualifications, track record, and tenure of the fund's manager. Successful funds have a record of management continuity.

Turnover   The annual turnover rate for portfolio investments will be listed. All other things being equal, buy the mutual fund with lower turnover.

Services   If there are services you consider important, such as check writing, free exchange between funds in the same mutual fund family, telephone exchange privileges, or automatic investing, check to make sure those services are listed in the prospectus.

Minimum   Most funds require a minimum investment to open an account. Some will agree to waive the minimum if you set up an automatic investment plan.

Rankings, Ratings, and Past Performance

The exploding popularity of mutual fund investing has been accompanied by another boom—the explosion of information about funds themselves. Many business and investment magazines offer special annual or quarterly issues devoted to mutual fund investing. Major newspapers carry multiple pages of daily fund price quotations. Specialized information services, including Lipper Analytical Services, Morningstar Mutual Funds, and the Value Line Mutual Fund Survey, generate huge amounts of comparative data about fund performance characteristics and portfolio investments.

This wealth of information enables investors to identify the group of funds that meets their own objective and then look for the one that appears most appropriate. You may be shopping for a growth fund, for example, and come across one with a strong 10-year performance record. But when you look it up in Morningstar Mutual Funds you discover the manager is new, meaning that the 10-year return belongs to someone else. Another fund may seem attractive, too, until you learn it has experienced much higher-than-average volatility when compared to its peers. These valuable information services are available at most public libraries.

The downside of the mutual fund information boom comes from the overuse of the rankings and ratings generated by investment publications and fund information services. Rankings are listings of funds in descending order, based on their total return over a particular period. Ratings are evaluations of funds. Morningstar Mutual Funds, for example, bases its ratings (5-Star = Highest, 1-Star = Lowest) on a fund's risk/reward ratio relative to other funds in its category.

Rankings and ratings such as these convey useful information, particularly as a starting point for evaluating a group of funds with a common investment objective, one that you have already decided is the appropriate objective for your needs. Morningstar, for example, says its ratings should not be used for one-shot investment decisions but rather as a first screen

WHAT A DIFFERENCE A DECADE MAKES

How the Top 20 Domestic Stock Funds from the 1970s
Performed during the 1980s

Fund Name	1970–1980		1980–1990	
	Rank	Average Annual Return	Rank	Average Annual Return
1. Twentieth Century Growth	1	27.12%	151	11.24%
2. Templeton Growth	2	22.34	101	12.68
3. Quasar Associates	3	20.56	161	10.99
4. 44 Wall Street	4	20.13	260	−16.83
5. Pioneer II	5	20.12	112	12.49
6. Twentieth Century Select	6	19.95	17	15.78
7. Security Ultra	7	19.74	249	2.22
8. Mutual Shares Corp.	8	19.52	29	15.23
9. Charter Fund	9	19.50	97	12.78
10. Magellan Fund	10	18.87	1	21.27
11. Over-the-Counter	11	18.13	210	9.24
12. American Capital Growth	12	18.11	243	4.90
13. American Capital Venture	13	17.97	136	11.75
14. Putnam Voyager	14	17.41	65	13.88
15. Janus Fund	15	17.29	18	15.74
16. Weingarten Equity	16	17.28	30	15.21
17. Hartwell Leverage Fund	17	16.92	222	8.44
18. Pace Fund	18	16.82	50	14.53
19. Acorn Fund	19	16.50	147	11.36
20. Stein Roe Special Fund	20	15.75	48	14.54
Average return of the 20 funds		19.01%		10.87%
Average return of equity funds		9.74		11.56
Return of S&P 500		8.45		13.87
Number of equity funds with 10-year records		211		260

Source: Burton G. Malkiel, *Returns from Investing in Equity Mutual Funds 1971–1991,* Center for Economic Policy Studies, Working Paper No. 15, Princeton University, 1993.

AND THE LAST SHALL BE FIRST

Average Total Return for Previous 5 Years

	As of 1989*	Rank	As of 1994*	Rank
International stock	20.6%	1	9.4%	6
Equity income	14.3	2	11.2	5
Growth and income	14.2	3	11.9	4
Growth	13.3	4	13.9	3
Small-company	10.3	5	15.9	2
Aggressive-growth	8.9	6	16.1	1

*February 28, 1989, and February 28, 1994.

Source: *Morningstar Mutual Funds,* Morningstar, Inc., Chicago, IL.

for the evaluation of a fund. The longer the period covered by a ranking or rating, the more meaningful it becomes.

Rankings and ratings, however, share a common weakness. They are based on past performance, and past performance is an unreliable predictor of future performance. Over short periods, such as a single quarter or year, the top performers tend to be highly volatile funds such as sector funds or aggressive growth funds. Odds are that in the next period these same funds will be among the worst performers because of their volatile nature. Even over longer time frames, however, past performance is an imperfect indicator. For example, out of the 20 top-performing stock funds during the 1970s, only 2 were able to stay on the top 20 list for the 1980s, according to a study by Burton G. Malkiel, professor of economics at Princeton University. Only 7 stayed in the top 100 performers, Malkiel found.

Over long economic and stock market cycles, which can last a decade or more, the relative performance of different categories of assets tends to rotate. For example, small-company stocks undergo long periods of under- and overperformance in relation to other types of investments. Their slump in the 1980s left the small-company and aggressive growth mutual funds that invest in these stocks with lowly rankings and ratings. As a result, many investors shunned them. Those investors lost out when the cycle turned. Small-company stocks rallied strongly at the beginning of the 1990s and returns from small-company and aggressive growth funds shot up.

ARE ALL-WEATHER FUND RATINGS MEANINGFUL?

The Long-Term Performance of *Forbes* Honor Roll of Mutual Funds

	Subsequent 10-Year Total Return of Honor Roll	Subsequent 10-Year Total Return of S&P 500	Ratio of Honor Roll's 10-Year Return to 10-Year Return of S&P 500
1976	392.20%	280.02%	1.40
1977	345.50	264.09	1.31
1978	344.65	312.62	1.10
1979	360.01	351.27	1.02
1980	320.66	401.22	0.80
1981	197.85	266.65	0.74
1982	294.23	402.61	0.73

	Subsequent 5-Year Total Return of Honor Roll	Subsequent 5-Year Total Return of S&P 500	Ratio of Honor Roll's 5-Year Return to 5-Year Return of S&P 500
1983	72.15%	113.64%	0.63
1984	58.45	103.24	0.57
1985	112.72	151.73	0.74
1986	61.49	85.28	0.72
1987	86.91	103.66	0.84

Source: Burton G. Malkiel, *Returns from Investing in Equity Mutual Funds 1971–1991*, Center for Economic Policy Studies, Working Paper No. 15, Princeton University, 1993.

The difficulty of drawing meaningful conclusions from past performance becomes even greater when performance in both bull and bear markets is being compared. Most stock funds do well in bull markets, because most stocks go up during those times. Conversely, most stock funds do poorly in bear markets. Further, those funds that do best in bull markets are probably investing in the type of stocks (i.e., volatile stocks) that will cause them to fare poorly in bear markets. Good bear market funds, on the other hand, those whose bear market losses are relatively low, will not recover sharply in a market rally.

The barriers to all-weather fund performance are reflected in the *Forbes* magazine rankings. Of the 465 stock funds that *Forbes* ranked for up and down markets in 1994, only one was able to stay in the top 20 percent among its peers during good times and bad. And only 43 of the 465 made it into the top 45 percent among peers in both up and down markets. Professor Malkiel of Princeton looked at the record of the *Forbes* all-weather honor roll funds from 1976 though 1990 and found that the performance of the magazine's selections lagged far behind the S&P 500 for most of that period.

This does not mean you should ignore past performance in selecting a mutual fund. We don't know the future, so all we have to go on is the past. Past performance can be a useful guide if it is not overemphasized and is used along with other relevant information when selecting a fund.

Selecting Mutual Funds

At first glance, selecting mutual fund investments appears to be an impossible challenge. With more than 5,000 funds now available, where do you start? Our approach here will be to begin with the asset allocation decision discussed in Chapter 5. Remember, more than 90 percent of the performance of your portfolio will be due to the mix of investments you select—your asset allocation—and less than 10 percent to the particular funds you choose. In other words, once you have determined the appropriate asset allocation, 90 percent of your investment decision is behind you. Here are the characteristics you should look for in selecting funds and completing the final 10 percent of the process.

1. **A fit with your asset allocation.** This is the starting point. You should be looking for funds that match your subcategory allocation.
2. **Above-average performance.** Compare the fund's return to the average return of its peer group over different time periods. Select a fund that beats the average over long periods.
3. **Below-average risk.** Likewise, look at risk ratings. Funds that beat the averages in terms of return are also likely to experience greater-than-average volatility, or risk. You want to find one with *above*-average return and *below*-average volatility.
4. **A consistent track record.** A fund whose returns have consistently placed it in the first or second quartile among its peers, and rarely in the bottom quartile, will be a better choice than an erratic up-and-down fund with the same overall average return.
5. **A complementary style.** Make sure your portfolio has a mix of styles. If you own two stock funds, for example, make sure one is a value style fund and the other is managed with a growth style. As you add stock funds, alternate between styles.

Focus on...

A Look at Closed-End Funds and Unit Investment Trusts

A closed-end fund is set up with a fixed number of shares, unlike a mutual fund, which issues and redeems shares on demand. The closed-end fund's sponsor sells these shares through underwriters at an initial public offering, in the same way that common stock of a corporation is issued. The underwriting is a onetime transaction that brings in a fixed amount of money for the fund to invest.

After that, the sponsor of the closed-end fund is not required to issue or redeem shares from investors. Instead, the shares trade on a stock exchange, where investors can buy or sell them at a price that may be above or below net asset value. In other words, a closed-end fund might have a net asset value of $10 a share, but investors might be willing to pay $12 a share for it, or they may be willing to pay only $9 a share.

Some fund companies use the closed-end fund as a vehicle to invest in securities that are not readily marketable. For example, the closed-end structure is often used for funds that invest in a single country such as Korea, Taiwan, Brazil, India, and Thailand, where stock markets are small and illiquid and local authorities may want to limit the amount of outside investment coming in.

The pros of closed-end funds include the following:

- Because the shares trade in the secondary market, which means on a stock exchange, the portfolio manager doesn't have to worry about new money coming in or about redemptions. That means he or she doesn't have to invest a big inflow of new cash, or keep cash on hand for a rash of redemptions. Instead, the manager can concentrate on investing a stable pool of assets to get the best return for the shareholder.
- Many of the closed-end funds offer the only opportunity to invest in special types of securities such as those of a single foreign country. There are about 20 closed-end funds that invest in only one country. Foreign investments in many of these countries are limited by their governments and these funds may provide the only opportunity to get into a fast-growing market.

And the cons:

- The fund's ability to sell at a discount or premium compared to its net asset value per share adds risk to the underlying investment.
- If you invest in a closed-end fund at the initial offering, you pay underwriting fees as well as a broker's commission. These fees typically range between 6 and 8 percent of your investment. So if you put $1,000 into the initial offering of a closed-end bond fund, perhaps $920 would actually be invested.

Focus on...

concluded

- If you buy a one-country fund, you are investing in a highly volatile instrument. The markets in many of these countries are small and they are dominated by a few large companies. Stocks may not be readily marketable. Trading volume may be thin and erratic. If the country faces a serious political problem and the stock prices fall at the same time the currency is devalued, your investment could be decimated.

The other relative of the mutual fund is the unit investment trust. A unit investment trust is a fund that has both a fixed number of shares and a fixed portfolio, usually composed of bonds. This fund is not managed. Instead the bonds are purchased and they remain in the fund until they mature. The investor who buys a slice of a unit trust gets a share of the income and appreciation in the securities. Although there is no secondary market for shares of a unit trust, it is usually possible to resell them to the broker.

6. **Below-average expenses.** Compare the expense ratio to the average for the fund's investment objective. Stick to funds with below-average expenses. Other things being equal, go with the fund that charges lower expenses.

7. **Consistency with investment objective.** Read the prospectus and check the composition of a fund's investment holdings to make sure the fund will focus on the asset category you want. For example, a growth fund may hold relatively large amounts of cash if the manager does not like the outlook for stocks. Or a domestic fund may invest heavily in foreign securities. If you already have an appropriate amount of cash or foreign securities in other funds, you may not want funds that stray from their objectives like this.

Following these steps is essentially the same approach used by the sponsors of huge pension plans. They hire money managers for a particular asset category. Then they insist that within that category the manager operates in a consistent, predictable fashion. If a manager hired to invest in large-company domestic stocks started buying shares in small European companies, he or she might generate great returns. But such a manager would also be quickly dismissed for violating the agreed-on guidelines. Lastly, sponsors of major pension plans insist on low fees and expenses from their managers, and so should you.

Focus on...

HIRING YOUR OWN MONEY MANAGER

Could you benefit from having your own money manager? Individual account management, once available only to the very wealthy, is a service that a growing number of investors now find affordable and worthwhile.

Individual account manager fees generally range from 1 percent to 3 percent of assets under management. That compares to an annual fee of about 1.5 percent charged by the average stock mutual fund. But individual account managers provide important additional services. They may custom-design an investment program for you, based on your own goals and risk parameters, then provide professional advice on asset allocation and handle selection of investments.

Individual account management services are available from a variety of sources, including independent money managers, trust or private banking departments at commercial banks, financial planners, and stockbrokers. Generally, clients must have at least $250,000 to invest, although some managers have higher minimums, such as $1 million or more.

Many managers use mutual funds as the vehicle for investing your money. You pay the manager's fee as well as the annual charges for expenses levied by the mutual funds. The total cost may still be modest if the manager uses funds with low expenses. For larger accounts, managers often establish common pools investing in individual securities for multiple clients with the same investment objective. Each client's gains or losses are based on his or her proportional share of the assets in the pool. For clients with greater wealth, managers assemble portfolios of individual stocks and bonds in segregated accounts.

Individual account management may be an appropriate choice for you under any of the following circumstances:

- You want to be able to control the timing of the sales of securities to match your own tax planning needs. For example, your money manager can work with you to realize capital losses at year end to offset gains realized earlier in the year. With a mutual fund, you as a shareholder have no control over the timing of such sales.
- You prefer to be the direct owner of bonds rather than own an interest in a fund that holds bonds.
- You want an investment portfolio precisely tailored to your own risk/reward profile. Or you have certain personal preferences about the types of investments you will make and cannot be assured that a mutual fund will follow them.
- You want the personalized advice and counsel that a money manager can provide to individual clients.

Focus on...

concluded

Selecting a money manager requires careful judgment and counsel from advisers such as your attorney, accountant, or financial planner. Get names of several prospective managers and interview them thoroughly. They must be able to provide you with detailed records of the investment performance for the assets they manage, as well as references from clients and professional background information about key personnel. Also important is the need for you to feel comfortable with the people who will handle your account and the process by which they make investment decisions. Taking time to pick the right manager will be a financially rewarding effort for you and your family.

Resources

Books and References

Bogle on Mutual Funds: New Perspectives for the Intelligent Investor. John C. Bogle. Burr Ridge, IL: Richard D. Irwin. 1994.

Directing Your Own Mutual Fund Investments. Kansas City, MO: Mutual Fund Education Alliance. With audiotape.

The Fidelity Guide to Mutual Funds: A Complete Guide to Investing in Mutual Funds. Mary Rowland. New York: Fireside/Simon & Schuster. 1990.

Funding Your Future: The Only Guide to Mutual Funds You'll Ever Need. Jonathan Clements. New York: Warner Books. 1993.

Grow Rich with Mutual Funds—Without a Broker. Stephen Littauer. Chicago: Dearborn Financial Publishing. 1994.

The Handbook for Low-Load Investors. Sheldon Jacobs. Irvington-on-Hudson, NY: The No-Load Fund Investor Inc. 1993.

The Individual Investor's Guide to Low-Load Mutual Funds. Chicago: American Association of Individual Investors. 1994.

Investor's Guide to Low-Cost Mutual Funds. Kansas City, MO: Mutual Fund Education Alliance. Updated semiannually.

The Investor's Series Educational Kit—Directing Your Own Mutual Fund Investments. Kansas City, MO: Mutual Fund Education Alliance. With audiotape.

The Mutual Fund Encyclopedia, 1994–1995 Edition. Gerald W. Perritt. Chicago: Dearborn Financial Publishing. 1994.

The New York Times Guide to Mutual Funds. Carole Gould. New York: Times Books. 1992.

The 1994–1995 Directory of Mutual Funds. Washington, DC: Investment Company Institute. 1993.

The Ultimate Mutual Fund Guide: 17 Experts Pick the 46 Top Funds You Should Own. Warren Boroson. Chicago: Probus Publishing Co. 1993.

Newsletters

5-Star Investor. Chicago: Morningstar, Inc. Subscription: 1 year (12 issues).

The No-Load Fund Investor. Irvington-on-Hudson, NY: The No-Load Fund Investor Inc. Subscription: 1 year (12 issues).

Rating and Data Services

(Available at many libraries.)

Morningstar Mutual Funds. Chicago: Morningstar, Inc. Subscription: 1 year (26 issues). Trial subscription: 3 months (7 issues).

The Value Line Mutual Fund Survey. New York: Value Line Publishing Inc. Subscription: 1 year (26 issues). Trial subscription: 3 months (7 issues).

LIFE EVENT
PLANNING

BEGINNING
THE
PROCESS

LIFE
EVENT
PLANNING

INTEGRATING
YOUR
PLANS

SAVING AND INVESTING

EDUCATION FUNDING

This chapter begins with a discussion of some fundamental truths about planning for education funding. One of those truths is that college costs have been increasing much faster than the general rate of inflation, indeed faster than after-tax investment returns. Another truth, paradoxically, is that it's easier than ever to finance a college education—through borrowing. But borrowing big to pay for college can be dangerous to the future financial health of your family—parents and children alike.

The chapter leads you through 10 key decisions you will have to make as you begin planning for college financing. It identifies and discusses the challenges involved in financing education. It also helps you analyze your own situation and your financial resources, then provides forms and coaching to help you set goals and determine priorities.

Myth vs. Reality

Myth: College costs $25,000 a year. There's no way we're going to be able to afford it.

Reality: Only a small number of private colleges cost that much. The average charge for tuition, fees, room and board for undergraduates at private four-year colleges for the 1994–95 school year was $16,685. For public four-year colleges, the average was $6,512, according to the College Board.

Myth: I make good money and my prospects for raises are excellent. I will be able to pay for college out of current income when tuition bills are due.

Reality: Maybe so, maybe not. As your income rises, you will likely be spending more money for such things as a bigger house and more expensive cars. So the amount left for college may be less than you expect. Then there is the possibility that job loss, disability, or premature death could cut off your income. A college savings fund will help ensure that some money is available no matter what the future brings.

Myth: College savings should be kept in a custodial account established in the child's name.

Reality: Custodial accounts can save taxes, particularly for families in the top tax brackets. However, many factors other than taxes affect their attractiveness. Custodial accounts may not be the best choice for you.

Myth: As parents, we have to make whatever sacrifices are needed to see that our kids get the best education possible.

Reality: Depleting savings and borrowing heavily for children's college education—to the point where you have jeopardized your basic financial security in retirement—are not in the best interests of you or your children.

Myth: I make too much money for my child to be eligible for financial aid.

Reality: Apply and see. You may be surprised. Families with incomes in excess of $100,000 can get aid. The aid is awarded based on a complex formula that includes the number of members in the household, the number of children in college, and the age of the oldest parent, as well as income and assets.

Myth: If we don't claim our child as a dependent on our tax return as college years approach, he will be eligible for more financial aid as an "independent" student.

Reality: Your child's tax return status is not an issue. To qualify as an independent student for federal financial aid purposes, the child must meet one of several specific requirements (see page 150). However, those requirements have nothing to do with whether your child is a dependent on your tax return.

Myth: My child will go to a state school and it won't cost much, so I don't need to be concerned about saving.

Reality: It's true that public colleges are cheaper than private colleges. But their costs recently have been rising much faster—10 percent annually in the last three years vs. 6.7 percent for private colleges—and that trend may continue. By the time your child is ready for college, the cost of a state school may be much higher, relative to your ability to pay, than it is now.

Myth: I don't want my child to borrow for college expenses and then start her working life saddled with debt.

Reality: A college education will significantly enhance your child's career earning potential. So it is not unreasonable to ask the child to contribute part of the cost of that education in the form of student loans to be repaid out of future career earnings. As with many other financial issues, each family must reach a comfortable balance regarding student borrowing.

Myth: The more you save for college, the more you are penalized when you apply for financial aid.

Reality: Financial aid formulas expect a much higher percentage of the child's assets to be used for college than they expect from the parents. If you are concerned that this may impact your child's eligibility for assistance, keep college savings funds in your own name. But by all means, be sure to save to pay for college.

Some Fundamental Truths about Paying for College

The high costs of higher education pose what is probably the most formidable financial planning challenge facing families today. The total price for four years at college has jumped to astounding levels—over $100,000 at the most expensive private universities, $70,000 at the average private college, and more than $30,000 at the average public college. Even after years of sharp annual increases, college costs continue to rise at twice the pace of inflation, as measured by the consumer price index. Their rate of growth has usually exceeded the after-tax rate of return on low-risk investments such as government bonds, meaning that conservative college savers have been falling steadily behind in terms of the tuition purchasing power.

It would be a stretch for many families, even with a planning horizon of 30 or 40 years, to save enough money for college, given the high current costs and their expected rate of increase. To accumulate that much money in the much shorter college planning horizon of 10 or 15 years that is typical for most families seems impossible.

In addition to the challenge of raising so much money in such a short time, planning for college also presents a number of pitfalls. For example, you may be tempted to overcommit yourself financially when it comes to college spending. You may think that college bills will arrive long before retirement, allowing you an opportunity to replenish your savings by the time your working years have ended. And besides, these are your

The high costs of higher education pose what is probably the most formidable financial planning challenge facing families today.

kids we're talking about and they deserve the best. If you don't stretch and sacrifice to send them through college, you will have failed them.

It's understandable for parents to think that way. But it can also be a serious mistake. Your college funding goals should be developed in concert with the rest of your financial goals. To reach those goals, as we saw in Chapter 1, you need to make trade-offs between spending now and spending later, and then between spending later on one goal vs. another. You may prefer to spend money on expensive colleges for your kids instead of spending it on retirement travel for yourself. That's a reasonable trade-off if you want to make it. But crippling yourself financially in retirement in order to spend extra money on college is not in your best interests.

While it is true that college costs are steep, it is not true that financing a college education is impossible or even all that difficult. Indeed, another pitfall has developed because it's become extremely easy to borrow to pay for college, perhaps too easy. Few of us are likely to overextend ourselves by borrowing heavily to pay retirement living expenses. Loans for such a purpose are simply not available. For better or worse, the same thing cannot be said of education loans.

Students, for example, can now borrow up to $65,000 in "unsubsidized" federal student loans (those available without regard to financial need) for undergraduate and graduate school. New rules also allow up to 30 years for certain student loans to be repaid. Another federal program

COLLEGE COST TRENDS

Increases in Undergraduate Tuition and Fees

Year	Two-Year College		Four-Year College		Consumer Price Index*
	Public	Private	Public	Private	
1987–88	5%	6%	6%	8%	3.6%
1988–89	4	7	5	9	4.1
1989–90	5	7	7	9	4.8
1990–91	5	8	7	8	5.4
1991–92	13	6	12	7	3.2
1992–93	10	6	10	7	2.9
1993–94	10	7	8	6	2.8
1994–95	4	5	6	6	2.7
Average	7.0	6.5	7.6	7.5	3.7

*For calendar year that starts school year.

College costs have long been increasing at a faster rate than inflation. This table shows the average annual percentage increase in tuition and fee expenses at public and private colleges, compared to inflation.

Source: "College Cost Trends," The College Board Annual Survey of Colleges 1994, press release entitled "State of Tuition Increases Drops at Most Colleges in 1994–95," Table 4 of addendum.

enables parents, again without regard to financial need, to borrow up to the full cost of undergraduate attendance, less any other assistance the student obtains. In addition to these federal programs, many private institutions offer extensive college financing to parents, on an unsecured basis or in the form of home equity loans. The danger is that parents and students will borrow too much, simply because it is available on favorable terms, and be overburdened with debt.

Another pitfall in planning for college is the failure to stay flexible and keep your options open. A child's education plans may change many times before he or she reaches college age. It will always be important for you to have a goal in mind to plan successfully. But it will be equally important for you to be able to change these goals as it becomes clear that the child's needs or your family's financial condition require such a change. Staying flexible means keeping your investments flexible as well. Many parents, for example, are concerned about the effect of taxes on college investments and automatically assume that custodial accounts are the best way to save because their children are in a lower tax bracket. In

SAMPLE STUDENT BUDGETS

1994–95 School Year

	Tuition and Fees	Books and Supplies	Room and Board	Transportation	Other	Total
Two-year public						
Commuter	$ 1,298	$566	$1,746	$934	$1,095	$ 5,639
Two-year private						
Resident	6,511	552	4,040	569	975	12,647
Commuter	6,511	552	1,850	908	1,192	11,013
Four-year public						
Resident	2,686	578	3,826	592	1,308	8,990
Commuter	2,686	578	1,684	892	1,314	7,154
Four-year private						
Resident	11,709	585	4,976	523	991	18,784
Commuter	11,709	585	1,809	844	1,123	16,070

Source: "Sample Student Budgets," The College Board Annual Survey of Colleges 1994, press release entitled "State of Tuition Increases Drops at Most Colleges in 1994–95," Table 3 of addendum.

reality, custodial accounts may not be the right choice, and one reason is that they reduce the amount of flexibility you have in using your family's college savings.

The biggest pitfall in college planning, however, is the danger of being overwhelmed by the enormity of the challenge at hand and simply giving up. Failure to plan adequately for the cost of college will yield predictable results. Either your children will not have the opportunity to attend the colleges of their choice because your family cannot afford to pay the bills. Or, to make up for savings shortfalls, you and your children will have to borrow substantial amounts to pay college bills, leaving you saddled with heavy debts.

> **The biggest pitfall of college planning is the danger of being overwhelmed by the enormity of the challenge at hand and simply giving up.**

Our suggestion: Get going, stay flexible, develop a college funding plan, and stick to it.

10 Decisions for College Planning

Decision No. 1   Will you provide any financial support for your children to attend college?

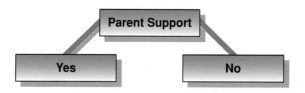

Most parents expect to help their children with college costs. To them, asking whether they will offer financial support or not may seem off the mark, or even off the wall. "Of course we will," they will say. "We'll do what we can."

The reality is, however, that many parents will not be providing money to their children for college, either out of necessity or through a deliberate choice. They may not have the wherewithal to offer even a token amount of money. The family's savings may have been drained or its future earnings power crippled, for example, by job loss, divorce, or disability. As a result, money for college may be out of the question unless it comes from outside financial assistance or the child's own earnings.

Then there are parents with available assets or borrowing capacity who nevertheless have decided not to provide college support for a particular child, or for any of their children. Maybe they don't see the value of higher education, as measured against the steep price of tuition today. Possibly they earned their own way through college without family support and believe their children should do the same. They may feel a certain child is not motivated to learn at this point and will spend four years and many thousands of dollars in college goofing off. Better, they conclude, to conserve the money so it can be used for a higher priority. Or perhaps the parents simply believe that paying for college is not a parental obligation, any more than buying an expensive new car for a child who reaches age 18 is a parental obligation.

Parents often skip this issue and focus solely on where they will get the money. Yet the question of providing support or not is a fundamental one. It should be considered at the outset of the college planning process—and periodically thereafter as the child nears college age. Is college going to be appropriate when the child finishes secondary school?

Can your family afford to provide financial support? If so, will the money be well spent? If the answer is not clearly yes, should the family's resources be allocated toward some other financial goal?

Maybe the child should get a job for a few years instead of going immediately to college. Another option is to live at home and attend college part time while also working part time to pay the expenses. Other alternatives, including military service, are available as well. Reserve officer training corps (ROTC) scholarships cover tuition, books, and fees in return for a tour of active military duty after graduation. The military services also offer educational benefits and incentive payments to active-duty personnel, as well as educational assistance programs to veterans.

Some caveats: If you are able to provide support but choose not to do so, your children will have trouble finding financial assistance on their own. Most assistance is "needs based" and predicated on an expected contribution from the parents determined by their level of income and assets. If the financial assistance formula calls for a certain parental contribution and you refuse to provide it, financial aid for your child will not be forthcoming under normal circumstances.

Moreover, refusal by parents to provide college support does not mean a child qualifies as an independent student, or one whose financial assistance needs are figured without regard to the parents' income and assets. To be considered independent for federal financial aid purposes, the student must meet any one of several tests. He or she must be at least 24 years old; a veteran of the armed forces; an orphan or ward of the court; married; a graduate- or professional-school student; or have legal dependents other than a spouse. Some private colleges may apply stricter standards than the federal guidelines in determining whether a student is independent for purposes of financial aid.

Our suggestion: Before you decide to provide support for a child's college education, look at all the factors involved.

Decision No. 2 Will you treat your children equally in terms of financial support?

No two children are the same. Siblings will differ, sometimes to a surprising degree, in terms of their personalities, social development, and athletic abilities, for example. Parents recognize the differences in their children and are accustomed to dealing with them as unique individuals. Yet when it comes time to plan for college, some parents feel they must treat each child in an identical manner. If we pay for Melissa to go to a private college, the parents may feel, then we owe the same to her younger brother Jonathan. Or, conversely, if we are sending Melissa to a state school, it won't be right to spend more money for Jonathan to attend a private college when it's his turn.

This reflects an admirable desire for fairness. However, it can complicate college planning and doesn't necessarily help you settle on the optimal educational experience for each child.

For example, take the complexity involved in trying to see that each child is treated exactly the same in terms of dollars and cents provided for college. If you decide to set aside identical amounts each year for children of different ages, the resulting accumulations will not be identical when the children are ready for college. If you start when one child is nine years old and the other is six, assuming an 8 percent investment return, the 6-year-old will have about one-and-a-half times as much available at age 18 as was available for the 9-year-old at age 18. Of course, you could calculate different annual savings amounts for each child to make their accumulations equivalent at age 18 in today's dollars. Inevitably, however, trying for equivalency will make the task more complex than it needs to be.

Much more important is the question of achieving the optimal educational experience for each child. As we noted above, siblings are different, and nowhere is that more evident than where educational needs and abilities are concerned. One child may thrive in a demanding, highly competitive college environment, while another may be turned off by intense competition and crave a different avenue for learning and accomplishment. One may need the range of options for specialized study available at a major state university while another is perfectly suited to the limited curriculum and cloistered setting of a small-town liberal arts college. It may be best for a particular child to stay home and commute to a nearby community college, with the intent of transferring to a four-year college and living away from home in a couple of years. That child's brother or sister, however, may be ready to leave home as a freshman and attend a four-year college hundreds of miles away.

Disparities such as these mean siblings are likely to need different educational experiences carrying different price tags. What's best for one may cost more, or less, than what's best for another. Sticking to the notion that you should spend the same amount on each child may needlessly complicate the decision-making process. You could end up paying more than you should, simply to equalize the college outlay among your children. Or worse, you could make the wrong choice simply because it comes with the same price tag carried by a sibling's college education.

Our suggestion: Make the best use of the funds you have allocated to provide for your children's educations. That doesn't mean spending the same dollar amount on college for each one.

Decision No. 3   How much money will you contribute toward college?

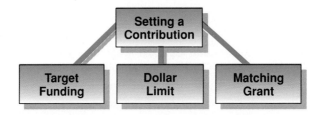

Skyrocketing tuition costs make funding college expenses appear especially daunting. How do you set a goal, given that college costs seem likely to double if your child will be enrolled 10 years from now, maybe even quadruple if your child will be in school 20 years from today? One way to simplify things is to plan in terms of today's dollars, or what college costs this year, not what it will cost in 10 or 20 years. The cost in today's dollars is easy to relate to your present level of income and savings. Future college costs will climb higher over the years in all likelihood, but so will your income and your capacity to save. By stripping inflation out of the planning equation and concentrating on purchasing power, you will have a more understandable gauge of the real resources needed to meet the college goal you choose.

Different approaches can be used to set your college funding goal. As mentioned earlier, we believe college decisions ought to be made as a family, with both parents and children involved. But let's assume you are starting to plan for college at the right time—when your kids are much too young to participate in the process. You as parents will set the planning goal on each child's behalf, with the expectation that your plan will likely be modified in the years ahead to reflect your children's own aspirations and academic plans.

Target Funding   With this method, you select a particular college or type of institution you would want your child to attend and use its total costs (tuition, room, board, books, and fees) in today's dollars for planning purposes. Which one do you pick? Say you and your spouse went to the same college. That might make it a logical choice. If the annual cost at your alma mater is now $15,000 a year, you could use that figure. Another way to select a funding target is to use the average cost of all colleges in a certain category. For example, if you expect your child to attend an Ivy League school but don't know which one, use $25,000, the current average for these elite schools. The average price tag for four-year private colleges in 1994–95 was $16,685. And the comparable figure for public colleges was $6,512.

If you decide it's reasonable to shoot for an average figure but are unsure whether to plan on the basis of private-college costs or public-college costs, we suggest you start using the average for private colleges. It will be easier in the coming years to scale back your savings if your child decides in favor of a public college than it will be to catch up to the higher rate that would be required for a private college. Or you could split the difference between the average figures for private and public colleges and use this midpoint as your funding target. Or you could set your target at half the average cost of private colleges: $8,300 in today's dollars. If you can fund half the cost of a private college education in advance for each of your children, you will be much more successful than most families in accumulating money for college.

Total Contribution Limit   With this approach, you set a fixed dollar amount as your college funding goal without regard to the cost of any particular college or group of colleges. You might decide, for example, that you will provide $40,000 in today's dollars for each of your two children for college. You can plan to accumulate the total amount through precollege saving or through a combination of precollege saving and annual contributions during the years your children are enrolled in college. You might even consider borrowing some of the required amount when the time comes, if that's what is needed to reach your contribution limit. But in any case, $40,000 in today's dollars will be the extent of what you provide for each child.

Where did that figure come from? Perhaps you simply have pegged your contribution at $10,000 per year of college per child in today's dollars. Or maybe $40,000 is the amount of your annual after-tax family income and you decided one year's worth of after-tax income is an appropriate amount to make available to each child for college. Then there is a third possibility: The figure of $80,000 in total college contributions was generated by developing a comprehensive financial plan for your family's future. After looking at your present and future financial resources and your goals, including retirement funding and paying for college, and after making the trade-offs needed to match your goals with your resources, you concluded $80,000 was the right college funding goal.

Matching Grant

This approach requires participation by your children, so you probably will have to wait until they reach junior high school before you can start using it. The idea is to offer an incentive in the form of a multiple match to encourage your children to save as much money as possible toward college. Part of their savings might come in the early years from the child's allowance, from payments for household chores, or from cash birthday gifts. As the child gets older, he or she might also be expected to save money from summer jobs and to work part time after enrolling in college.

You might structure your matching grant formula, for example, by offering to contribute $5 toward college for every $1 your child contributes from savings or earnings. You could supplement that by agreeing further to contribute $1 for every $1 the child borrows for college. As an alternative formula, you might offer to pay the cost of tuition if your child covers all other expenses, including room, board, fees, and books. Or you could turn that arrangement around and offer to pick up all other expenses while your child is responsible for tuition. (At private colleges, tuition represents about 60 percent of total costs, while at public colleges tuition makes up about 30 percent of the total.)

Grandparents who are interested in giving money toward college may find that the matching grant approach offers attractions. They may prefer a formula that pegs their contribution to the child's contribution, say $1 for every $1 the child saves. As an alternative, the grandparents might offer to match some percentage of the family's total contribution, say $1 for every $5 that the parents and child together pay toward college.

Each of these methods for determining your total college contribution has advantages and drawbacks. The target funding approach, for example, helps you identify and plan for a realistic college funding goal. It's also a good way to get the planning process started when your kids are still very young. But you may find after a few years that the target you have chosen is not the appropriate one for your child, so you need to pick a new one. Or you may have to downsize your target to divert more savings toward meeting your other financial goals, such as a particular level of retirement funding. The total contribution approach, on the other hand, may fit well with your other goals but may not deliver the right level of college funding when your child is ready to enroll. For its part, the matching grant approach provides savings incentives and encourages a commitment from your child but doesn't enable you to start early enough. For most families, it can function best as a supplement to one of the other approaches.

Our suggestion: Start with the target funding approach when your children are young. If need be, switch to the total contribution approach to integrate your college funding plan with your other financial goals. As they grow up, get your children involved and committed toward saving for college by offering some kind of matching grant incentive.

Decision No. 4   How much will you expect your children to contribute toward college?

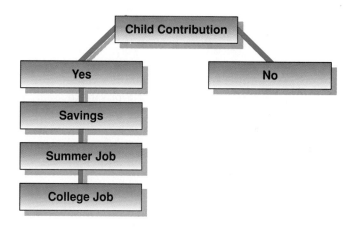

Working your way through college was once an accustomed means for many students to pay for higher education. Now it seems like just another old-fashioned notion that went out of style sometime in the 1950s or 1960s. As growth in college costs has outpaced wage increases over the years, the portion of a typical tuition bill that can be paid out of part-time or summer employment earnings has declined.

That does not mean it's not worth the trouble for a college-bound student to work and contribute to his or her own education. Student earnings can have a big impact in helping families meet overall college costs. For example, a student who can pay for room and board through part-time work during the school year will be meeting more than a quarter of the total cost of the average private college. The impact is even bigger at a public college. There a student earning room and board is covering almost 60 percent of the total annual cost. Let's say that in addition to earning room and board the student also makes $3,000 in take-home pay from a summer job to contribute to the next year's tuition. At the average private college, that student is paying about 48 percent of total costs for tuition, fees, room, and board. At a public college, he or she is covering all costs. Clearly, the child's contribution can make a difference when it comes time to pay college bills.

Many parents believe there's more than just money involved in having children contribute toward college. Willingness to earn money and build a college savings fund is a measure of commitment. The more committed children are to helping pay for their educations, the thinking goes, the more committed they will be to studying hard and making the most of their college experience. This same attitude is reflected in the student aid policies at most colleges. They typically require students receiving scholarships to make a contribution of their own, often through a work-study program offering part-time employment.

Our suggestion: Expect your child to earn and save enough money to make a meaningful contribution toward his or her college costs. That might mean 10 to 20 percent of the cost of a private college, and 30 percent or more of the expense of a public college.

Decision No. 5 Will you seek financial aid, and if so how much will be available for each of your children?

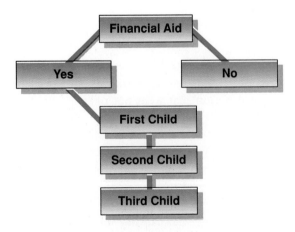

As college costs have grown, so has the availability of student financial assistance. For example, the Higher Education Act of 1992 significantly expanded eligibility for federal financial aid, raised borrowing limits, and provided for extended repayment terms of up to 30 years. Many states have their own assistance programs, and colleges themselves provide financial help in

As college costs have grown, so has the availability of student financial assistance.

the form of scholarships and loans. Most financial assistance available to college students is based on need. If your family income and assets exceed certain levels, you will not qualify, although the ceilings may be higher than you expect. For example, families with incomes of $100,000 or more may be eligible for assistance under certain circumstances, particularly if they have two children in college at once.

To determine how much a family can afford to pay for college in a given year, colleges conduct a needs analysis, using a formula that considers the income and assets of the parents and student, family size, the number of children attending college, and certain other factors. The result is a dollar figure known as the expected family contribution. The difference between the cost of attending a particular college for the year and the expected family contribution equals the student's "need," or the amount of financial assistance for which he or she is eligible. If your family will have two children in college during the same year, your expected family contribution for each child would be half the amount determined by the formula.

The federal government's formula for expected family contribution is used to determine need for assistance for all federal student aid programs including Pell grants, federal supplemental educational opportunity grants, Perkins loans, Stafford loans, and federal work-study programs. Most public colleges use the same federal formula in awarding assistance. When awarding financial aid from their own funds, many private colleges modify the formula in ways that increase the expected family contribution. The federal formula, for example, does not count as a parental asset the value of equity in a home and considers only the income of the custodial parent when a student's parents are divorced. A private college formula may include home equity as well as the income of the noncustodial parent, raising the expected family contribution and thus reducing the amount of aid available.

To figure your exact expected family contribution under the federal formula, obtain a publication called *Expected Family Contribution Formulas* from the U.S. Department of Education. This booklet contains tables, worksheets, and instructions to calculate expected family contribution. It can be ordered at no charge by calling the Federal Student Aid Information Center at 800-433-3243.

If your child would be eligible for financial assistance now, it's reasonable to assume for planning purposes that he or she would be eligible for a similar amount of aid in today's dollars on reaching college age. Keep in mind, however, that this may not necessarily be the case. Congress may reverse course and decide it's time to cut back on student aid programs instead of making them more generous. Or your income in the coming years may move up at a faster rate than the eligibility limits for financial aid. If so, you will have to be prepared to pay for college out of your own family resources or with loans or financial aid that are not need-based. On the other hand, the availability of aid may continue to expand, as it has in recent years. And you may find through circumstances—such as a year or two of overlap with two children in college—that you are eligible for a substantial amount of assistance.

What importance is there now in having an estimate of the amount of assistance your child might receive in 10 or 15 years when he or she enters college? It's worth knowing for several reasons. If your family clearly does not qualify for assistance, that fact should be a strong wakeup call. You need to get started by setting a college funding goal and developing a strategy to reach that goal. If you don't have adequate savings when your child is ready for school, your only alternative may be to borrow heavily to pay college tuition bills. On the other hand, if you do qualify for assistance, having an estimate of your expected family contribution may help you in refining your education funding goal and setting the amount of your annual savings. It will be particularly useful if you expect to have more than one child enrolled in college in the same year.

Our suggestion: Assess your expected future college costs to determine whether you will need financial assistance. Learn the complex rules governing financial aid if you expect to apply for it.

Decision No. 6   Will you or your children borrow to meet college costs?

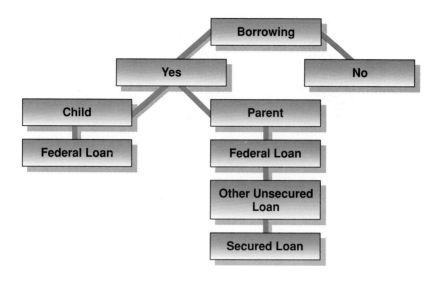

If you begin planning for college when your children are young, there should be no reason to include a provision for future borrowing as part of your plan. One purpose of setting educational funding goals and developing a strategy to accomplish them is to avoid borrowing to pay for college. Loans add substantially to the cost of education and drain resources that could help you accomplish other important family goals, such as saving for retirement or purchasing a vacation home. As a result, borrowing is best viewed as a last-minute alternative, to be used sparingly and only if necessary.

If borrowing is required to meet college costs, the first and most important decision is who should borrow the money, you or your child? In most cases, the answer is the child. There are several reasons for this. First, the rates and terms for loans to students are much more attractive than those offered on loans available to parents. For example, the variable interest rate for Stafford loans is now capped at 8.25 percent. Students eligible for subsidized Stafford loans, those based on financial need, are not required to make interest or principal payments until six months after leaving school. Those with unsubsidized Stafford loans, which are available regardless of need, can add the interest that accrues while they are in school to the principal of the loan and also avoid repayment until after graduation. Stafford loans obtained through banks and other financial

STUDENT LOAN LIMITS UNDER
FEDERALLY SPONSORED PROGRAMS

	Limit
Stafford loans (subsidized and unsubsidized)	
First year	$ 2,625
Second year	3,500
Undergraduate after second year	5,500
Graduate students	8,500
Total undergraduate	23,000
Total graduate (including undergraduate)	65,500
Supplemental Loans for Students (SLS Loans)	
First and second year	$ 4,000
Undergraduate after second year	5,000
Graduate students	10,000
Total undergraduate	23,000
Total graduate (including undergraduate)	73,000
PLUS loans for parents	Cost of attendance less other aid

Source: Student Loan Marketing Association, "Student Loan Limits under Federally Sponsored Programs," press releases entitled "More Funds Available in Federally Sponsored Student Loans," 1993, updated August 1994.

institutions carry 10-year maturities, but loans made under the government's Direct Student Loan Program are now available with maturities up to 30 years.

No other types of loans for college, be they private or federal, secured or unsecured, are as attractive as the federally sponsored student loan programs in terms of rates, repayment features, and availability of credit. As a result, it's preferable for borrowing to be done by the student. If you as a parent feel that student loans will result in an undue burden, consider giving money each year after graduation for your child to repay student loan balances, rather than borrowing the money yourself. Another point: Because of financial assistance formulas, which penalize students with money in the bank during college years, it may be advisable for grandparents or others outside the immediate family who want to help with college bills to wait until after graduation and assist the child in repaying student loans, rather than giving money before tuition bills are due.

If the parent must borrow, the cheapest form of debt may be a home equity loan. Proceed carefully, however. These loans are secured by your property. If you default, you may lose your home. The chief advantage of home equity borrowing is that the interest is generally tax deductible if the loan is secured by your primary residence or second home. The maximum amount of home equity debt on which interest is deductible is the lesser of these two figures: (1) $100,000 or (2) the fair market value of your home after subtracting the current balance of the debt you incurred to purchase or improve your home. Consult your tax adviser to determine whether home equity loan interest is deductible. If so, the after-tax cost of the loan is figured by subtracting your tax bracket expressed as a decimal fraction from 1, then multiplying the result by the loan's interest rate. For example, if your marginal tax rate is 31 percent and your loan interest rate is 10 percent, you would subtract 0.31 from 1 ($1 - 0.31 = 0.69$) then multiply the result times the interest rate (0.69×10 percent). Your after-tax borrowing cost would thus be 6.9 percent.

Our suggestion: Avoid borrowing to pay for college if you can. Borrowing by the student is generally preferable to borrowing by the parent. Parents or grandparents can help students repay their loans after graduation.

Decision No. 7   How much will you set aside each year toward college?

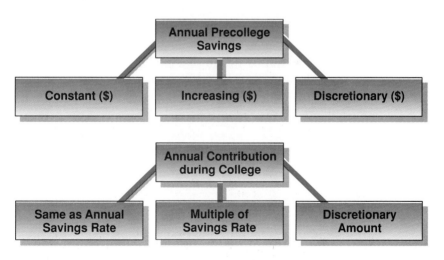

Once you have decided the total amount you will contribute toward college, the next step is to figure how that contribution will be divided over the years. How much will you save each year? (A constant amount in today's dollars? An increasing amount?) Will you contribute the same amount (More? Less? None?) during the years when your child is enrolled is college? It is worthwhile to examine the trade-offs among these alternatives.

Many families plan to save a certain amount every year and then stretch their budgets as much as possible to contribute a larger back-end amount, say two or three times as much, during the four years when the child is enrolled in college. However, to minimize the total savings required and maximize the benefit of compounding, you will be better off to "front-end" your contributions instead. Let's look at an example.

Say you're starting from scratch and your goal is to finance an education costing $58,000 for a child who is now age 3. (All figures in this example are in terms of today's dollars and ignore taxes.) You expect that during the child's four years in college you will be able to stretch your budget and provide $6,000 annually toward tuition out of current-year earnings. To accumulate the difference ($58,000 − $24,000 = $34,000) you would need to save about $1,600 a year, assuming an 8 percent investment return and 4 percent rate of inflation.

What if you decided to accumulate the entire $58,000 by saving before college begins? You would need to set aside $2,800 a year, using the same assumptions for investment return and inflation. In that case your total outlay would be $42,000 ($2,800 × 15), a total of $6,000 less. Even better, you would be able to use the $24,000 you planned to stretch out of your budget during college for something else, such as retirement savings. You would also have the $58,000 in college money safely in the bank at the start of freshman year and be able to earn an extra $3,500 (assuming a 4 percent return) on the unspent balance before the last tuition installment was due. The lesson: You're much better off to stretch somewhat at the start than to stretch a lot when the time for college arrives.

In addition to deciding how to apportion your college contribution between precollege savings and outlays from current income during the college years, you should also consider how you will set the annual amounts. One option is to pick a dollar figure and save that amount every year. The problem with this approach over time is that inflation causes the value of your annual amount to decrease. For example, say you are putting aside $2,000 a year toward college. At a 4 percent rate of inflation, the amount you are saving will decline each year in real terms. The third year, for example, it will be worth only $1,770. By the fifth year, it will be down to $1,600 and in year 10 will have dropped to $1,350. Because inflation causes money to decline in value over time, to keep future amounts constant in terms of purchasing power they must be increased by the rate of inflation. For example, to save $2,000 a year in today's dollars, assuming an inflation rate of 4 percent, you would set aside $2,000 the first year, $2,080 the second year, $2,160 the third year, and so forth, the next year's contribution always being 1.04 times this year's amount.

Saving a constant amount in today's dollars means you are staying even in terms of purchasing power. If you are getting big raises and the purchasing power of your income is advancing each year, in other words growing greater than inflation, you might consider increasing your college savings at that faster rate. Let's say you can afford a $2,000 annual savings amount today for college but your income is rising at 10 percent a year, six percentage points greater than inflation. If you saved $2,000 the first year and raised the amount saved each year by 10 percent, you would accumulate $60,000 in today's dollars after 15 years, as compared to $41,000 if you increased your annual savings by the rate of inflation, assuming an 8 percent return on your invested funds.

Our suggestion: Don't "back-end" your college contributions by planning large expenditures out of current income in the years when your children are in college. Instead, plan to accumulate the money in advance. Focus on the purchasing power of the money you are saving and investing to make sure it is growing according to your plan.

Decision No. 8   Will you use a family account to invest for college, or child-specific accounts, or both?

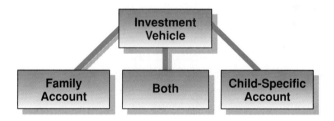

You have several options for managing college investments. One is simply to lump college money together in a common account with other family investments you are making for such purposes as retirement or a down payment on your next car. This catchall approach avoids the cost of establishing a separate account and allows maximum flexibility in using your money as needed in the future. But it will likely prove to be an unsatisfactory way to manage college investments over time.

Not segregating college funds makes it difficult to monitor the portion of your money intended for college savings. Are you saving enough? Are your college investments maintaining their purchasing power? Is the mix of asset categories appropriate for your college planning time horizon? Are you doing the best job you can of reducing the tax bite on your college investment returns? If your college money is kept in the same pot with your other family investments, you will probably have trouble answering any of those important questions.

A more effective approach is to set up a family college fund for all of your children, or individual college funds for each child. For now, let's assume in either case that the money would remain in the parents' names; therefore, no issues arise regarding the federal gift tax, the "kiddie tax" on investment income of children under 14, or over control of the money. The family fund or child-specific college funds would be owned and controlled by the parents; investment income from the funds would be reported on their tax return.

The benefits of establishing college funds are several. First, you can keep better track of your progress toward reaching your college funding goal. You can easily measure the investment return and see how your college money is doing relative to inflation.

A college fund also makes it easier to tailor the mix of your assets depending on the time remaining before your child enters college. For example, when your children are young, you might want to invest in growth stock mutual funds offering relatively high returns and generating little or no current taxable income. As the freshman year nears, you can gradually switch the money into municipal bond funds offering tax-exempt income and less price fluctuation.

A family college fund also makes it easier to stick to a disciplined savings program. You can arrange for automatic transfers of monthly savings from your checking account to your college fund. That will ensure that your savings program stays on track and will also enable you to take advantage of the benefits provided by dollar-cost averaging.

Finally, having the investments segregated in a college fund makes it less tempting to tap into college money for some unplanned expenditure. The money is available, of course, in case of a financial emergency. But having it socked away in a college fund means you are less likely to use it for noncollege purposes such as a vacation or kitchen remodeling job.

Which is better, a family college fund or child-specific funds? As long as the money remains in the names of the parents, it probably doesn't make much difference. You may find it easier to manage investments in separate funds for each child. On the other hand, when it comes time to withdraw cash to pay college tuition bills, a family fund may turn out to be more flexible than multiple funds. Some parents use both a family fund and separate child-specific funds, finding it to be the most convenient approach.

Our suggestion: Start when your kids are young by establishing a family college fund. Make sure the financial institution you choose offers a range of investment options, such as a number of mutual funds with different investment objectives. After a few years, if you find a reason to do so, set up child-specific funds to replace or supplement your family college fund.

Decision No. 9   For child-specific accounts, will you shift ownership of assets to the child?

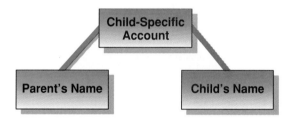

You can reduce the tax bite on college investments by shifting ownership of the money to your children. That usually means establishing a custodial account in the child's name with you as custodian under provisions of the Uniform Transfer to Minors Act (UTMA) or Uniform Gift to Minors Act (UGMA) of your home state. You then make gifts to the account on the child's behalf. The custodian manages the assets until the money is needed to pay college expenses.

The tax savings from shifting assets can be significant because, as a general rule, your child will be in a lower tax bracket than you are. If, as is likely, your child falls in the 15 percent bracket, taxes will take about $1 out of every $7 of the child's investment income. If you are in the 36 percent tax bracket, taxes will take about $2.50 out of every $7 of your investment income. The higher your tax bracket, the bigger the advantage.

If gifts are made to custodial accounts in the form of appreciated property, capital gains taxes can also be reduced. Say you own shares of stock that have increased in value from $20 to $100 a share. If you sold

100 shares, your gain would be $8,000 and you would owe capital gains tax of $2,240. If you gave the 100 shares to a child who is in the 15 percent capital gains tax bracket and the child sells shares, the child pays only $1,200 in capital gains tax.

Despite the tax advantages, however, shifting college money to your children can have many drawbacks. First, the tax breaks on unearned income (such as interest, dividends, and capital gains) are strictly limited until the child reaches age 14. For children under 14, the first $650 of unearned income is tax free and the next $650 is taxed at the child's rate, probably 15 percent. All unearned income over $1,300 is taxed at the parents' marginal tax rate. That means the maximum annual tax savings from income shifting to a child younger than 14 would be about $266 for parents in the 36 percent tax bracket. (These figures assume you file a separate tax return for your child. If you report the child's income on your own return, the limits are lower.)

There are other disadvantages to income shifting as well. Gifts to a child under UTMA or UGMA are irrevocable. You can't change your mind years later and take the money back. And in most instances you can't use income from a custodial account to pay any of the child's routine living expenses. If income from a custodial account is used for support, then under current law that income is taxable to you.

In general, custodial account assets must be turned over to the child and the custodial account closed once the child reaches the age of majority. The age of majority varies by state, ranging from 18 to 21 years of age. In certain states, custodianship of assets can be continued until age 21 even though the child reaches the legal age of majority at 18 or 19.

The final and perhaps most important drawback to transferring assets to your child comes into play if you apply for college financial aid. Financial aid formulas expect a much higher percentage of the child's assets to be used for college than they expect from the parents. It works like this: parents are expected to use up to about 6 percent of their savings each year during college to meet tuition bills and other expenses under the formula for expected family contribution. Students, on the other hand, are expected to use 35 percent of the assets in their names each year for college. As a result, if you are eligible for aid, having college savings in a child's name reduces the amount of aid you will receive and raises your cost of college.

There are ways to minimize or defer taxes on college money that do not require shifting assets to your child. You might consider, for example, selecting investments that don't generate currently taxable income, such as growth stocks that don't pay dividends or tax-exempt municipal bonds.

Focus on...

CUSTODIAL ACCOUNTS: THE PROS AND CONS

Advantages

- Under age 14: No income tax on the first $650 of unearned income, with the next $650 taxed at the child's rate, probably 15 percent. Unearned income above $1,300 is taxed at the parent's rate.
- Age 14 and older: All income is taxed at the child's rate.
- Can be used to give the child appreciated property, such as stocks that have risen in value. When the property is sold, the capital gain is taxed at the child's lower rate.

Disadvantages

- Money is given irrevocably to the child. If income is used for routine support of the child, it is taxable to you, not the child.
- Assets must be turned over to the child when he or she reaches the age of majority and cannot be used for a sibling's education.
- College financial aid formulas penalize savings in the child's name.

Interest on Series EE U.S. Savings Bonds, if used for college expenses, is fully tax free for individuals filing singly with incomes up to $42,300 or for couples with incomes up to $63,450. The benefit is phased out as incomes rise and eliminated for single taxpayers earning above $57,300 and couples making more than $93,450.

Our suggestion: If you qualify for any financial aid on the basis of your situation today, you might want to avoid the use of custodial accounts or other methods of shifting assets to your children. On the other hand, a higher-income family that will not be eligible for financial aid can clearly benefit by shifting assets to children for college saving.

Decision No. 10   How will you allocate your college investments among different categories of investment assets?

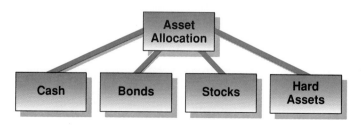

Focus on...

THE TAX RULES FOR GIFTS TO CHILDREN

Parents and grandparents often consider making gifts to children to help finance college education. Here are some points to remember about the tax rules and legal requirements covering gifts.

- Gifts are subject to tax under federal law. The federal gift tax is levied at the same rate as the tax on estates. That's because gift and estate taxes are two sides of a coin, known as the unified estate and gift tax. The gift tax covers property given away before death and the estate tax applies to property you own at the time of death. Gift/estate tax rates rise to 55 percent on transfers of more than $3 million.
- Up to certain dollar limits, however, gifts are exempt from tax. Two principal rules apply. One is a lifetime exemption of $600,000 that is applied against gifts or the assets in your estate at death. The second is the annual exclusion of up to $10,000 per donee on gifts to as many persons as you wish, free of tax. Married couples can give up to $20,000 a year to an unlimited number of persons without tax. Amounts given under the $10,000 annual exclusion do not count against the $600,000 lifetime exclusion.
- There is a third gift tax exclusion intended specifically for those who want to pay college tuition expenses for a student. An unlimited amount can be given to the student free of tax if the funds are paid directly to an educational institution for tuition and related fees. Room, board, and other expenses, such as books and travel, are not covered. Grandparents may find this exclusion particularly attractive.
- If a child is a minor under state law, a parent has an obligation to support the child. Several court cases have held that college expenses are support; therefore, they would not be considered a gift.
- In general, minors cannot own property outright. Gifts of cash or other valuable assets to a child must be held by a custodian or trustee for the child's benefit. Income from property held by a custodian is taxable to the child; income from trust assets is generally taxable to the trust.
- The most common method of holding assets in a child's name is a custodial account, established under terms of your home state's Uniform Transfer to Minors Act (UTMA) or the Uniform Gift to Minors Act (UGMA). Provisions of these laws are generally similar. UTMA laws provide more flexibility in the types of property that can be given to children. UTMA states allow gifts of interests in real estate, for example, while UGMA laws do not.

Focus on...

concluded

Uniform Transfer to Minors Act (UTMA) states are Alabama, Alaska, Arizona, Arkansas, California, Colorado, District of Columbia, Florida, Georgia, Hawaii, Idaho, Illinois, Indiana, Iowa, Kansas, Kentucky, Louisiana, Maine, Maryland, Massachusetts, Minnesota, Missouri, Montana, Nebraska, Nevada, New Hampshire, New Jersey, New Mexico, North Carolina, North Dakota, Ohio, Oklahoma, Oregon, Pennsylvania, Rhode Island, South Dakota, Tennessee, Utah, Virginia, Washington, West Virginia, Wisconsin, Wyoming.

Uniform Gift to Minors Act (UGMA) states are Connecticut, Delaware, Michigan, Mississippi, New York, South Carolina, Texas, Vermont.

• Another method of handling a gift to a child is to establish a minor's trust. The two types, 2503(b) and 2503(c) trusts, are named after the sections of the Internal Revenue Code governing them. Funds are given to the trust on the child's behalf and invested until they are needed to pay college expenses. Normal gift tax rules apply, meaning you can give up to $10,000 a year to the trust ($20,000 for couples) without incurring federal gift tax. The trustee has the power to distribute the income or principal of the trust on the child's behalf.

In the case of the 2503(b) trust, the child must receive and pay tax on all the income generated by the trust assets each year. With 2503(c) trusts, the income is retained by the trust and taxed at rates that escalate quickly. The first $1,550 of trust taxable income is taxed at 15 percent. The next tax brackets are 28 percent (income from $1,550–$3,700); 31 percent (income from $3,700–$5,600); 36 percent (income from $5,600–$7,650) and 39.6 percent (income over $7,650).

You should consider use of a minor's trust only if you are in the top tax brackets. Consult your tax adviser to see if a minor's trust could benefit you.

If you have a long planning horizon for college, that is, 10 years or more until you need your funds, it makes sense to invest most of your college money in assets that provide substantial possibilities for growth, such as common stocks or growth-stock mutual funds. Also consider keeping a small portion of your savings (10 percent or less) in hard assets such as real estate, oil stocks, or gold stocks as an extra hedge against a possible flare-up of inflation. Keep in mind that stocks are the only class

ASSET ALLOCATION STRATEGIES FOR COLLEGE INVESTMENTS

Years until Money Is Needed	Cash	Bonds	Stocks	Hard Assets
15	0%	20%	70%	10%
10	0	30	60	10
3	20	50	30	0
2	70	30	0	0

of investment asset that has been able to keep pace in recent years with the average rate of increase in college costs.

With a long enough time horizon, you will have plenty of opportunity to weather any short-term dips in value that may occur by holding these more volatile types of investments. As the child nears the start of college, however, you have less tolerance for price fluctuations. Once tuition bills arrive, you will want to be sure you can count on a particular amount being available. When the child reaches age 14 or so, you should begin to move the bulk of your college money into nonvolatile investments such as money market funds, certificates of deposit, and short-term bonds. They offer more price stability as well as higher current income than stocks.

College Planning Example—The Powers Family

Richard and Jill Powers have started to save for college for their two children, Melissa, 9, and Jonathan, 6. Their goal is to be able to send both children to private colleges for four years. In particular, they want to be able to pay about 75 percent of total costs at an average-priced private college ($16,685 in 1995). The children will finance the remaining 25 percent of their college costs through student loans and part-time work before and during college years.

The parents expect college costs to increase at a 6 percent annual rate. They also expect a 10 percent average return on their college investments. So far, the Powers have accumulated $24,000 in college investments and want to know how much they need to be saving each year to meet their goal. Using the college worksheet and tables in

Section I: College planning example

GATHERING THE BASIC
INFORMATION

	Child's Name Melissa Powers	Child's Name Jonathan Powers
1. Current age	9	6
2. Age at first year of college	18	18
3. Number of years in college	4	4
4. Years until first year of college (Line 2 − Line 1)	9	12
5. Years until last year of college (Line 4 + Line 3)	13	16
6. Estimated annual rate of increase in college costs	6%	6%
7. Estimated real rate of increase in college costs (Line 6 − 4% inflation rate)	2%	2%
8. Annual college costs in today's dollars	$16,685	$16,685
9. Student employment, financial aid, and loans per year in today's dollars	$4,000	$4,000
10. Adjusted college costs in today's dollars (Line 8 − Line 9)	$12,685	$12,685
11. Current college investments	$12,000	$12,000
12. Estimated annual investment return	10%	10%
13. Estimated real annual investment return (Line 12 − 4% inflation)	6%	6%

Appendix 3 (see pages 336–42), they determine the adjusted four-year college costs in today's dollars for Melissa and Jonathan are $62,537 and $66,343, respectively. After factoring in the future value of their $24,000 in current investments, they determine they need to be saving $5,367 a year for Melissa's education and $4,138 for Jonathan. To maintain the purchasing power of their annual savings, they will need to increase those amounts by 4 percent each year.

Section II: College planning example   ESTIMATING FUTURE COSTS

Melissa Powers

	Year 1	Year 2	Year 3	Year 4
Years until start of this college year	9	10	11	12
	Item 4	Item 4 + 1	Item 4 + 2	Item 4 + 3
Adjusted annual college costs in today's dollars	$12,685	$12,685	$12,685	$12,685
	Item 10	Item 10	Item 10	Item 10
Growth factor for real cost of college (from Table A page 339)	1.20	1.22	1.24	1.27
Growth factor × Adjusted cost = Future costs in today's dollars	$15,222	$15,476	$15,729	$16,110
Adjusted total college expense (Sum of future costs for years 1–4 in today's dollars)				$62,537

Jonathan Powers

	Year 1	Year 2	Year 3	Year 4
Years until start of this college year	12	13	14	15
	Item 4	Item 4 + 1	Item 4 + 2	Item 4 + 3
Adjusted annual college costs in today's dollars	$12,685	$12,685	$12,685	$12,685
	Item 10	Item 10	Item 10	Item 10
Growth factor for real cost of college (from Table A page 339)	1.27	1.29	1.32	1.35
Growth factor × Adjusted cost = Future costs in today's dollars	$16,110	$16,364	$16,744	$17,125
Adjusted total college expense (Sum of future costs for years 1–4 in today's dollars)				$66,343

Section III: College planning example — ESTIMATING THE VALUE OF CURRENT SAVINGS

	Melissa Powers	Jonathan Powers
1. Current college investments (Item 11)	$12,000	$12,000
2. Years to start of college (Item 4)	9	12
3. Estimated real investment return (Item 13)	6%	6%
4. Growth factor from Table B page 340	1.69	2.01
5. Line 4 × Line 1 = Value of current college investments at start of college in today's dollars	$20,280	$24,120

Section IV: College planning example — DETERMINING HOW MUCH MORE IS NEEDED

	Melissa Powers	Jonathan Powers
6. Adjusted total college expense in today's dollars	$62,537	$66,343
7. Additional capital needed at start of college (today's dollars) (Line 6 − Line 5)	$42,257	$42,223
8. Required annual savings (today's dollars) (Line 7 × Factor from Table D page 342)	$5,367	$4,138
	Factor: .127	Factor: .098

To maintain the constant purchasing power of the amount you save, this should be increased by 4% each year.

	Melissa Powers	Jonathan Powers
9. Required annual savings next year (Line 8 × 1.04)	$5,582	$4,304

Resources

Books and References

The As and Bs of Academic Scholarships. Debra L. Wexler. Alexandria, VA: Octameron Press. 1994.

The Best 306 Colleges. Tom Meltzer, Zachary Knower, Edward T. Custard, and John Katzman. New York: Villard Books/The Princeton Review Books. 1994.

College Costs and Financial Aid Handbook. New York: College Board Publications.

The College Handbook. New York: College Board Publications.

Don't Miss Out, The Ambitious Student's Guide to Financial Aid. Robert and Anna Ledier. Alexandria, VA: Octameron Press. 1994.

Earn & Learn: Cooperative Education Opportunities Offered by the Federal Government. Joseph M. Re. Alexandria, VA: Octameron Press. 1994.

Financial Aid Officers: What They Do to You—And for You. Donald Moore. Alexandria, VA: Octameron Press. 1994.

Loans and Grants from Uncle Sam: Am I Eligible and for How Much? Alexandria, VA: Octameron Press. 1994.

Paying for College 1994 Edition. Kalman Chany with Geoff Martz. New York: Villard Books/The Princeton Review Books. 1994.

Paying for College: A Guide for Parents. Gerald Krefetz. New York: College Board Publications. 1994.

Paying Less for College 1994, The Complete Guide to Over $30 Billion in Financial Aid. Princeton, NJ: Peterson's Guides Inc. 1994.

Peterson's Competitive Colleges 1994–1995. Princeton, NJ: Peterson's Guides Inc. 1994.

Peterson's Guide to Four-Year Colleges. Princeton, NJ: Peterson's Guides Inc. 1994.

Peterson's Guide to Two-Year Colleges. Princeton, NJ: Peterson's Guides Inc. 1994.

Peterson's Sports Scholarships and College Athletic Programs. Princeton, NJ: Peterson's Guides Inc. 1994.

Winning Money for College, A High School Student's Guide to Scholarship Contests. Alan Deutschman. Princeton, NJ: Peterson's Guides Inc.

Newsletters

The College Planning Quarterly. Information on admissions and financial aid issues for prospective students and parents. South Orange, NJ: College Planning Quarterly.

Solutions: Octameron Associates' College Planning Newsletter. Information on admissions and financial aid issues for prospective students and parents. 10 issues per year. Alexandria, VA: Octameron Press.

Software

College Explorer Plus. Offers a wide range of data including tuition and fee information for 2,800 undergraduate colleges and 1,200 graduate schools. For IBM PCs and compatibles. Requires DOS 3.2 or higher. New York: College Board Publications.

Federal Methodology. Calculates expected family contribution toward college costs using federal student aid standards. For IBM PCs and compatibles. Requires DOS 3.30 or higher. Alexandria, VA: Octameron Press. 1994.

Price Waterhouse Education Funding System. Projects college costs, funding requirements, annual contribution amounts, and funding shortfalls or excesses.

Answers "what if" questions based on changes in cost/contribution variables. Microsoft Windows™ (Version 3.1 or higher) and DOS (Version 2.0 or higher). Chicago: Price Waterhouse LLP.

Videotapes

How to Pay for College. 40-minute videotape with 72-page guidebook. Alexandria, VA: Octameron Press. 1994.

Financing a Future: Paying for College Costs. 10-minute videotape. New York: College Board Publications.

Financial Aid Worksheet

"Expected Family Contribution Formulas." Washington, DC: U.S. Department of Education, Student Financial Assistance Programs. Booklet contains tables, worksheets, and instructions to calculate expected family contribution for determining college financial aid. Can be ordered at no charge by calling the Federal Student Aid Information Center, 800-433-3243.

RETIREMENT PLANNING

This chapter begins with a discussion of some fundamental truths about retirement. One of those truths is the changing nature of retirement. Longer life expectancies and more career options have an impact on retirement financing. The chapter identifies and discusses the challenges involved by leading you through 10 key decisions you will have to make. Along the way, it explores the personal and family issues that need to be faced in retirement planning. It also helps you analyze your own situation and financial resources and then provides forms and coaching to help you set goals and determine priorities.

The chapter looks at retirement living costs and helps you consider your retirement lifestyle expectations. It covers basic facts about employer-sponsored plans and offers tips on maximizing the benefits that they provide, such as by making optional after-tax contributions where permitted. Finally, the question of how to invest your retirement savings is addressed.

Myth vs. Reality

Myth: I'll retire with plenty of money from my company pension—Part I.

Reality: Not if you change jobs several times in your career. Traditional pension plans are heavily "back-loaded," with much larger benefits going to longer-term employees. Those who switch jobs and thus have a relatively short tenure with each employer will get less, even if they collect several pension checks.

Myth: I'll retire with plenty of money from my company pension—Part II.

Reality: Not if you expect to maintain the purchasing power of your income. Most pensions are fixed monthly amounts. After 10 years, the purchasing power of your pension dollar will decline to 68 cents, assuming 4 percent inflation. After 20 years, it will be down to 46 cents.

Myth: I will collect full Social Security benefits at age 65.

Reality: Not if you were born after 1937. The normal retirement age for receiving full benefits will be increased gradually starting in the year 2003. It will become 65 and a fraction of a year for those born in 1938–42, 66 for those born in 1943–54, age 66 and a fraction of a year if you were born in 1955–59, and 67 for everyone born after 1959.

Myth: Retirement will be a short period of time at the end of my life.

Reality: You may spend a third of your life in retirement.

Myth: Social Security will provide my retirement income.

Reality: If so, prepare to live frugally. The average benefit for a worker retiring at age 65 and spouse is about $14,000 in today's dollars. The maximum benefit is $21,600 for a worker and spouse retiring at 65 where the worker's career earnings have equaled or exceeded the Social Security taxable wage ceiling ($61,200 in 1995).

Myth: I will be in a lower tax bracket once I retire.

Reality: Not necessarily. Remember, pensions are fully taxable, and up to 85 percent of Social Security is also subject to tax. In retirement, you will probably have little in the way of tax deductions for such items as mortgage interest or business-related expenses. The result? Your effective tax rate may not decline. It may even go up.

Myth: Congress is not going to tinker with Social Security.

Reality: Social Security will require some major changes within the next decade or so. Taxes may be raised, and benefits for higher-income retirees may be reduced. The result: Social Security will provide a smaller measure of future income for retirees relative to other income sources.

Myth: My salary will keep rising at the same rate for the rest of my career. That means I'll be bringing in plenty of money in my 50s and 60s to sock away for retirement.

Reality: Middle managers who are "downsized" often find their salaries at new jobs to be 40 to 50 percent less than previously. For financial planning purposes, it's best to assume that future increases in your earnings will equal or only slightly exceed the rate of inflation.

Myth: Once I become an officer in my company, I'm set for life.

Reality: Things change. You may opt for another job or another career in a few years. Your company may dramatically change directions and you may choose to leave or the company may ask you to leave. The point is, you should not be relying solely on your employer to provide your retirement nut.

Myth: Old age is old age. There is no great difference between people who are 65 and those who are 75 or 85.

Reality: These three retirement-age groups differ dramatically in terms of their goals, activity levels, and financial needs. Those differences are important enough so that it makes sense to plan separately for each of the three phases of retirement: the early years (65 to 75), the middle years (75 to 85) and the later years (85 and older).

Myth: My company benefits will take care of me for the rest of my life.

Reality: Most companies today don't have traditional pension plans. The trend is toward employee contributory plans, where you share part of the burden of funding your own retirement account.

Some Fundamental Truths about Retirement

The nature of retirement is changing. In part, this is because the nature of employment and careers has changed. Previously, the norm for most workers was a long career at a single company, ending with retirement and a full pension at 65. Now, job changes are more frequent and may be involuntary. Older workers are sometimes forced into second careers or self-employment.

The downside of these developments is a loss of job security and diminished or less-certain pension benefits. There may be an upside, however, in that older workers will have more options going into their retirement years. For example, an employee forced to find a second career at age 55 because of corporate cutbacks may choose a job that offers the flexibility of part-time work that can be continued well past the normal retirement age. Clearly, there is no longer a sharp age boundary between full-time work and no work. Instead, semiretirement is likely to become an increasingly common transition period between a career and retirement.

HOW CAREERS AND RETIREMENT ARE CHANGING

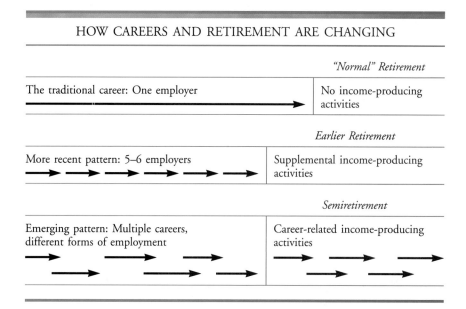

	"Normal" Retirement
The traditional career: One employer	No income-producing activities

	Earlier Retirement
More recent pattern: 5–6 employers	Supplemental income-producing activities

	Semiretirement
Emerging pattern: Multiple careers, different forms of employment	Career-related income-producing activities

Corporate restructurings have a further impact: They prompt people to switch jobs. And the more job changes your career endures, the lower your pension benefit is likely to be at retirement. Today, the average American worker changes jobs once every 5.7 years. This results in a lower pension benefit because defined-benefit plans reward long-term employees with much larger retirement benefits. Thus, those who switch jobs several times during their careers find themselves penalized.

Consider the case of two employees who start at $25,000 a year and work for 40 years, both getting the same 5 percent salary increases every year. The long-term employee stays at the same company for 40 years and has a defined-benefit pension of $80,000. The job switcher works for five different companies, each for eight years, working just as long as the long-term employee and making exactly the same career earnings. But the job switcher's five defined-benefit pensions add up to only $42,000. (Of course, if the job switcher had managed to land a substantially higher salary with each new job, the difference in total pension benefits would be less.)

Retirement is also getting longer. Two factors contribute to this change: the decades-long trend toward early retirement and the longer life spans enjoyed by Americans. Waves of corporate downsizings and cutbacks in recent years have swelled the ranks of those who leave their jobs before the

THE COST OF SWITCHING JOBS

		Years of Service	Final Salary	Annual Pension Benefit*
Long-term employee		40	$168,000	$80,000
Job switcher	Job 1	8	35,000	$3,400
	Job 2	8	52,000	5,000
	Job 3	8	77,000	7,300
	Job 4	8	113,000	10,700
	Job 5	8	168,000	16,000
	Total	40		Total $42,400

*Annual defined-benefit pension = .0125 × Average salary in last three years × Years of service. Assumes full vesting in all benefits.

normal retirement age of 65. Company pension plans often provide incentives for early retirement. And many employers have sweetened those incentives in recent years with early retirement windows offering extra benefits to workers who agree to take a gold watch and leave before age 65. More than half (55 percent) of men covered by Social Security now begin drawing retirement benefits at age 62, the earliest year of eligibility. And only one-third of the men age 60 or older are working today, compared to 1930, when two-thirds of that group were still in the labor force.

Increased longevity is the other factor. Today, 65-year-old men can expect to live to age 80. Women will live to about age 85. Although these figures represent averages, people who stay healthy and physically fit may live significantly longer.

Because of early retirement trends and increased longevity, Americans will be spending roughly a third of their lives in retirement. Living longer in retirement means your money will have to last longer to maintain your targeted lifestyle. For example, to provide a $2,000 monthly income for 10 years requires a nest egg of $173,000, assuming a 7 percent investment return. To generate $2,000 a month for 20 years, you would have to start retirement with a nest egg of $259,000.

Longer retirements and changing retirements have implications for financial plans and income needs. In the out years of a long retirement, for example, the real value (after inflation) of a fixed pension benefit is substantially diminished. Your financial plan needs to reflect the likelihood of this greater long-term income need.

THE TREND TOWARD EARLY RETIREMENT

Men 55 and Older in the Work Force

	Age 55–64	Age 65 and Over
1970	83%	27%
1980	72	19
1990	68	16
1993	67	16

Source: U.S. Bureau of Labor Statistics Bulletin 2307, Employment and Earnings Monthly, January 1995.

Threats to Retirement Security

Much has been written already about a retirement crisis that will confront members of the baby boom generation sometime after the turn of the century. Much more will be written by the time the first wave of baby boomers begins retiring around 2010. You don't have to be an alarmist to agree that there is significant cause for concern. Signs of weakness are apparent in each of the legs of the "three-legged stool" that has up to now supported retirees: employer pensions, Social Security, and individual savings. The number of employees covered by traditional pension plans is shrinking, and some of the remaining plans have become underfunded.

Meanwhile, Social Security is headed for trouble. Experts agree that Social Security payroll taxes will have to be raised and growth of benefits will have to be trimmed over the coming decades; the great debate is over how much and when. To offset pension and Social Security shortcomings, individuals ought to

A LONGER LIFE REQUIRES A BIGGER RETIREMENT NEST EGG

	Monthly Withdrawal		
	$1,000	$2,000	$3,000
Years	Amount Needed		
10	$ 87,000	$173,000	$260,000
15	112,000	224,000	336,000
20	130,000	259,000	390,000
25	142,000	285,000	427,000

Table shows the total sum you would need at retirement to make monthly withdrawals for indicated number of years. It assumes a 7 percent return on the remaining amount and an ending balance of zero.

be saving more. But they aren't. The personal savings rate declined sharply beginning in the early 1980s from a previous range of about 9 percent of national income to about 3 percent today.

On the macro level, these developments add up to a changing picture of future retirement security for Americans. But how will your ability to achieve your retirement goals be affected? As you might expect, the impact on individuals is difficult to gauge, making retirement planning a challenge.

> **Because of early retirement trends and increased longevity, Americans will be spending roughly a third of their lives in retirement.**

The retirement time horizon extends decades into the future because you can't predict your retirement date or life expectancy. You also can't know what future inflation rates or investment returns will be. As a result, you don't know how much money you will need to meet living expenses in retirement. And you don't know what your financial resources will be or how long they will last.

Our suggestion: Realize that you, not your employer or the government, will be responsible for providing your retirement security. Don't count too much on a pension or Social Security for retirement income.

10 Decisions for Retirement Planning

Decision No. 1   Will you retire at all?

Retirement is no longer the sharp break it once represented between working and not working. Instead, retirement is evolving as a transition period, meaning a change in careers or a move to part-time work or self-employment.

Will you retire at all? The question may seem silly, but it bears asking. "Absolutely," you may respond, "and the sooner the better." Your eagerness would be understandable. The popular image of retirement is often painted as a time of ease and enjoyment. After decades of work, you gather the fruits of your labor and use them to support a new lifestyle, one that is lived at a less-hurried, even leisurely, pace.

It sounds good, but that image doesn't square with the way we actually think and talk about retirement. In common parlance, retirement is defined by what it's not. It means *not* being in the labor force, *not* working, *not* going to the office, *not* getting a paycheck. All those nots add up to a lot of negatives. To retire, says the dictionary, is to give up or withdraw from one's work, business, or career, especially because of age. Viewed in a single sentence, the words give up, withdraw, and because of age seem less than triumphant. If your feelings of self-worth depend on what you do each day in your workplace, business, or profession, retirement may even trigger a full-fledged identity crisis. In this light, the whole notion of retirement can quickly lose its appeal.

Instead of asking the question, "Why retire at all?" the more relevant question would have been, "Will you be able *not* to retire?" In other words, have you managed your career so that you have the skills, the experience, and the job connections to give you adequate income-producing opportunities as you get older? And do you have the financial resources that may be needed to tide you over and help you make the transition from one income-producing activity to another?

Recall in Chapter 1 the discussion of financial equilibrium and the importance of being reasonably prepared for what life will throw at you. One way to make sure you maintain financial equilibrium is to keep your retirement options open. Will you retire at all? Yes, you may say, but it will be when you are 70, not 62. Should your employer disagree and present you with an exit offer at age 62, you should expect to be ready with a strategy for pursuing some other employment activities for the next eight years.

Our suggestion: Don't assume you must retire or you must retire at a particular date set by someone else. If the prospect of retirement holds no appeal, prepare a strategy that will enable you to work as long as you want to.

Decision No. 2   When will you retire?

Your ability to pay for the retirement lifestyle you want will be largely determined by these four factors:

• When you start saving regularly for retirement.
• The amount you save relative to your income.
• Long-term investment return.
• How old you are when you retire.

Each factor is important. For example, starting to save early in your career makes a big difference. As we saw in Chapter 4, for every dollar you don't save for retirement by age 35, you will need to put aside $3.90 at age 55. Obviously, the *amount* of money you save each year also makes a difference. Double your savings rate and you will double your investment income in retirement. It's that simple.

Long-term investment return has a big impact as well. Invest an amount at a 5 percent rate of return and you will have a 60 percent gain after 10 years. Double your return to 10 percent and you will have a 160 percent gain, or two and a half times the gain at 5 percent.

Last, but probably most important, is the timing of your retirement. That decision determines: (1) how long your current lifestyle will be supported by your paycheck; (2) how many more years you will be

---

THE IMPACT OF THE TIMING
OF YOUR RETIREMENT

Life
Expectancy

Retirement

Saving   Spending

Retirement

Saving   Spending

•••••••••

Early retirement means "double-whammy" years (•••••) when you are spending—and not saving.

DELAYING RETIREMENT

A Few Years Can Dramatically Reduce the Amount of Savings
Required to Support Your Lifestyle

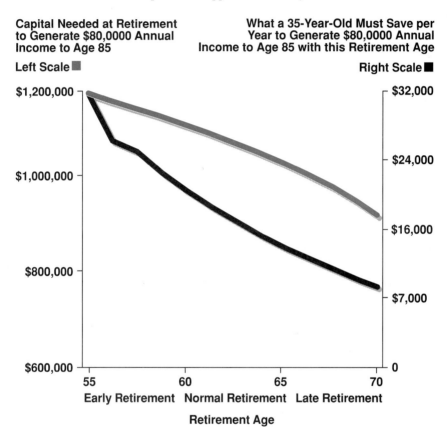

**Capital Needed at Retirement
to Generate $80,0000 Annual
Income to Age 85**

Left Scale ■

**What a 35-Year-Old Must Save per
Year to Generate $80,0000 Annual
Income to Age 85 with this Retirement Age**

Right Scale ■

able to save; and (3) how long—given your life expectancy—your assets
will support your postretirement lifestyle. Because it affects both the
amount of money you will have and the amount you will need, the timing of your retirement has a dramatic impact on your ability to make
ends meet.

Retiring early requires substantially more money to support a given
lifestyle; retiring later means you will need substantially less. For example, if
you retire at age 60, it will take about $1.1 million to generate an $80,000

PENALTIES FOR CLAIMING BENEFITS EARLY

Age You Retire	Percent of Your Social Security Benefit You Will Receive	Percent of Employer Pension Benefit You Will Receive with Full Actuarial Reduction for Early Retirement*
65	100%	100%
64	93	90
63	87	81
62	80	73

*Based on Unisex Projected Mortality Table (1984) and 6 percent interest rate assumption.

Note: Many employer pension plans provide for normal retirement before 65 and may give other incentives for retirement before that age. In such instances, reductions in pension benefits, if any, would be less than the full actuarial reductions shown here.

annual income through age 85, assuming a 6 percent investment return. Retiring at 65, you would need $972,000 to generate the same income through age 85, while retiring at 70 would require only $824,000. Translate that into what you have to save each year and the differences are much more dramatic. To provide an $80,000 income from age 60 through 85, a worker who is now 35 would have to save $18,600 a year until retirement. Delaying that worker's retirement until 65 drops the required savings to $11,600. And if the 35-year-old retires at 70, he or she needs to save only $7,000 a year.

Other factors add to the financial impact of the timing of your retirement. For example, Social Security and the defined-benefit pensions offered by many employers are permanently reduced if you retire before the normal retirement age. Most men (55 percent) and women (60 percent) now begin receiving Social Security retirement benefits during the first year they are eligible, at age 62. But there's a price for starting benefits before Social Security's normal retirement age of 65. For example, your benefit at age 62 will be 20 percent less than your age-65 benefit. If you start getting Social Security at 63½, your benefit will be reduced by 10 percent. The reductions are slightly larger for spouses of retired workers who start receiving their spousal benefits at age 62. Currently, they face a reduction of 25 percent. The early retirement penalty will be increased as the normal retirement age is gradually raised to 67 beginning in 2003. Eventually, for everyone born after 1959, the penalty for claiming benefits at age 62 will be a permanent 30 percent reduction in benefits. For spouses, the penalty will be 35 percent.

Timing of Retirement: Stopgap Measure or Long-Term Goal?

As we have seen, the timing of your retirement has great dollars-and-cents impact. Think of it as a lever. Pull the lever in the direction of retiring early, and the cost of your retirement rises sharply. Push it the other way, toward a later retirement, and the cost drops. If you have waited until age 50 to start saving for your later years, delaying your retirement is likely to be the *only* financial strategy that will make a big difference in your ability to pay for the retirement lifestyle you want. By then, whatever you can manage to save each year will certainly help, but it won't have time to compound and grow by very much before you need to spend it. In that sense, the longer you wait, the more the timing of your retirement becomes a stopgap measure instead of a goal in itself. You will have the option of delaying your retirement to make the numbers add up, but the option of earlier retirement may be financially unobtainable.

Our suggestion: Start planning early so that the timing of your retirement is something you can control.

Decision No. 3   What are your goals for the three phases of your retirement years?

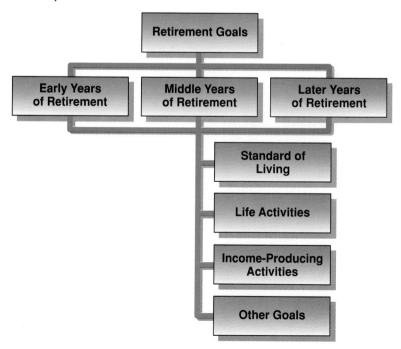

No single decision about retirement is meaningful for the entire span of years involved. In many ways, the three phases of your retirement will be as different from each other as they are from the earlier stages of your life. In each, you will have different goals, different activities, different income needs, and a different level of energy and physical stamina. So it makes sense to separate them for planning purposes. For each phase, ask yourself:

- What do I plan to do?
- What will my lifestyle be?
- What will be my spending goals?
- What income-producing activities will I undertake?
- What career management do I need to prepare myself?

Recall from Chapter 2 how you can formulate planning goals in steps, going from a general statement to one that focuses on a measurable attainment expressed in terms of today's dollars.

Retirement Goals

Retire with enough money to live comfortably.

Revision 2

Retire at age 65 with enough income to maintain our current lifestyle in a less-expensive community, and be prepared to retire earlier if necessary.

Revision 3

Retire at age 65 with 80 percent of our current income in today's dollars for 25 years. Be prepared to retire at age 60 with 70 percent of our income in today's dollars for 30 years.

As a rule of thumb, you will need about 60 to 80 percent of your preretirement income to support yourself once you retire and maintain the same standard of living. Your requirements will be less for several reasons.

- **Savings.** You will no longer be saving for retirement, so the share of your previous income that went to retirement savings won't be needed. Of course, you may want to continue saving whatever is possible, but the commitment to savings as a portion of your total income will drop.
- **Spending.** Employment-related costs such as commuting, union dues, clothing for work, and other such expenses will disappear.
- **Debt.** By retirement, your mortgage may be paid off and your monthly housing costs will drop significantly as a result.

Retirement planning worksheet   ESTIMATE YOUR SPENDING
GOALS (TODAY'S DOLLARS)

	Today	*Retirement Years*		
	Today	Early	Middle	Later
Mortgage or rent	$ _____	$ _____	$ _____	$ _____
Home upkeep, taxes	_____	_____	_____	_____
Utilities	_____	_____	_____	_____
Auto expenses	_____	_____	_____	_____
Medical, dental	_____	_____	_____	_____
Insurance				
Household	_____	_____	_____	_____
Medical/Medigap	_____	_____	_____	_____
Life	_____	_____	_____	_____
Long-term care	_____	_____	_____	_____
Food	_____	_____	_____	_____
Clothing	_____	_____	_____	_____
Recreation, travel	_____	_____	_____	_____
Family gifts	_____	_____	_____	_____
Charitable gifts	_____	_____	_____	_____
Loan payments	_____	_____	_____	_____
Other expenses	_____	_____	_____	_____
Total annual spending	_____	_____	_____	_____

Our suggestion: Don't assume a big drop in the amount you will
spend for current consumption after you retire. Medical and prescription
costs, in particular, are likely to be greater.

Decision No. 4   Where will you live in retirement?

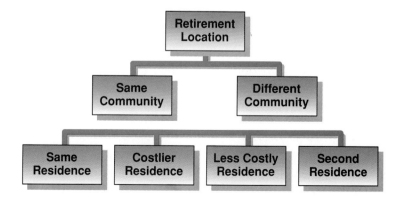

Some retirees can't wait to pack up and move to the Sun Belt. They may buy a retirement residence years in advance and use it as a vacation home until they are ready to stop working and relocate. Others take the opposite view. They wouldn't dream of pulling up stakes and leaving family, friends, and neighborhood just because they are retiring. Their mortgage will be paid off and they will be perfectly happy to stay put in the comfort of their longtime homes.

Why move? There are many good reasons to consider doing so. You may yearn for a warmer climate where golf, tennis, fishing, or gardening can be enjoyed throughout the year. Or you may want to leave behind the fast-paced atmosphere of a big city and move to a small town or rural area. You may like the idea of a retirement community, particularly if friends have already relocated there or plan to do so. Or you may want to move closer to children who have made their home in another part of the country. One of the attractions of retirement is the change in lifestyle, and that could mean moving to a new location.

Several issues are involved in moving. By far the most important one relates to family and friends. You may be hesitant about leaving a community where you have lived for decades, with relatives and friends near. The idea of moving to a warmer climate in a Sun Belt state may offer appeal; lower taxes may make that appeal almost irresistible. But the reality of a strange new home away from family and lifelong acquaintances may turn out to be much less attractive. In addition to family and friends, there are other ties to your home community that you might also be reluctant to sever. The social organizations, religious activities, and entertainment choices you now enjoy may be lacking at a new location.

Despite the drawbacks, there may also be good dollars-and-cents reasons for moving. For example, your residence may be bigger than you need. Buying a smaller retirement home will enable you to save on maintenance, utilities, taxes, and insurance. Also, the cost of living varies significantly among different areas of the country. The chief factors behind those differences are housing costs and taxes. Buying a less-expensive residence in a less-expensive area, particularly one where there is no state tax on pension benefits, can dramatically improve the standard of living you can maintain on a given income. On the other hand, if you intend to continue working part time or to retain ownership of a business during retirement, moving may not be possible, at least until you give up those activities.

If in balancing the pros and cons, you decide you still want to move to achieve a significantly lower cost of living, make sure the move will accomplish that goal. As noted above, taxes and housing expenses are responsible for most of the variations in living costs among different geographic areas. Unless you can be assured of paying lower taxes and housing expenses, moving may not leave you better off financially.

The median price of houses in the 100 largest metropolitan areas was $111,000 in 1994, but wide variations exist. For example, an average-priced house in the Boston area costs 2.3 times as much as the average house in San Antonio. You could sell an average-priced Boston-area house, use the proceeds to buy a comparable house in San Antonio, and have $100,000 left (before any sales costs or taxes) to invest for retirement income. Housing

The biggest single asset of most retirees is the value of the equity in their residences.

prices in a new location are fairly easy to analyze and compare. Real estate agents can give you an accurate picture of the purchase costs and ongoing expenses of home ownership in a particular community. You will want to visit and spend a substantial amount of time in the location where you plan to relocate. This will afford you plenty of opportunity to assess local real estate costs to see how much you could gain by changing residences.

State tax issues, in contrast, are much more complex and difficult to analyze. For example, some states exempt all or part of pension benefits from state income taxes. The rules, however, are not uniform. Private-employer pensions, public-employer pensions, annuity payments, IRA withdrawals, and lump-sum pension distributions may be treated differently, even though they are all essentially the same thing: retirement income. One state may tax all these income sources, another may tax some, and a third may not tax any. Further, some states attempt to tax pension benefits earned during your career as a state resident, even if you subsequently retire in a different state. In the event that your retirement income is subject to such out-of-state tax claims, moving may not save you as much in taxes as you expected.

There are other wrinkles as well. For example, some states collect taxes based on the value of tangible personal property, such as automobiles and boats, or the value of investments such as stocks or bonds. If your retirement income is derived from Social Security and an employer pension, these taxes will not be significant; if your retirement is largely financed from your own investment portfolio, they may turn out to be more meaningful.

STATE TAXES ON PENSIONS AND PERSONAL INCOME DIFFER WIDELY

	Maximum Personal Income Tax Rate	Pension Amount Exempt from State Income Tax			Maximum State/Local Sales Tax
		Private	State	Federal	
Alabama	5.0%	100%	100%	100%	12.0%
Alaska	—	—	—	—	7.0
Arizona	6.9	0	$2,500	$2,500	8.5
Arkansas	7.0	$6,000	$6,000	$6,000	7.5
California	11.0	0	0	$40	8.25
Colorado	5.0% of FIT	$20,000	$20,000	$20,000	8.5
Connecticut	4.5	0	0	0	6.0
Delaware	7.7	$3,000	$3,000	$3,000	—
Florida	—	—	—	—	7.0
Georgia	6.0	$11,000	$11,000	$11,000	6.0
Hawaii	10.0	Partial	Partial	Partial	4.0
Idaho	8.2	Partial	Partial	Partial	7.0
Illinois	3.0	100%	100%	100%	8.75
Indiana	3.4	0	0	Partial	5.0
Iowa	9.98	0	0	0	6.0
Kansas	7.75	0	100%	100%	7.4
Kentucky	6.0	0	100%	100%	6.0
Louisiana	6.0	$6,000	100%	100%	10.75
Maine	8.5	0	0	0	6.0
Maryland	6.0	Partial	Partial	Partial	5.0
Massachusetts	5.95	0	0	0	5.0
Michigan	4.4	Partial	Partial	Partial	6.0
Minnesota	8.5	Partial	Partial	Partial	7.5
Mississippi	5.0	100%	100%	100%	7.25
Missouri	6.0	0	Partial	Partial	7.725
Montana	11.0	Partial	Partial	Partial	—
Nebraska	6.99	0	0	0	6.5
Nevada	—	—	—	—	7.0
New Hampshire	5.0*	—	—	—	—
New Jersey	6.65	Partial	Partial	Partial	6.0
New Mexico	8.5	0	0	0	6.5
New York	7.875	Partial	100%	100%	8.5
North Carolina	7.75	$2,000	$4,000	$4,000	6.0

	Maximum Personal Income Tax Rate	Pension Amount Exempt from State Income Tax			Maximum State/Local Sales Tax
		Private	State	Federal	
North Dakota	12.0	0	Partial	Partial	6.0
Ohio	7.5	Partial	Partial	Partial	7.0
Oklahoma	10.0	0	$5,500	$5,500	10.5
Oregon	9.0	Partial	Partial	Partial	—
Pennsylvania	2.8	100%	100%	100%	7.0
Rhode Island	2.75% of FIT	Partial	Partial	Partial	7.0
South Carolina	7.0	$10,000	$10,000	$10,000	6.0
South Dakota	—	—	—	—	6.0
Tennessee	6.0*	—	—	—	8.75
Texas	—	—	—	—	8.25
Utah	7.2	Partial	Partial	Partial	7.125
Vermont	9.0	0	0	0	5.0
Virginia	5.75	Partial	Partial	Partial	4.5
Washington	—	—	—	—	8.2
Wash. D.C.	9.5	0	$3,000	$3,000	5.75
West Virginia	6.5	0	Partial	Partial	6.0
Wisconsin	6.93	0	Partial	Partial	5.5
Wyoming	—	—	—	—	6.0

FIT = Federal income tax.

*Only on interest and dividends.

Note: When there is a difference in the tax rate or exemption between single and married filing jointly, table lists the figure for married filing jointly. When level of exemption varies by age, the maximum exemption is listed. Partial exemptions are those that are subject to a formula. Sales tax may vary by county within a state.

Sources: Maximum personal income tax rates—Chart of State Taxes, Commerce Clearing House, 1994; Pension tax information—Individual state tax returns; and State and local sales tax—*National Sales Tax Directory,* Vertex Systems Inc., 1995.

If you do move, or you plan to maintain residences in two states, it will be important to establish your legal domicile if you don't want to risk being taxed as a resident of both states. As usual, each state has its own residency provisions. In general, steps to establish legal domicile in another state include:

- Changing your driver's license, car titles, and registration.
- Registering, voting, and paying taxes from your new address.

COMPARING HOUSING PRICES ACROSS THE UNITED STATES

Metropolitan Area	Median Home Price (1994)	Percent of National Median Home Price
Akron	$ 84,000	76%
Albany/Schenectady, N.Y.	111,000	100
Albuquerque	109,000	98
Allentown/Bethlehem, Pa.	96,000	86
Atlanta	92,000	83
Augusta, Ga.	74,000	66
Austin, Texas	97,000	88
Bakersfield, Calif.	142,000	128
Baltimore	118,000	106
Baton Rouge	79,000	71
Bergen/Passaic, N.J.	195,000	176
Birmingham, Ala.	102,000	91
Boston	181,000	162
Buffalo	85,000	76
Charleston, S.C.	91,000	82
Charlotte, N.C.	104,000	93
Chicago	146,000	132
Cincinnati	98,000	88
Cleveland	94,000	85
Columbia, S.C.	85,000	76
Columbus, Ohio	98,000	88
Dallas/Fort Worth	98,000	89
Dayton, Ohio	87,000	78
Denver/Boulder	117,000	105
Detroit	84,000	76
El Paso, Texas	74,000	67
Flint, Mich.	66,000	60
Fort Lauderdale, Fla.	107,000	96
Fort Wayne, Ind.	86,000	78
Fresno, Calif.	111,000	99
Gary/Hammond, Ind.	87,000	78
Grand Rapids	78,000	70
Greensboro/Winston Salem, N.C.	97,000	87
Greenville/Spartanburg, S.C.	88,000	79
Harrisburg, Pa.	90,000	81
Hartford, Conn.	134,000	120

Metropolitan Area	Median Home Price (1994)	Percent of National Median Home Price
Honolulu	361,000	325
Houston	84,000	76
Indianapolis	95,000	85
Jacksonville, Fla.	81,000	73
Jersey City	90,000	81
Johnson City/Kingsport, Tenn.	70,000	63
Kansas City, Mo.	88,000	79
Knoxville, Tenn.	89,000	80
Lansing, Mich.	76,000	68
Las Vegas	113,000	102
Little Rock, Ark.	75,000	68
Los Angeles	187,000	168
Louisville, Ky.	79,000	71
Memphis	88,000	79
Miami	103,000	92
Middlesex/Somerset, N.J.	171,000	154
Milwaukee	112,000	101
Minneapolis/St. Paul	102,000	91
Mobile, Ala.	71,000	64
Monmouth/Ocean counties, N.J.	143,000	128
Nashville	96,000	86
Long Island, N.Y.	163,000	147
New Haven, Conn.	141,000	127
New Orleans	78,000	70
New York City	177,000	159
Newark, N.J.	192,000	173
Norfolk/Virginia Beach, Va.	109,000	98
Oklahoma City	69,000	62
Omaha, Neb.	76,000	68
Orange County, Calif.	214,000	192
Orlando, Fla.	91,000	82
Philadelphia	115,000	103
Phoenix	92,000	83
Pittsburgh	84,000	75
Portland, Ore.	115,000	103
Providence, R.I.	117,000	105
Raleigh/Durham, N.C.	113,000	101
Richmond, Va.	95,000	86

Metropolitan Area	Median Home Price (1994)	Percent of National Median Home Price
Riverside, Calif.	130,000	117
Rochester, N.Y.	87,000	78
Sacramento, Calif.	127,000	114
St. Louis, Mo.	86,000	78
Salt Lake City	98,000	88
San Antonio, Texas	79,000	71
San Diego	173,000	156
San Francisco/Oakland, Calif.	255,000	230
San Jose, Calif.	223,000	201
Scranton/Wilkes-Barre, Pa.	82,000	74
Seattle/Everett, Wash.	145,000	131
Springfield, Mass.	110,000	99
Stockton, Calif.	102,000	92
Syracuse, N.Y.	83,000	75
Tacoma, Wash.	119,000	107
Tampa/St. Petersburg, Fla.	76,000	69
Toledo, Ohio	75,000	67
Tucson, Ariz.	81,000	73
Tulsa, Okla.	74,000	67
Vallejo, Calif.	114,000	103
Ventura, Calif.	151,000	136
Washington, D.C.	162,000	145
West Palm Beach, Fla.	116,000	104
Wichita, Kan.	74,000	66
Wilmington, Del.	128,000	116
Youngstown/Warren, Ohio	66,000	59
National median home price	$111,000	100%

Source: Excerpted by permission from the January 1995 issue of *Kiplinger's Personal Finance Magazine.* Copyright © 1995 The Kiplinger Washington Editors, Inc.

- Filing an official declaration of domicile with states such as Florida that offer such forms.
- Changing bank, brokerage, and credit card accounts.
- Executing a will in the new state in which you refer to your domicile.
- Renting a safe deposit box at the new location and moving your valuables.

- Resigning from business, social, and religious organizations at your old location, or seeking nonresident or inactive membership status.
- Spending more time in the new state than the old one.

Turning Home Equity into an Income-Producing Investment

One compelling reason to move is to capture some or all the financial value of the equity in your residence and invest it to augment your retirement income. Moreover, because of the onetime $125,000 capital gains tax exclusion available to those 55 or older, you may be able to trade down to a smaller home and free a substantial amount of money from the proceeds of the sale to add to your retirement investment portfolio. As noted above, you could sell an average-priced house in an expensive region, buy an average-priced house in a lower-cost area of the country, and have money left to invest.

This trading down strategy doesn't necessarily require a move to a different part of the country. Moving to a less costly residence can make sense, even if you want to stay in the same general area. For example, let's assume you live in Chicago and your house is worth about one and a half times the average price of houses there. You could sell it and use the proceeds to buy another house in Chicago valued at 75 percent of the metropolitan-area average ($146,000 per accompanying chart). You would have about $110,000 left to invest, before any sales costs and taxes.

This strategy is particularly attractive for those age 55 and older because they can take advantage of a onetime tax exclusion on capital gains of up to $125,000 from the sale of a home. Generally, to be eligible, neither you nor your spouse can have used the exclusion before and the home must have been your principal residence for at least three of the five years before the sale date. To defer any gain over the $125,000, the price of the new residence must be equal to or greater than the price of your old residence, after adjustment for the age 55 exclusion and for selling expenses. Additionally, you must buy and occupy the new residence within 24 months before or after selling your old one.

Here is an example of the tax calculation for an owner 55 or older who sells a house for $250,000 that he purchased for $95,000. The mortgage has been paid off and there are $15,000 in selling expenses. He buys a new house for $170,000.

SELLING A RESIDENCE WITH THE AGE 55 EXCLUSION

Step 1

Sales price	$250,000
Cost basis	95,000
Gain	$155,000
Age 55 exclusion	125,000
Gain not covered by exclusion	$ 30,000

Step 2

Sales price	$250,000
Age 55 exclusion	(125,000)
Selling expenses	(15,000)
Adjusted sales price	$110,000
Cost of new residence	170,000
Gain recognized and subject to tax	$ 0

Step 3

Cost of new residence		$170,000
Less difference between the gain on sale of old residence not covered by exclusion and the gain recognized	$30,000 0	
		30,000
Cost basis of replacement house (with $30,000 of the gain deferred until the new house is sold)		$140,000

Here is how such a sale unlocks cash for investment: The proceeds from the first house would be $235,000 ($250,000 less $15,000 in selling expenses) because no capital gains tax is due. If the second house were purchased for cash, $65,000 would be available for investment. If the second house were purchased with a 25 percent down payment ($42,500) and the remainder financed with a mortgage, the cash available for investment would be $192,500. Assuming a 7 percent rate of return, that amount would generate about $13,500 per year in income. The combined use of the $125,000 exclusion and the deferral of gain on the sale and replacement of a residence represent—literally—a once-in-a-lifetime opportunity. Plan carefully to maximize their usefulness to you.

Our suggestion: Consider separately the question of whether to move or not after retirement for each of the three phases of your retirement years. You may want to stay put during the active early years of retirement to continue your income-producing activities, for example, then move later to another location. Or you may like the idea of planning to keep your present home until the later years of retirement, then moving to a retirement community offering special-care facilities.

Focus on...

A LOOK AT REVERSE MORTGAGES

The biggest single asset of most retirees is the value of the equity in their residences. But that value is locked in. Normally, it can't be spent unless the residence is sold. Second mortgages or home equity loans offer a way of borrowing against the value of a home to get cash. But they generally aren't available unless you have sufficient employment income, a requirement that puts them out of reach for the typical retiree.

To help retirees who want to tap the value of their home equity without selling or moving, some financial institutions now offer a form of loan called a reverse mortgage. These loans actually work in reverse, when compared to the traditional mortgage. With a traditional mortgage, your monthly payments gradually repay the principal that you borrowed, building up your equity. With a reverse mortgage, the lender makes payments to you in the form of loan advances. As the accrued principal and interest grow from these outstanding loan advances, your equity in the residence is drawn down. When you move or die, and the residence is sold, the balance of the reverse mortgage is repaid to the lender from the proceeds of the sale.

Reverse mortgages offer a variety of income options. You can receive monthly payments for life, or for a certain period of time, say 10 years. You can also choose a lump sum payment or a credit line against which you can withdraw money when you want it. The size of the reverse mortgage you can obtain depends on your age, prevailing interest rates, and the value of your equity in your residence. To qualify, you must be at least 62 years old and there must be little or no debt outstanding against your property. Other qualifications vary depending on whether your reverse mortgage is federally guaranteed or issued under a private lending program. The Federal Housing Administration guarantees reverse mortgage loans ranging up to a maximum of $124,875.

For information about reverse mortgages, contact:

- The National Center for Home Equity Conversion, 1210 E. College, Suite 300, Marshall, MN 56258 (507-532-3230).
- American Association of Retired Persons, Home Equity Information Center, Consumer Affairs Section, 601 E. Street, N.W., Washington, DC 20049 (202-872-4700).

Decision No. 5   How much should you expect from Social Security?

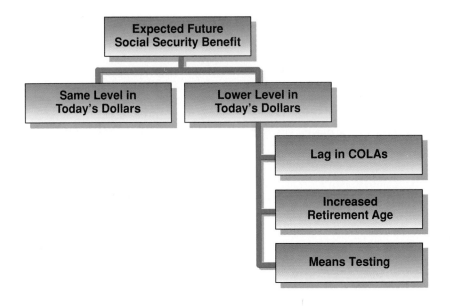

Social Security provides a basic retirement income with one particularly valuable feature: benefits that keep pace with inflation. Most employer pensions, in contrast, pay fixed monthly benefits for life. As a result, the value in "real" terms of fixed employer pensions—in other words, their purchasing power—steadily declines because of inflation.

That's not the case with Social Security. The purchasing power of your Social Security benefits remains constant as long as you live, thanks to the decision by Congress in the 1970s to increase benefits in line with the growth in consumer prices. As a result, even if Social Security initially provides only a small portion of your total retirement income, its relative importance will grow over the years as the purchasing power of your employer pension benefit declines.

The retirement benefit you will receive from Social Security is based on your career earnings. The maximum benefit in 1995 was $14,388 for a worker and $21,576 for a worker and spouse receiving a spousal benefit. Benefits are increased each year, as is the maximum amount of income subject to Social Security tax ($61,200 in 1995). Because of the cap, and because the benefit formula is more generous to lower-income

SHARE OF EARNINGS REPLACED BY SOCIAL SECURITY

| | *Percent Replaced by Social Security* | |
Annual Earnings	Individual Worker	Individual and Nonworking Spouse
$20,000	44%	66%
30,000	40	60
40,000	32	47
50,000	28	40
60,000	24	35
70,000	21	30
80,000	18	27
90,000	16	24
100,000	14	22

Percentages are approximate. Assumes raises equal to the U.S. average throughout career and retirement this year at age 65.

THE SOCIAL SECURITY "BONUS" FOR CLAIMING BENEFITS LATE

Year You Reach Age 65	Social Security Benefit Increase for Each Year You Delay Retirement after Age 65 (up to Age 70)
1992–93	4.0%
1994–95	4.5
1996–97	5.0
1998–99	5.5
2000–01	6.0
2002–03	6.5
2004–05	7.0
2006–07	7.5
2008 and after	8.0

workers, the higher your earnings, the smaller the portion of your salary that will be replaced by Social Security. For example, Social Security will replace about 40 percent of income for someone retiring this year at 65 with $30,000 in annual earnings. For someone making $70,000, Social Security benefits will replace about 21 percent of earnings.

To be eligible for Social Security benefits, you must have at least 40 credits, or quarters of covered employment. You gain one credit each time you earn a particular amount, up to a maximum of four credits each year. That amount of money, $630 in wages or self-employment income for 1995, is raised annually. In 1995, therefore, if you earned $2,520 or more ($630 × 4), you would receive four credits. The monthly Social Security benefit you will receive is known as your "primary insurance amount" and is based on the year of your birth and lifetime contributions to Social Security. Your spouse can receive a spousal benefit equal to one-half of your benefit on reaching age 65, although your spouse can't draw spousal benefits before you do. If both spouses are entitled to benefits on their own, they can receive them independently. Or one spouse can begin receiving his or her own benefit, then switch to a spousal benefit

HOW CREDIT FOR DELAYING SOCIAL SECURITY BEYOND AGE 65 WILL BOOST BENEFITS AFTER THE YEAR 2008

Years Delayed after 65	Annual Pension Benefit	Percent Increase in Benefit from Delaying Retirement
0	$14,388*	—
1	15,539	8%
2	16,782	16
3	18,124	26
4	19,574	36
5	21,141	47

*Maximum individual benefit in today's (1995) dollars.

when the other spouse retires if it provides a higher total monthly payment.

Workers who wait until after 65 to receive Social Security get a credit that slightly increases the amounts they are paid each month. For those age 65 in 1994 or 1995, for example, the increase is 4.5 percent each year for waiting until age 70 to start collecting benefits. The extra amount does not currently make up for the payments retirees lose by not starting to collect Social Security checks until after normal retirement age. But the credit is being raised so that it will amount to 8 percent per year of delay for those born after 1942.

Working during Retirement

You can plan to continue working full time during the early phase of retirement, or you can plan to collect Social Security benefits right away. But you shouldn't plan to do both. If you work after starting to receive Social Security, your benefits will be reduced once your employment income reaches a certain limitation, depending on your age. If you are under the normal retirement age (currently 65), you will start to lose Social Security benefits after your earnings exceed $8,160 (for 1995). For every $2 you earn above that amount, you lose $1 in benefits. For those 65 to 69, the (1995) limitation is $11,280. In this age group, for every $3 you earn above the limitation, your benefits are reduced by $1. The limitations are raised each year based on the change in average wages for all employees. After age 70, your Social Security benefits will not be reduced no matter how much you earn. The same rules apply to self-employment income, but not to investment income or other forms of unearned income.

HOW WORKING
REDUCES YOUR SOCIAL
SECURITY BENEFIT

Earned Income	*Social Security Benefit after Earnings Penalty*	
	Age 62–64	Age 65–69
$ 0	11,510	14,388
10,000	10,590	14,388
20,000	5,590	11,481
30,000	590	8,148
40,000	0	4,815
50,000	0	1,481
60,000	0	0

Table assumes you are eligible for the (1995) maximum individual benefit.

For those collecting Social Security, the earnings limitation functions as a tax on benefits that rises fairly quickly along with earned income to an effective rate of 100 percent. Thus, someone in the 62–64 group would lose all benefits when earnings pass $30,000. That threshold for the 65–69 group is an earnings level of just over $50,000. Clearly, it makes no sense to collect benefits while working and simultaneously to lose most or all of those benefits to the earnings limitation penalty. If you plan to work more than part time during retirement, don't count on getting Social Security benefits until age 70, when the earnings limitation is lifted.

Once you have started receiving Social Security, you can return to work and suspend your benefits. If you are under 65 and you repay the amount you have received, the reduction you took for retiring early will be canceled, and you will be eligible for full benefits reflecting your additional earnings at 65. If you suspend your benefits without repaying what you have received, you can have them recalculated when you reach 65 and will lose credit only for the period when you collected them.

The Future of Social Security

There is little doubt that Social Security will be around and will still be paying benefits when you are ready to retire. But there is also little doubt that Congress will be forced to change the Social Security system sometime within the next decade or so. The result is likely to be less purchasing power than would be projected today.

The reason? Social Security faces a looming financial shortfall because of changing demographic patterns. Over the next 35 years, the baby boom generation (those born from 1946 to 1964) will retire, while the smaller contingent of baby busters meets the Social Security payroll taxes. Forty years ago, 16 workers were contributing to Social Security for every recipient drawing benefits. Today the ratio is 3.3 to 1. Forty years from now, there will be only two workers paying for each retiree. The result will be bigger retirement bills and fewer workers to pay them.

Congress completed an overhaul of Social Security in 1983, pushing the normal retirement age to 67 by 2010, instituting a tax on Social Security retirement benefits, and raising Social Security taxes so they now generate a surplus each year. These surpluses are earmarked for a trust fund that is expected to swell to $3 trillion and then be depleted by 2029 as it is liquidated to pay benefits for retiring baby boomers. However, amounts credited to the trust fund are actually being invested in U.S. Treasury bonds and used to help finance the government's budget deficit. When it comes time to spend the trust fund for retirement benefits, the government will have to raise taxes to generate the cash needed to retire the bonds and provide Social Security with money to pay benefits.

With no changes in the current levels of benefits and taxes, Social Security will fall short in its ability to pay promised benefits. Estimates of the shortfall vary, but it seems at this point likely to be between 20 and 35 percent. Congress is expected to close the shortfall by raising taxes and cutting benefits. Among the ways that benefits could be trimmed: reducing cost-of-living increases, raising the normal retirement age to 70, and introducing a "means test" that would phase out benefits for upper-income retirees.

Our suggestion: Don't count on Social Security to replace the same portion of your income that it replaces for those in your earnings bracket who are retiring today.

Decision No. 6   How much will you set aside each year toward retirement?

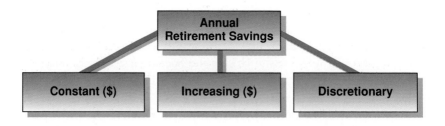

Once you have set your retirement goals, you are ready to analyze your financial resources and then determine what shortfall, if any, will have to be made up with additional annual savings. It's possible that your intended retirement lifestyle can be financed without any extra savings.

For example, you may expect a sizable pension benefit and may have built up a large balance over the last decade in your employer's 401(k) plans. Or you may plan to live simply in retirement on half your income in today's dollars, so that your living expenses can be supported by your pension and Social Security. Or both you and your spouse work and expect to collect substantial pensions. In short, you may be home free.

For most of us, however, the numbers will show a shortfall in expected retirement resources. If that's the case for you, it will be necessary either to increase your annual retirement savings, revise your spending goals, increase your investment return, retire later, or some combination of actions.

Your retirement resources will come from:

- An employer pension.
- Social Security.
- Retirement investments.
- Income-producing activities such as part-time work or self-employment.
- Other assets, such as the equity in your residence.

When you have refined your retirement goal and stated it in terms of the percentage of your income in today's dollars that you want to replace, say 70 percent, you are ready to use the worksheet on pages 344 and 345 to figure out how much you will set aside each year for retirement, also in today's dollars. Saving a constant amount in today's dollars means you are staying even in terms of the purchasing power that you are putting away for retirement. For example, to save $3,500 a year in today's dollars, assuming an inflation rate of 4 percent, you would set aside $3,500 the first year, $3,640 the second year, $3,786 the third year, and so forth, next year's contribution always being 1.04 times this year's amount.

Alternatively, if your income is experiencing steady growth year after year, you may want to increase your savings by more than the annual rate of inflation. If you saved $3,500 this year and raised that amount each year by 10 percent, you would accumulate $178,000 in today's dollars after 20 years, as compared to $106,000 if you increased your annual savings by the assumed 4 percent rate of inflation (assuming an 8 percent investment return).

A third approach is to budget your savings year by year on a discretionary basis. You may own a business and your income may be highly uneven, up one year and down the next. Or you may have little money available now to save for retirement but expect big gains in savings power down the road when your children have finished college or your mortgage has been paid off. In the examples here, we assume you save a constant amount in today's dollars. To plan for increasing savings or discretionary amounts, you will need the help of a financial planner or a financial planning computer program capable of handling uneven savings cash flows.

Planning Example 1—Jim and Mary Freeman

Jim and Mary Freeman are both 45 and want to retire when they reach 65. Jim makes $95,000 today and Mary has no earned income. Their goal is to replace 70 percent of Jim's salary, which means they will need annual income of about $66,500 in today's dollars during retirement.

Jim and Mary will be entitled to Social Security benefits of $21,600 in today's dollars. But they expect the purchasing power of their Social Security benefit to be reduced by about 25 percent by the time they retire, so they have decided to plan for a benefit in today's dollars of $16,000.

Jim has a pension from a previous employer that will be worth $5,000 a year in today's dollars at retirement and expects a pension of

---

Retirement planning example   GATHERING THE BASIC INFORMATION

Example 1—Jim and Mary Freeman	Jim	Mary
1. Current age	45	45
2. Retirement age	65	65
3. Life expectancy	85	90
4. Years until retirement	20	20
5. Years in retirement	20	25
6. Current annual income	$95,000	
7. Retirement income replacement ratio	70%	
8. Annual retirement income goal (today's dollars)	$66,500	
9. Estimated Social Security benefits (today's dollars)	$16,000	
10. Estimated pension income (today's dollars)	$30,000	
11. Value of investments available to fund retirement	$91,000	

Retirement planning example

HOW MUCH DO I NEED TO SAVE EACH YEAR TO MEET MY RETIREMENT GOAL?

Example 1—Jim and Mary Freeman

1. Annual retirement income goal (today's dollars)			$66,500
2. Estimated Social Security benefits (today's dollars)			$16,000
3. Estimated pension income (today's dollars)			$30,000
4. Income needed from investments (today's dollars) (Line 1 – Line 2 – Line 3)			$20,500
5. Income needed from investments at retirement (Line 4 × Factor from Table 1 page 346)	Factor: 2.19		$44,895
6. Capital needed to fund income from investments (Line 5 × Factor from Table 2 page 347)	Factor: 16.49		$740,319
7. Income needed to maintain purchasing power of pension (Line 3 × Factor from Table 1 page 346)	Factor: 2.19		$65,700
8. Capital needed to fund income to maintain purchasing power of pension (Line 7 × Factor from Table 3 page 347)	Factor: 4.96		$325,872
9. Total capital required at beginning of retirement (future dollars) (Line 6 + Line 8)			$1,066,191
10. Value (in today's dollars) of investments available to fund retirement (401(k), IRA, profit sharing, deferred compensation, and personal investments)			$91,000
11. Value of investments at retirement (future dollars) (Line 10 × Factor from Table 4 page 348)	Factor: 4.66		$424,060
12. Write in amount from Line 9			$1,066,191

If Line 11 is greater than Line 12, you do not need to save any more for retirement. If Line 12 is greater than Line 11, enter difference between the two on Line 13.

13. Additional capital needed at retirement (future dollars) (Line 12 – Line 11)			$642,131
14. Additional capital needed at retirement (today's dollars) (Line 13 divided by Factor from Table 4 page 348)	Factor: 4.66		$137,796
15. Required annual savings (today's dollars) (Line 14 × Factor from Table 5 page 349)	Factor: .075		$10,335

Each year, to maintain the constant purchasing power of the amount you save, this should be increased by 4%.

16. Required annual savings next year (Line 15 × 1.04)			$10,748

$25,000 a year from his current employer. Both pensions will pay fixed monthly benefits.

Jim expects to live to age 85 and Mary to age 90. They now save about $850 a month for retirement, mostly through Jim's 401(k) savings plan at work, and their retirement investments total $91,000. They expect to earn an 8 percent return on their retirement investments.

The worksheet shows that Jim and Mary have a shortfall in retirement investment funds of $137,796 in today's dollars. To close that gap, they need to be saving about $10,300. At the current rate of $850 a month, their savings are nearly adequate to close that gap. To stay on track, they need to increase their savings next year to about $895 a month.

Planning Example 2—Johanna Quint

Johanna Quint, 35, wants to retire at age 60 with an income in today's dollars of about $44,000, or 80 percent of her current $55,000 salary. She expects $14,000 in Social Security benefits and a pension of $21,000 in today's dollars from her employer, a large hospital. Johanna's retirement investments total about $37,000, and she now saves about $200 a month toward retirement. She expects an 8 percent return on her retirement investments.

Retirement planning example	GATHERING THE BASIC INFORMATION

Example 2—Johanna Quint

1. Current age	35
2. Retirement age	60
3. Life expectancy	90
4. Years until retirement	25
5. Years in retirement	30
6. Current annual income	$55,000
7. Retirement income replacement ratio	80%
8. Annual retirement income goal (today's dollars)	$44,000
9. Estimated Social Security benefits (today's dollars)	$14,000
10. Estimated pension income (today's dollars)	$21,000
11. Value of investments available to fund retirement	$37,000

Retirement planning example   HOW MUCH DO I NEED TO SAVE
EACH YEAR TO MEET MY
RETIREMENT GOAL?

Example 2—Johanna Quint

1.	Annual retirement income goal (today's dollars)	$44,000
2.	Estimated Social Security benefits (today's dollars)	$14,000
3.	Estimated pension income (today's dollars)	$21,000
4.	Income needed from investments (today's dollars) (Line 1 − Line 2 − Line 3)	$9,000
5.	Income needed from investments at retirement (Line 4 × Factor from Table 1 page 346) Factor: 2.67	$24,030
6.	Capital needed to fund income from investments (Line 5 × Factor from Table 2 page 347) Factor: 18.30	$439,749
7.	Income needed to maintain purchasing power of pension (Line 3 × Factor from Table 1 page 346) Factor: 2.67	$56,070
8.	Capital needed to fund income to maintain purchasing power of pension (Line 7 × Factor from Table 3 page 347) Factor: 6.14	$344,270
9.	Total capital required at beginning of retirement (future dollars) (Line 6 + Line 8)	$784,019
10.	Value (in today's dollars) of investments available to fund retirement (401(k), IRA, profit sharing, deferred compensation, and personal investments)	$37,000
11.	Value of investments at retirement (future dollars) (Line 10 × Factor from Table 4 page 348) Factor: 6.85	$253,450
12.	Write in amount from Line 9	$784,019

If Line 11 is greater than Line 12, you do not need to save any more for retirement. If Line 12 is greater than Line 11, enter difference between the two on Line 13.

13.	Additional capital needed at retirement (future dollars) (Line 12 − Line 11)	$530,569
14.	Additional capital needed at retirement (today's dollars) (Line 13 divided by Factor from Table 4 page 348) Factor: 6.85	$77,455
15.	Required annual savings (today's dollars) (Line 14 × Factor from Table 5 page 349) Factor: .065	$5,035

Each year, to maintain the constant purchasing power of the amount you save, this should be increased by 4%.

16.	Required annual savings next year (Line 15 × 1.04)	$5,236

The worksheet shows Johanna with an investment shortfall of $77,455 at retirement in today's dollars, indicating she needs to be saving $5,035 a year, or $420 a month, to close the gap. That amounts to 9 percent of her pretax income, and Johanna thinks saving this would be too much of a stretch. However, she is determined to retire at 60. One way to keep her retirement plan on track is to reduce her income goal to $40,000 in today's dollars, or about 73 percent of her income. Redoing her worksheet calculations using the new goal, her investment shortfall declines to about $49,000 in today's dollars, a gap she can close by saving $3,200 a year, or $265 a month. By reducing her current consumption and saving another $65 a month, Johanna decides, her new plan will work.

Planning Example 3—Bruce and Virginia Bledsoe

Bruce Bledsoe, 48, is an independent manufacturer's representative who owns his own business. Virginia Bledsoe, 42, graduated from law school when she was 33 and now is a partner in a successful law firm. Bruce wants to sell his business and retire by 65, but he can't count on being able to realize any particular amount of proceeds from the sale. Virginia has no interest in retirement and plans to work at least to age 70.

Retirement planning example	GATHERING THE BASIC INFORMATION	

Example 3—Bruce and Virginia Bledsoe	Bruce	Virginia
1. Current age	48	42
2. Retirement age	65	70
3. Life expectancy	85	90
4. Years until retirement	17	28
5. Years in retirement	20	20
6. Current annual income	$175,000	$120,000
7. Retirement income replacement ratio	75%	75%
8. Annual retirement income goal (today's dollars)	$131,000	$90,000
9. Estimated Social Security benefits (today's dollars)	—	—
10. Estimated pension income (today's dollars)	$65,000	$55,000
11. Value of investments available to fund retirement	$155,000	$155,000

Retirement planning example   HOW MUCH DO I NEED TO SAVE EACH YEAR TO MEET MY RETIREMENT GOAL?

Example 3—Bruce and Virginia Bledsoe	Bruce	Virginia
1. Annual retirement income goal (today's dollars)	$131,000	$90,000
2. Estimated Social Security benefits (today's dollars)	—	—
3. Estimated pension income (today's dollars)	$65,000	$55,000
4. Income needed from investments (today's dollars) (Line 1 − Line 2 − Line 3)	$66,000	$35,000
5. Income needed from investments at retirement (Line 4 × Factor from Table 1 page 346)	$128,700 Factor: 1.95	$105,000 Factor: 3.00
6. Capital needed to fund income from investments (Line 5 × Factor from Table 2 page 347)	$1,841,697 Factor: 14.31	$1,502,550 Factor: 14.31
7. Income needed to maintain purchasing power of pension (Line 3 × Factor from Table 1 page 346)	$126,750 Factor: 1.95	$165,000 Factor: 3.00
8. Capital needed to fund income to maintain purchasing power of pension (Line 7 × Factor from Table 3 page 347)	$468,975 Factor: 3.7	$610,500 Factor: 3.7
9. Total capital required at beginning of retirement (future dollars) (Line 6 + Line 8)	$2,310,672	$2,113,050
10. Value (in today's dollars) of investments available to fund retirement (401(k), IRA, profit sharing, deferred compensation, and personal investments)	$155,000	$155,000
11. Value of investments at retirement (future dollars) (Line 10 × Factor from Table 4 page 348)	$573,500 Factor: 3.70	$1,337,650 Factor: 8.63
12. Write in amount from Line 9	$2,310,672	$2,113,050
If Line 11 is greater than Line 12, you do not need to save any more for retirement. If Line 12 is greater than Line 11, enter difference between the two on Line 13.		
13. Additional capital needed at retirement (future dollars) (Line 12 − Line 11)	$1,737,172	$775,400

Retirement planning example
concluded

HOW MUCH DO I NEED TO SAVE
EACH YEAR TO MEET MY
RETIREMENT GOAL?

Example 3—Bruce and Virginia Bledsoe	Bruce	Virginia
14. Additional capital needed at retirement (today's dollars) (Line 13 divided by Factor from Table 4 page 348)	$469,506	$89,850
	Factor: 3.70	Factor: 8.63
15. Required annual savings (today's dollars) (Line 14 × Factor from Table 5 page 349)	$39,438	$5,481
Each year, to maintain the constant purchasing power of the amount you save, this should be increased by 4%.	Factor: .084	Factor: .061
16. Required annual savings next year (Line 15 × 1.04)	$41,016	$5,700

Their combined income is about $295,000, and they believe they could live comfortably in retirement with 75 percent of that amount in today's dollars. They estimate their pensions will total about $120,000 in today's dollars and don't expect to receive any Social Security benefits because of the level of their incomes. They have about $310,000 in investment assets and assume an 8 percent return on their retirement investments. Because Bruce is a business owner and Virginia is a law firm partner, both are contributing to their pensions through their firms, but are not saving anything each year in addition to that.

Their worksheet shows that Bruce and Virginia have a total shortfall in retirement investment funds of about $559,000 in today's dollars. They can make it up by saving $44,900 a year, which equals about 15 percent of their current combined pretax incomes. Instead, Bruce and Virginia decide to invest more aggressively and take on the greater risk that will come with seeking a 10 percent return on their retirement investments. They figure the greater risk is warranted because of their high incomes and degree of control over their retirement dates. With a 10 percent investment return, the couple needs to be saving about $23,100 a year, or $1,930 a month toward retirement.

Our suggestion: Start setting aside enough now to reach your retirement goal. Each year, increase the amount you save by 4 percent, an amount that will comfortably retain the purchasing power of the amount you are setting aside, based on historical levels of inflation.

Decision No. 7   Will you make your retirement investments on a taxable or tax-deferred basis?

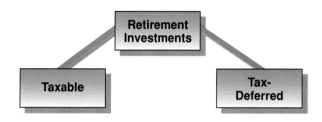

Congress has built incentives into the tax laws to encourage saving for retirement. Money placed in retirement plans, individual retirement accounts, and annuities grows without being taxed until withdrawal. The advantages of this tax deferral, as we saw in Chapter 4, can be compelling. Allowing income to compound without losing a portion of your return to taxes each year means your money can grow much faster. Tax deferral is particularly valuable in helping you reach your retirement goal because the long time horizon gives tax-deferred compounding an extended opportunity to work in your favor.

Be aware, however, that the benefits of tax deferral come with a price. Tax-deferred investments offer less flexibility and impose more recordkeeping burdens than taxable investments. A more important drawback: Tax-deferred investments may be subject to withdrawal penalties. Other restrictions and penalties may apply as well, depending on the type of account. Here is a look at some of them:

The Penalty for Withdrawing Too Soon   If you withdraw money from a tax-deferred account before age 59½, you normally must pay a 10 percent penalty plus income tax on the amount withdrawn. No IRS penalty or tax is due on withdrawals of nondeductible, or after-tax, contributions. In addition, some types of tax-deferred investments such as annuities carry their own penalties in the form of surrender charges applied to any amounts withdrawn within a certain initial period, typically the first seven years or so after purchasing the annuity.

The Penalty for Withdrawing Too Little

Once you reach age 70½, you must start taking out a minimum amount of money each year from tax-deferred accounts, including employee savings plans and individual retirement accounts. (This rule does not apply to individual tax-deferred annuities.) If you take out too little, you must pay a penalty equal to 50 percent of the amount of the underwithdrawal.

The Penalty for Withdrawing Too Much

If you withdraw more than $150,000 in one year from your retirement plans—including any pension, 401(k), IRA, or employee stock ownership plans—you must pay a penalty in the form of a 15 percent excess distributions tax on the amount over $150,000. Social Security benefits are not included, nor are any after-tax contributions that you withdraw from your retirement plans. You face the same penalty on any portion of a lump-sum distribution from a qualified retirement plan that is greater than $750,000. (Again, this rule does not apply to individual tax-deferred annuities.)

When a Tax Deduction Is Available, Tax Deferral Makes Sense

The point here is not to play down the attractiveness of tax-deferred investing vs. taxable investing for retirement. But you shouldn't automatically assume that a tax-deferred investment is a better choice than a taxable one. Tax deferral clearly has its advantages. In fact, when tax *deferral* is coupled with a tax *deduction* for your contribution to a retirement account, it will almost always be a better choice. With a deductible contribution, not only does your investment compound without tax until withdrawal, but also the deduction helps you finance the contribution. How? The amount of tax you save because of the deduction in effect becomes an interest-free loan from the government. And you don't have to repay the loan until your contribution is withdrawn many years in the future.

Tax deductions are available to individuals for contributions to several types of retirement accounts.

Individual Retirement Accounts

You can deduct up to $2,000 a year from earned income for contributions to an individual retirement account if neither you nor your spouse are eligible to participate in an employer-sponsored retirement plan. (The limit is $2,250 for a spousal IRA, which can be used if one spouse has no earned income.) If you or your spouse are eligible for a retirement plan at work, you can still deduct up to $2,000 in IRA contributions if your income is less than $25,000 for an individual or $40,000 for a couple filing a joint tax return. IRA deductions are phased out as income reaches $35,000 for a single individual or $50,000 for a couple.

Employee Savings Plans (Corporate)

If you participate in your employer's 401(k) savings plan, you can currently defer up to $9,240 in earnings each year. That amount is indexed to inflation but is adjusted upward only when the cumulative growth in the consumer price index is large enough to cause the deferral limit to increase by $500. The actual annual limit on deferrals may be lower than the legal limit for some plans or some employees. Many employers will match some or all of your contribution up to a certain limit—for example, 6 percent of your salary.

Employee Savings Plans (Nonprofit)

If you work for a non-profit organization, such as a hospital, university, or public school, you are eligible for something similar, a 403(b) plan. Your employer may sponsor a 403(b) or, if not, you may be able to arrange for an individual 403(b) plan through an insurance company or mutual fund company. As with a 401(k), your salary is reduced by the amount of your contribution to a 403(b) plan. The annual contribution limit is 25 percent of salary up to a ceiling of $9,500. That ceiling will be adjusted upward for inflation once the 401(k) contribution ceiling (currently $9,240) catches up with it. In certain circumstances, employees nearing retirement age may be entitled to exceed these contribution limits in 403(b) plans. Nonprofit employers may also make matching contributions to 403(b) plans.

Self-Employed (Keogh) and Simplified Employee Retirement Plans (SEPs)

Self-employed individuals can choose among several types of retirement plans offering deductible contributions. Keogh profit-sharing plans and SEPs, for example, allow deductible contributions of up to $22,500, or 15 percent of income, whichever is less. If you are self-employed, the effective contribution limit is $19,560 or 13.04 percent of self-employment earnings after deduction for one-half of individual self-employment taxes, whichever is less. However, you can contribute

INDIVIDUAL CONTRIBUTION LIMITS
FOR TAX-DEFERRED INVESTMENTS

Tax-Deferred Investment	Individual Deductible Contribution/ Limit	Individual Nondeductible Contribution/ Limit
Company savings plan or 401(k)	Up to $9,240*	May be possible
Employer pension plan	Not applicable	May be possible
Nonprofit employer (403(b)) plan	Up to $9,500	May be possible
Individual retirement account	Up to $2,000†	Up to $2,000
Self-employed (Keogh) pension	Various limits	May be possible
Individual tax-deferred annuity	Not applicable	No legal limit

*Limit may be less for particular plans or employees.

†Neither you nor your spouse can be eligible to participate in an employer-sponsored retirement plan. For others, deduction is phased out at $35,000 for singles and $50,000 for couples.

less than the maximum, or even zero, in any year if you choose. This flexibility makes a Keogh profit-sharing plan or SEP attractive if your self-employment income varies substantially year to year.

Another type of plan, known as a money purchase plan, lets you contribute up to 25 percent of earnings or $30,000—again, whichever is less. (For the self-employed, the effective limit after deduction of self-employment taxes is 20 percent of salary or $30,000.) However, you must commit to contributing a fixed percentage of salary every year, with a 10 percent penalty levied by the IRS on any amount you should have contributed but didn't.

You can also combine the features of profit-sharing and money-purchase plans into what is known as a paired plan. With a paired plan, you commit to contributing a certain percentage of salary each year and can make additional variable annual contributions as well. The ceiling for total contributions is set at 25 percent of earnings or $30,000, whichever is less (20 percent or $30,000 of income after self-employment taxes).

With No Deduction, Does Tax Deferral Still Make Sense?

What if you aren't eligible for a tax-deductible retirement contribution? Let's say you have a pension plan at work, but no 401(k) plan. If your

HOW THE IRA DEDUCTION IS PHASED OUT AS INCOME RISES

Single/Married Income	Maximum IRA Deduction for Workers Eligible to Participate in Employer-Sponsored Retirement Plan
$25,000/$40,000	$2,000
26,000/ 41,000	1,800
27,000/ 42,000	1,600
28,000/ 43,000	1,400
29,000/ 44,000	1,200
30,000/ 45,000	1,000
31,000/ 46,000	800
32,000/ 47,000	600
33,000/ 48,000	400
34,000/ 49,000	200
35,000/ 50,000	0

income is above $50,000 for a married couple, you can't deduct an IRA contribution and probably don't have access to any other type of deductible retirement investment. Or perhaps you have a pension and 401(k) plan at work but have contributed the maximum amount to the 401(k) and still want to invest more for retirement this year. What are your options?

Tax deferral is still available, but only for amounts that are invested on a nondeductible, or after-tax, basis. One possible option is to make after-tax contributions to your employer's retirement plan. Some employer plans permit after-tax contributions by employees up to certain limits. In these instances, employees can use the employer plan as a kind of tax-deferred retirement savings account. Another option is to contribute up to $2,000 on a nondeductible basis to an IRA. A third option is to invest in an individual deferred annuity. Deferred annuities are a type of insurance contract that offers tax deferral of investment earnings and a minimum death benefit. There is no legal limit on the amount you can invest.

But without a deduction, does tax deferral still make sense? Or would you be better off simply investing on a fully taxable basis? The answer will depend on your own circumstances, particularly your tax bracket, your investment time horizon, and the type of investment income you intend to seek. Here's why.

Your tax-deferred income may end up being taxed at a higher rate. All income withdrawn from a tax-deferred account is taxed as ordinary income (maximum rate 39.6 percent) even if it resulted from long-term capital gains (otherwise taxed at a maximum rate of 28 percent). For example, let's say your tax rate for ordinary income is 31 percent, or three percentage points higher than the 28 percent maximum rate for long-term capital gains income. If you sold an investment that had

INVESTING ON A FULLY TAXABLE BASIS
SOMETIMES MAKES SENSE

Ordinary income = Income from such sources as wages, salaries, self-employment, dividends, and interest.

Long-term capital
gains income = Gains from the sale of capital assets such as stocks, bonds, or real estate that have been owned for at least one year.

	For Taxable Income above These Amounts	
Tax Rates for Ordinary Income	Single	Married
28%	$ 23,350	$ 39,000
31	56,550	94,250
36	117,950	143,600
39.6	256,500	256,500

Maximum tax rate for long-term capital gains income: 28%

increased in value by $1,000 over several years, the income would be considered a long-term capital gain and your tax would be $280. However, if the investment had been owned in a tax-deferred account such as an IRA, the $1,000 gain would be considered ordinary income even though it was derived from the gain on the sale of your investment. The result: Your tax at withdrawal would be $310. As the example above shows, there may be circumstances where you are better off investing on a fully taxable basis outside a tax-deferred account.

Let's look at the effect of the differential between the tax rate on long-term capital gains and the rates on ordinary income. Say you invest $1,000 in a tax-deferred account and another $1,000 on a fully taxable basis. In each case, you use the money to buy stocks that appreciate in price by 6 percent a year and generate 2 percent a year in dividend income. For the taxable account, you pay taxes each year on the 2 percent dividend income at your ordinary income tax rate and reinvest the remainder. For the tax-deferred account, the dividends are reinvested without tax. After 10 years, you sell the stocks in both accounts, withdraw the money, and pay all taxes due.

Which approach provides the better return? It depends first on your tax rate. The higher your tax bracket—and thus the larger the spread

TAXABLE VS. TAX-DEFERRED GAIN FROM
$1,000 STOCK INVESTMENT OVER 10 YEARS

Tax Bracket	Fully Taxable Gain	Tax-Deferred Gain	Ratio of Tax-Deferred Return to Taxable Return
28%	$751	$834	1.11
31	741	800	1.08
36	724	742	1.02
39.6	713	700	0.98

Assumes 8% total return, 6% from unrealized long-term capital gains and 2% from dividends. Investments sold, funds withdrawn, and deferred taxes paid at the end of the 10-year period. Capital gains tax rate is 28%.

TAXABLE VS. TAX-DEFERRED GAIN FROM
$1,000 BOND FUND INVESTMENT OVER 10 YEARS

Tax Bracket	Fully Taxable Gain	Tax-Deferred Gain	Ratio of Gain Tax-Deferred/Fully Taxable
28%	$457	$696	1.52
31	416	667	1.60
36	352	619	1.76
39.6	310	584	1.88

Assumes 7% total return, all from interest income. Investments sold, funds withdrawn, and deferred taxes paid at the end of the 10-year period.

between the rate you pay on ordinary income and the rate you pay on long-term capital gains income—the more attractive it will be for you to invest for capital appreciation on a fully taxable basis outside a tax-deferred account. Here is what your gain would be net of taxes after 10 years, depending on your tax bracket.

Second, as we have seen, the taxable vs. tax-deferred equation depends on the type of asset in which you are investing. If the income generated by your investments is ordinary income—not subject to the

TAXABLE VS. TAX-DEFERRED GAIN
FROM $1,000 STOCK INVESTMENT OVER 10 YEARS
NET OF 1.3% AVERAGE ANNUAL FEE FOR VARIABLE ANNUITY

Tax Bracket	Fully Taxable Gain	Tax-Deferred Gain	Ratio of Gain Tax-Deferred/Fully Taxable
28%	$751	$657	0.87
31	741	630	0.85
36	724	584	0.81
39.6	713	551	0.77

Assumes 8% total return, 6% from unrealized long-term capital gains and 2% from dividends. Also assumes return is reduced by an annual expense of 1.3%, the average fee charged by tax-deferred variable annuities. Investments sold, funds withdrawn, and deferred taxes paid at the end of the 10-year period.

more favorable long-term capital gains tax rate—then tax deferral may be more attractive. Let's take the example of an investment in a bond fund with a 7 percent return consisting of dividends taxed at ordinary income rates. In this case, the higher your tax bracket, the more attractive tax deferral becomes.

A third factor is the extra cost, if any, that accompanies tax deferral. In many cases, that cost will be negligible. For example, you may have to pay a slightly higher annual fee to maintain an IRA account than you would pay for a comparable taxable account. Fees for accounts such as Keogh plans will be more substantial because of additional recordkeeping and reporting requirements. But in either case the amounts involved will be relatively small.

In other instances, however, fees associated with tax deferral can become significant. Let's look at one popular tax-deferred investment, variable annuities, and see how they illustrate the impact of fees on returns.

Variable annuities can be thought of as tax-deferred mutual funds. They typically offer a choice of several mutual fund-like "subaccounts" with different investment objectives such as growth, growth and income, and so forth. (For a more detailed discussion of annuities, see page 225 in this chapter.) Like mutual funds, variable annuities levy annual fees for

TAXABLE VS. TAX-DEFERRED GAIN FROM $1,000 BOND FUND INVESTMENT OVER 10 YEARS NET OF 1.3% AVERAGE ANNUAL FEE FOR VARIABLE ANNUITY

Tax Bracket	Fully Taxable Gain	Tax-Deferred Gain (w/1.3% Fee)	Ratio of Gain Tax-Deferred/Fully Taxable
28%	$457	$533	1.17
31	416	511	1.23
36	352	474	1.35
39.6	310	447	1.44

Assumes 7% total return, all from interest income. Also assumes return is reduced by an annual expense of 1.3%, the average fee charged by tax-deferred variable annuities. Investments sold, funds withdrawn, and deferred taxes paid at the end of the 10-year period.

investment management and administrative costs. And because they offer a death benefit, variable annuities charge an additional fee to cover the death benefit and related insurance costs. These additional fees average about 1.3 percent a year, according to Morningstar, Inc. The higher the fee, the less attractive such annuities will be when compared to fully taxable investments.

A fourth factor in deciding whether to invest on a taxable or taxdeferred basis is your investment time horizon. If there is much likelihood that you will need the money before retirement, then the 10 percent penalty for withdrawals before age 59½ will make tax deferral much less attractive. Likewise, if the tax-deferred investment you are considering also carries a surrender charge in the initial years after your purchase, as is the case with most deferred annuities, it becomes even less advantageous for anything but a lengthy investment time horizon.

On the other hand, the longer you keep your money in a taxdeferred investment, the more time there will be for the benefits of tax deferral to outweigh any extra costs that may be involved. In the case of a deferred annuity, for example, you can estimate the length of the holding period that will be required before the tax benefits of deferral will outweigh the added insurance-related costs posed by the annuity. That

BREAK-EVEN PERIODS FOR VARIABLE ANNUITIES

Stock Investments

Return (Capital Gain % Return + Dividend % Return)

Tax Rate	7% (5% + 2%)	8% (6% + 2%)	9% (7% + 2%)	10% (7% + 3%)	
28%	49 years	32 years	23 years	18 years	Break-even
31	—	35	26	20	period for
36	—	39	31	23	variable
39.6	—	42	34	25	annuity

Variable annuity insurance expense of 1.3%

With stock investments, the higher your tax rate, the longer it takes for a variable annuity to break even.

Bond Investments

Return (Consists of Ordinary Interest Income)

Tax Rate	7%	8%	9%	10%	
28%	49 years	32 years	23 years	18 years	Break-even
31	39	27	20	17	period for
36	30	21	16	13	variable
39.6	26	19	14	11	annuity

Variable annuity insurance expense of 1.3%

With bonds, the higher your tax rate, the sooner a variable annuity breaks even.

break-even holding period will vary depending on your tax bracket, the assumed investment return, and the expense charged by the insurance company offering the annuity. The charts for this illustration show various break-even holding periods for investments made in a tax-deferred variable annuity. They assume investment gains are realized each year and funds are withdrawn from the annuity at year end. They also assume no withdrawals before age 59½.

As the charts show, break-even periods vary significantly depending on your tax bracket and whether the investments generate ordinary income or long-term capital gains income. With stock investments, the

HOW LOWER EXPENSES AFFECT BREAK-EVEN PERIODS

Stock Investments in Variable Annuities

Return (Capital Gain % Return + Dividend % Return)

Tax Rate	7% (5% + 2%)	8% (6% + 2%)	9% (7% + 2%)	10% (7% + 3%)	
28%	29 years	20 years	15 years	12 years	Break-even
31	31	23	18	14	period for
36	36	28	23	18	variable
39.6	39	31	26	20	annuity

Variable annuity insurance expense of 1.0%

Lower expenses shorten the break-even period for variable annuities.

Bond Investments in Variable Annuities

Return (Consists of Ordinary Interest Income)

Tax Rate	7%	8%	9%	10%	
28%	29 years	20 years	15 years	12 years	Break-even
31	24	18	14	11	period for
36	20	15	11	9	variable
39.6	17	13	10	8	annuity

Variable annuity insurance expense of 1.0%

Particularly for variable annuities invested in bonds.

higher your tax rate, the longer it takes for a variable annuity to break even. In contrast, with bond investments, the higher your tax rate, the sooner a variable annuity breaks even. Break-even holding periods are shorter if the insurance costs are reduced.

Our suggestion: First, use all tax-deductible opportunities for retirement investing. If your employer matches part of your contribution, contribute enough to get the maximum available match. Once you have used up your tax-deductible retirement investing opportunities, carefully weigh the costs and potential advantages of making further tax-deferred investments on a nondeductible, or after-tax, basis.

Decision No. 8   Should you take an annuity or a lump-sum distribution from your company's retirement plan?

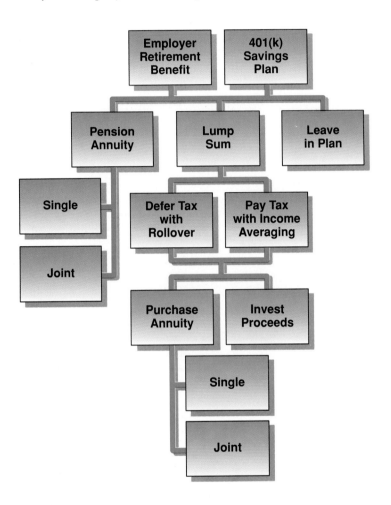

At retirement, you will probably face a decision about the payout of your retirement plan benefits. For example, you may be able to choose between a fixed monthly pension benefit for life and a lump-sum distribution of part or all of your retirement plan balance. The idea of the pension may appeal to you because it's a guaranteed monthly payment that you cannot outlive. Choose this option and you will then have to decide between a monthly benefit amount that will end at your death and a lower level of benefit that will continue as long as you *or* your spouse is alive.

On the other hand, you may find the lump sum appealing. It affords more flexibility and control, as well as the possibility of inflation protection if you invest the money for growth. Elect the lump sum and you must choose whether to pay taxes on it at a favorable onetime rate or to keep the money at work tax-deferred by rolling it over into an individual retirement account. The choices involved are complex and often your selection of a pension plan distribution option is irrevocable; you don't get a chance to change your mind after a year or two. Make the wrong move and you can find yourself stuck with an unexpected tax bill or with a pension plan payout that does not meet your needs.

Choosing between a Pension Annuity and a Lump-Sum Payout

Whether you have a choice between a pension annuity and a lump sum will depend on your employer's retirement plan. Traditional employer pension plans, known as defined-benefit plans, all offer a pension annuity; some also give you the option of a lump-sum distribution. In contrast, 401(k) savings plans all offer a lump-sum distribution. But they may also give you the option of keeping your money in the plan after retirement or of converting your plan balance to a pension annuity. As a result, if you participate in both a defined-benefit plan and 401(k) plan at work, you may be faced with two annuity vs. lump-sum decisions.

Your pension annuity over your life expectancy and an optional lump sum are designed to have the same value, or be "actuarially equivalent." That means the present value of your expected future annuity payments (assuming you live to exactly your predicted life expectancy) should equal the value of the lump sum. To figure that value, your employer will start with the amount of the monthly benefit you have earned, then factor in your life expectancy and an assumed rate of investment return. The life expectancy will project the number of payments you would receive if you chose the pension annuity. And the assumed investment return will be used to figure the present value of each of your future monthly payments. The total of those present values should be the amount of your lump sum.

In practice, employers have some leeway in choosing the investment return assumptions used to figure lump sums for all but the highest-paid employees. (After 1999, the investment return rate used to calculate lump sums will be tied to 30-year Treasury bond rates.) As a result, the lump-sum option you are offered may be more or less "generous" in relation to

Focus on...

WHAT ABOUT TAX-EXEMPT INVESTMENTS?

Another way to manage the tax exposure of your retirement portfolio is to invest the bond portion in municipal bonds. Interest from these securities, issued by state and local governments, is not generally subject to federal income taxes and may be free of state and local taxes as well. The same is true of dividends from mutual funds and unit trusts that invest in municipal bonds.

What's the catch? Municipal bonds offer lower yields than taxable bonds of comparable maturities and credit quality. For example, if a U.S. Treasury bond yields 7.5 percent, a high-quality municipal bond of the same maturity might yield 6 percent. How do you compare tax-exempt and taxable yields? Would it be better, for example, to choose a tax-free investment yielding 6 percent or a taxable investment with a 7.5 percent yield? It depends on your tax bracket. You can make the comparisons yourself using two simple calculations.

To convert a tax-exempt yield to the equivalent taxable yield, divide the tax-exempt yield by 1 minus your federal income tax rate, expressed as a decimal fraction. If your federal tax rate is 28 percent, you would use .28. Here is an illustration using a 6 percent tax-exempt yield:

$$\frac{6\ percent}{(1-.28)} \quad or \quad \frac{6\ percent}{.72} \quad = \quad 8.3\ percent \qquad \begin{array}{l}Equivalent \\ taxable\ yield\end{array}$$

In other words, you would need to obtain an 8.3 percent yield on a taxable investment to match a 6 percent tax-exempt yield.

To convert a taxable yield to a tax-exempt yield, multiply the taxable yield by 1 minus your tax rate. In this example, let's say your tax rate is 31 percent and you are considering the purchase of a taxable security yielding 7.5 percent.

7.5 percent × (1 − .31) or 7.5 percent × .69 = 5.2 percent   Equivalent
                                                             tax-free
                                                             yield

This means a tax-exempt investment yielding 5.2 percent would have the same after-tax return for you as the taxable investment yielding 7.5 percent. A warning: When deciding between taxable and tax-exempt investments, make sure credit quality and maturity are comparable. Longer-term investments, and those with lower credit quality, may offer higher returns, but they will also pose greater risks.

HOW TO COMPARE TAX-EXEMPT AND TAXABLE YIELDS

	Tax Bracket				
Tax-Exempt Yield	28%	31%	36%	39.6%	
4.0%	5.6%	5.8%	6.3%	6.6%	Equivalent
4.5	6.3	6.5	7.0	7.5	taxable yield
5.0	6.9	7.2	7.8	8.3	
5.5	7.6	8.0	8.6	9.1	
6.0	8.3	8.7	9.4	9.9	
6.5	9.0	9.4	10.2	10.8	
7.0	9.7	10.1	10.9	11.6	

the value of your monthly pension benefit, depending on the investment return assumption your employer uses. The higher the return, the less your lump-sum value will be; the lower the return, the bigger your lump sum. That's because a greater return will generate a larger amount of income from any given lump-sum amount. If your lump sum is assumed

TRANSLATING AN ANNUITY INTO A LUMP SUM

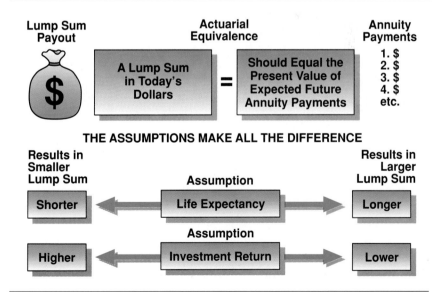

to earn more, it doesn't have to be as large to provide you with a given amount of income.

Deciding between a pension annuity and a lump sum is likely to be difficult. Keep in mind that the income from the annuity is guaranteed. You don't have to worry about managing the investments backing the annuity or outliving the payments it will provide. If your family has a history of longevity and you are in good health, you can probably count on collecting benefits for more years than the life expectancy tables would predict, making the annuity a better deal for you. Likewise, women may find annuities more attractive than lump sums because the lump-sum calculation is based on unisex life expectancy tables, and women live longer on average than the unisex life expectancy. The annuity payout option will be a compelling choice if the employer's policy is to provide cost-of-living pension adjustments or health-care benefits for retirees.

Yet there are a number of advantages to the lump-sum payout option. The chief one is flexibility. You have the flexibility to pay tax on the lump sum at a favorable rate if you are age 59½ or older. Or you can defer all taxes by rolling over the distribution into an individual retirement account.

With a lump sum, you take control of the investment decisions. Instead of receiving your retirement benefit as a fixed income stream— the pension annuity option—you can direct your lump amount toward growth investments that should do a better job of staying ahead of inflation. If you feel comfortable managing your own investments, a lump sum could be the right choice for you.

Finally, if you are undecided but are leaning toward the lump-sum option, remember that you can use part or all of your lump sum to purchase an annuity from an insurance company at the time of retirement or later. The annuity will provide a guaranteed lifetime income, just like your employer's pension annuity.

If You Choose an Annuity Payout

The pension annuity choice requires one or two subsequent decisions. The first issue is whether you will choose a single-life annuity with payments that stop at your death or a joint-and-survivor annuity with payments that go to you and your spouse (or other joint annuitant) as long as either of you live. If you elect the joint-and-survivor annuity, then you have another decision: What percentage of your benefit will go to your

---

RETIREMENT PLAN PAYOUT OPTIONS

Pension Annuity	Lump Sum
Guaranteed income for life	You bear risk of investment loss
Generally, no inflation protection	Can be managed for growth
No access to principal	Full flexibility in use of funds
Cannot be left to heirs	Available to heirs if unspent
All defined-benefit plans	Some defined-benefit plans
Some 401(k) plans	All 401(k) plans

---

survivor. The greater the percentage going to your survivor (up to 100 percent) the lower your initial monthly payment.

Why is that? As in the case of the annuity vs. the lump sum, your annuity choices will be actuarially equivalent. In other words, the benefits will be set so that if you and your spouse both live to your normal life expectancies, the pension plan will pay out the same total amount under either the single-life option or the joint-and-survivor option. The joint-and-survivor benefits are lower but will be paid over a longer period of time, making the two types actuarially equivalent. For example, if you choose single-life annuity—let's say your benefit is $2,400 a month—the benefits stop when you die. With a 50 percent joint-and-survivor option, your benefit would be less, probably around $2,160, but your survivor would receive half of that amount ($1,080) monthly for life in the event of your death. With a 100 percent joint-and-survivor annuity, your benefit might be reduced to $1,750 but that amount will be paid every month as long as either you or your spouse live.

In general, if you are married, a joint-and-survivor annuity will be the better choice if your spouse will need retirement income. By law, if you choose a single-life annuity, your spouse has to give his or her consent, and this consent must be in the form of a notarized waiver that both of you must sign. A joint-and-survivor annuity may also be the better choice if your employer provides medical benefits to pensioners and their spouses. Without the joint annuity, medical coverage for your spouse might end along with your monthly pension payment when you die. The joint-and-survivor annuity will be particularly attractive if your employer's pension plan offers a benefit that is higher than the actuarial equivalent of the single-life benefit.

However, a joint-and-survivor annuity is not necessarily the best option for a married worker. If each spouse has pension income, for example, choosing single-life annuities will provide a bigger total monthly benefit. A single-life annuity also makes sense if you expect to live much longer than your spouse. A healthy woman whose husband is much older or in poor health, for example, might find a single-life annuity more attractive.

If You Choose a Lump-Sum Payout

In addition to their other advantages, lump-sum distributions are eligible for favorable tax treatment. You have two options: rolling over the distribution into an IRA (or your new employer's plan) without paying any current taxes, or paying taxes now using a favorable tax treatment known as forward averaging. To qualify for treatment as a lump-sum distribution, a payout from a retirement plan has to meet several requirements. It must be made from a qualified retirement plan in which you have been a participant for at least five years. It must also be paid as the result of retirement or other separation from service, death, disability, or attaining age 59½. The distribution also must represent your entire interest in the plan and be made to you within a single tax year.

By rolling over your lump sum into an IRA, you maintain tax-deferred status of the amount. Further, you can control how the money is invested. If you are not yet retired and have no plans to spend the money currently, the IRA rollover will usually be a better decision than forward averaging. Remember to have your lump sum transferred directly to your IRA or new employer's plan. Otherwise 20 percent of the distribution will be withheld for taxes.

Forward averaging enables you to pay less than your current tax rate on money you receive as a lump-sum distribution from a qualified retirement plan. You must be at least 59½ and have been a plan participant for at least five calendar years when the distribution is received. One method, five-year averaging, allows you to figure your tax as if the lump sum were distributed over five years, using current tax rates. Those born in 1936 or later may use five-year averaging once they reach 59½. Taxpayers who were born before 1936 are eligible for 10-year forward averaging. Ten-year averaging treats the distribution as if it occurred over 10 years, using tax rates that were in effect in 1986. In addition, 10-year averaging offers a favorable 20 percent capital gains treatment for the portion of your distribution that represents pre-1974 plan participation. Take note: Five- and 10-year averaging are methods for computing the

10-YEAR VS. 5-YEAR
COMPARING INCOME-
AVERAGING METHODS

Effective Tax Rates

Lump Sum	10-Year Averaging	Five-Year Averaging
$ 20,000	5.5%	7.5%
50,000	11.7	13.8
100,000	14.5	15.0
200,000	18.5	21.4
300,000	22.1	24.1
400,000	25.7	25.8
500,000	28.7	26.9

tax payable in the year you receive a lump-sum distribution. They do not permit you to spread out payment of that tax over a 5- or 10-year period.

Ten-year averaging is generally more advantageous for lump-sum amounts up to just over $400,000. For larger distributions, five-year averaging yields a lower tax bill.

Our suggestion: Don't make decisions about your retirement plan distributions one at a time or at the last minute when you are ready to retire. Keep your overall financial picture in mind. It may make sense, in the interest of hedging your bets, to arrange for part of your retirement money to be placed in an annuity that you can't outlive and to invest the remainder to keep pace with inflation.

Decision No. 9   How much of your money will you spend each year in retirement?

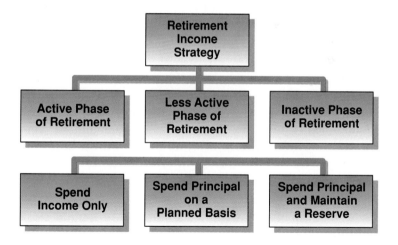

Financial planners typically recommend that you should expect to spend the principal as well as the income from your investment assets in retirement. The reason is simple: It requires much greater assets to meet retirement living expenses if you spend income only. Not spending principal means you will need a substantially larger retirement nest egg. For example, let's say you need to generate $40,000 a year from your investments to supplement your pension and Social Security benefits in retirement and can earn an 8 percent pretax return. If you are willing to spend down your principal on a planned basis over 25 years, you could generate that $40,000 with a nest egg of about $427,000. If you are unwilling to spend principal and insist on generating the $40,000 entirely from income, you would require about $500,000. At a 6 percent pretax rate of return, you would need a nest egg of $511,334 if you spend down principal, or about $670,000 if you do not.

Taking anticipated inflation into consideration, your savings will need to be much greater. For example, at an 8 percent pretax return coupled with 4 percent inflation, you would need a nest egg of $625,000, if you planned to spend down your principal, or $1 million if you did not.

Recall in Chapter 1 when we talked about the trade-offs between present consumption and future consumption. Your investments are nothing more than deferred consumption, plus the compounded earnings on that deferred consumption. Nonetheless, many retirees are reluctant or unwilling to spend principal. They may fear they won't have sufficient money available to meet an emergency, or they will simply outlive their assets and become a burden on relatives. These fears are understandable. As you reach retirement, your financial options narrow.

Unlike workers who are accumulating money for future needs, retirees don't have the options of saving more out of each paycheck, working overtime, or finding a better-paying job. Your ability to earn extra money may be limited. Likewise, you don't have the luxury of extended time frames that dampen risk for long-term accumulation investors. With a narrower range of alternatives, retirees investing for income find themselves making difficult trade-offs among four primary risks: (1) inflation risk, (2) investment risk, (3) the risk of having insufficient current income, and (4) the risk of being forced to spend down principal on an unplanned basis, or what might be called legacy risk. (Principal that has been spent cannot be left to heirs.)

The decision about whether to spend principal or live just on current income has implications for your retirement investment strategy. Investing to maximize current income means favoring higher-yielding assets such as bonds and avoiding or minimizing investments in assets with growth potential like stocks.

THE INVESTMENT TRADEOFFS FACING RETIREES

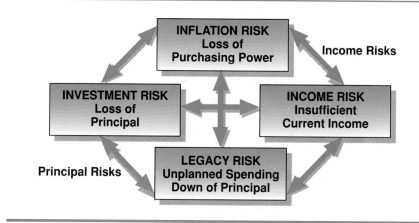

An income portfolio by definition will offer less protection of your purchasing power because its assets will not grow. It is also likely to offer much less in the way of total return because total returns for stocks have averaged about 10 percent, while returns for bonds have been around 5 percent. If you emphasize stocks and invest for total return, rather than favoring bonds and investing for current income, you may be able to spend a portion of your principal each year and still come out ahead.

The accompanying table (page 234) shows the potential benefit of investing for total return and spending principal during retirement. Let's say your time horizon is 20 years, your retirement funds amount to $500,000, and the inflation rate is 4 percent. In the first example (Column A), let's also assume you are unwilling to spend any principal. By using income-oriented investments such as bonds, you should be able to generate an after-tax current income of about $20,000 a year. Although you wouldn't have spent any principal, your nest egg would decline in terms of its purchasing power to $228,000 over 20 years.

What if you were willing to spend some of your principal each year and invest in stocks? You could significantly improve your standard of living. Let's look at what would happen (Column B) if you set aside $100,000 of your nest egg as a reserve, investing the money in bonds with an after-tax return of 4 percent, and spending neither principal nor

WHY IT PAYS TO INVEST FOR TOTAL RETURN
AND BE WILLING TO SPEND PRINCIPAL IN RETIREMENT

	Column A	*Column B*
	Spend Income Only	Spend Principal on Planned Basis, Maintain Reserve
Investment assets		$400,000 Portfolio
	$500,000	100,000 Reserve
Time until principal = 0	Principal not spent	20 years Portfolio Reserve not spent
After-tax return	4% bonds	6% Portfolio 4% Reserve
Total income	$20,000	$24,000 Portfolio 4,000 Reserve
Total spent each year	$20,000	$33,000 Portfolio 0 Reserve
Principal spent each year	0	$9,000 Portfolio 0 Reserve
Total spent over 20 years	$400,000	$660,000 Portfolio 0 Reserve
Amount remaining after 20 years in today's dollars	$228,000	0 Portfolio $100,000 Reserve

income for 20 years. The remaining $400,000 you invest in stocks with a 6 percent after-tax return (2 percent current income and 4 percent appreciation) and "annuitize" it, or plan to spend it at a rate so that this portion of your money will be reduced to zero after 20 years. That would enable you to spend $33,000 annually for 20 years, more than one and a half times the amount you would have available by spending income only. At the end of the period, your reserve would still be worth $100,000 in today's dollars.

Our suggestion: If you are not comfortable with the idea of spending your assets in retirement on a planned basis, plan to create a reserve that will be invested in cash equivalents to maintain its value in today's dollars.

HOW LONG WILL YOUR WITHDRAWALS LAST?

This table shows how many years your withdrawals will last for different rates of return and annual percentage withdrawals.

Percentage of Original Amount Withdrawn Each Year	Percentage Rate of Return							
	4%	5%	6%	7%	8%	9%	10%	
15%	8	8	9	9	10	11	12	Years
14	9	9	10	10	11	12	13	your
13	9	10	10	10	11	12	13	money
12	10	11	12	13	14	16	19	will
11	12	12	14	15	17	20	25	last
10	13	14	16	18	21	27		
9	15	17	19	22	29			
8	18	20	24	31				
7	22	26	33					
6	28	37						
5	41							

Decision No. 10   How will you allocate your retirement investments among different categories of investment assets?

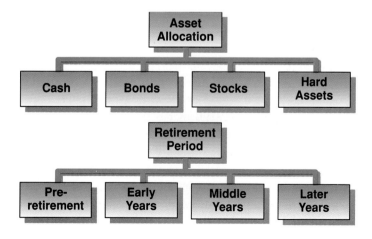

ASSET ALLOCATION

Investing for Retirement

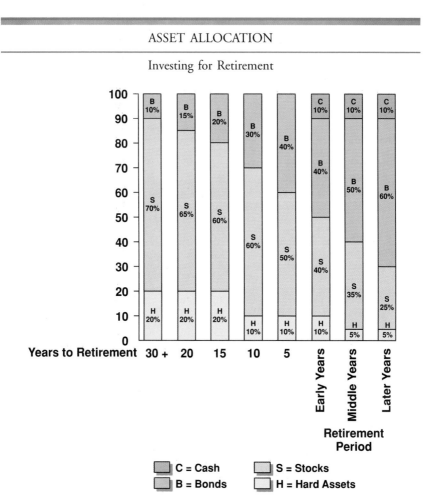

In Chapter 5, we introduced the concept of asset allocation and rec-ommended how to allocate your retirement investments. Let's review those recommendations now. Recall that your investment time horizon depends on your present age and your life expectancy. You may not need to start consuming your retirement investments for 25 or 30 years, and then you may need them for another 25 years or more after you retire.

In our view, investments in equities and hard assets offering inflation protection are of paramount importance for long-term retirement investors. Cash and bond investments should be given relatively little weight until

INVESTING FOR RETIREMENT: SUBCATEGORY ALLOCATIONS

	Years to Retirement					Retirement Period		
	30 or more	20	15	10	5	Early Years	Middle Years	Later Years
Bonds	10%	15%	20%	30%	40%	40%	50%	60%
Short term*	0	0	0	0	10	10	10	20
Intermediate term†	10	15	20	30	30	30	40	40
Stocks	70%	65%	60%	60%	50%	40%	35%	25%
Growth and income	0	0	0	5	10	10	15	15
Growth	20	20	20	20	15	10	10	5
Aggressive growth	25	20	20	15	10	10	5	0
International	25	25	20	20	15	10	5	5

* 1–3-year maturity.
† 3–10-year maturity.

you approach the years you plan to retire. Someone with 30 years until retirement, for example, would want 70 percent of his or her investment assets in stocks, 20 percent in hard assets, and 10 percent in bonds. Even in retirement, it will be important for you to maintain a meaningful portion of your asset location in equity and hard-asset investments to protect the purchasing power of your funds during retirement. For retirees, playing it too safe where investment volatility is concerned can mean losing purchasing power to inflation over the long term. During retirement, your asset allocation should vary depending on whether you are in the early years (65 to 75), the middle years (75 to 85) or the later years (85 and older).

As we suggested in Chapter 5, you should also allocate your investments within the larger categories of stocks and bonds. The subcategories we recommend for bonds are short-term (one- to three-year maturity) and medium-term (3- to 10-year maturity). Stock investments should be split among domestic and international stocks. We suggest three types of mutual funds to use for your suballocations to domestic stocks: growth and income, growth, and aggressive growth.

Remember, too, that these allocations are only guidelines. Your individual circumstances may provide many reasons to modify them. For example, suppose the largest portion of your retirement income is derived from a fixed pension and Social Security. In that case, you might want to give relatively more weight than we recommend here in allocating your investments to stocks and hard assets. A fixed pension and Social Security benefits represent "bond-like" assets. As a result, you may find yourself too heavily weighted in bonds.

Or perhaps you have a certain percentage of your portfolio that you have earmarked for your heirs and have even taken steps, such as splitting your investments into multiple IRAs and designating a grandchild as beneficiary of each, to convey that property to them. (For more information on this issue, see Chapter 10.) Again, you should consider weighting these investments more heavily toward stocks because their time horizon now becomes the point at which they will be consumed by your heirs, hopefully many years in the future.

Our suggestion: Pay close attention to the allocation of your retirement investments. It will be the most important decision you make in determining your investment returns over the years. In particular, remember the risks of long-term inflation. Short-term safety of principal may mean long-term sacrifice of purchasing power.

Resources

Books, Booklets, and References

Don't Work Forever! Simple Steps Baby Boomers Must Take to Retire. Steve Vernon. New York: John Wiley & Sons. 1995.

Guide to Social Security and Medicare. Louisville, KY: William M. Mercer Inc. Updated annually.

How to Plan for Your Retirement Years. Great Barrington, MA: American Institute for Economic Research.

Retirement in the 21st Century: Ready or Not? Washington, DC: Employee Benefit Research Institute.

T. Rowe Price Retirement Planning Kit. Baltimore, MD: T. Rowe Price Associates.

T. Rowe Price Retirees Financial Guide. Baltimore, MD: T. Rowe Price Associates.

The Price Waterhouse Retirement Planning Adviser. Burr Ridge, IL: Irwin Professional Publishing.

The Vanguard Retirement Investing Guide. Valley Forge, PA: The Vanguard Group.

Where to Get Help with a Pension Problem. Washington, DC: The Pension Rights Center.

Organizations

American Association of Individual Investors. Chicago. 312-280-0170.

American Association of Retired Persons. Washington, DC. 202-872-4700.

National Research Center for Women and Retirement Research. Long Island University, Greenvale, NY. 800-426-7386.

The 401(k) Association. Langhorne, PA. 215-579-8830.

Software

Fidelity Retirement Planning Program Thinkware. Boston, MA: Fidelity Investments. Microsoft Windows™ (Version 3.1 or higher). 800-544-3703.

Price Waterhouse Retirement Planning System. Chicago: Price Waterhouse LLP. Microsoft Windows™ (Version 3.1 or higher) and DOS (Version 2.0 or higher). 800-752-6234.

T. Rowe Price Retirement Planning Kit. Baltimore, MD: T. Rowe Price Associates. DOS (Version 2.1 or higher). 800-541-8460.

The Vanguard Retirement Planner. Valley Forge, PA: The Vanguard Group. 800-876-1840. Microsoft Windows™ (Version 3.1 or higher) and DOS (Version 3.0 or higher). 800-876-1840. ⚖

DISABILITY PLANNING

The chapter begins with a discussion of the fundamental truths about planning for disability. One of those truths, for example, is that your chance of being permanently disabled before age 65 is much greater than the chance that you will die prematurely. The chapter identifies and discusses the issues involved in planning for disability. It will help you analyze and project your income replacement needs in the event of disability during the years before and after your expected retirement age. Then it provides forms and coaching to help you set goals and determine priorities. The chapter shows you step by step how to plan for the risk of becoming disabled and explains the features of disability income policies. Finally, the chapter looks at long-term care needs and the features of long-term care insurance policies.

Myth vs. Reality

Myth: If I am disabled, I can live on Social Security disability payments.

Reality: Most claims for Social Security disability benefits are denied because of the strict rules for proving that you are unable to earn any income. If you manage to obtain benefits, they may be less than you need to live on. The maximum Social Security disability benefit, for example, is currently about $1,400 a month for an individual or $2,100 a month if you qualify for family benefits.

Myth: I have disability coverage at work, so I don't need a disability income insurance policy of my own.

Reality: Many employer disability policies offer short-term coverage for only 60 or 90 days. If long-term disability insurance is part of your benefit package, it probably will not be portable. When you leave your job, coverage stops.

Myth: Disability benefits are tax free.

Reality: Benefits are free of tax only if you have paid the insurance premiums from your own after-tax income. If your employer pays the premiums or you pay them on a pretax basis through a plan offered by your employer, benefits are fully taxable.

Myth: I'm healthy and I work in an office, so my chances of being disabled are relatively small.

Reality: That may be true. But you are still roughly three times more likely to be disabled than to die before age 65.

Myth: Women live longer than men and are less likely to be disabled.

Reality: The first statement is accurate, but not the second. Depending on age, women are almost twice as likely as men to be disabled before age 65.

Myth: If I am disabled, my living costs will drop substantially. Taxes will be lower and I won't have any work-related expenses.

Reality: If you suffer a disability, your basic daily living costs may go up, not down. Disabled workers often face large expenses for ongoing medical care and rehabilitation.

Myth: I can always buy disability income insurance later.

Reality: Disability insurance becomes progressively more costly as you get older. And if you experience a future health problem, your chances of subsequently buying disability coverage will be slim.

Myth: Disability income policies replace 60 to 70 percent of your compensation.

Reality: Insurance is available only to replace base salary, not bonuses or other forms of compensation. In addition, there is a dollar limit, typically $12,000 to $15,000, on the monthly disability benefit an insurance company will offer, no matter how high your base salary.

Myth: Disability benefits are adjusted for inflation.

Reality: Not necessarily. It is true that Social Security disability payments are increased as the cost of living rises. But disability benefits provided by your employer probably are not adjusted for inflation. Inflation protection is available at extra cost when you buy an individual disability policy.

Myth: Buy the most expensive disability income policy you can find.

Reality: Benefits are limited to no more than 60 to 70 percent of your earned income. Therefore, extra-cost policy options that don't add anything to the basic monthly benefit may not be worth the money.

Some Fundamental Truths about Disability Planning

What's your most valuable asset? Your home, you would probably say. Odds are, however, that you are overlooking an asset worth many times the value of a typical home: your future earning power. For most workers, the stream of earnings generated over the remainder of their careers is by far the most valuable asset they have. If you earn $75,000 a year, for example, and expect raises averaging 5 percent annually until you retire in 25 years, your earnings over that period will total more than $3.57 million.

Like any valuable asset, your earning power needs protection. If your house is worth $150,000 or your new car has a value of $25,000, for example, odds are that you have them fully insured to protect against such hazards as fire or collision. And most of us understand the need to provide protection against the risk of premature death by means of life insurance and the risk of disability by having disability income insurance.

Too often, however, disability protection gets short shrift. For example, New York Life Insurance Co. found that 95 percent of respondents to a 1993 telephone survey agreed that it was important to maintain an insurance policy that would cover their loss of income in the event of a disabling accident or illness. How many actually owned a disability policy? Only about half of those responding said they actually carried disability income insurance. The unfortunate truth is that most of us don't have adequate protection against the possibility of long-term disability.

WILL YOU BE DISABLED?

Odds of Being Disabled for at Least 90 Days before Reaching Age 65

Current Age	Likelihood of Disability Occurring by Age 65	
	Men	Women
30	33%	57%
35	31	52
40	29	45
45	26	38
50	23	29
55	18	21
60	11	12

Source: "Will You Be Disabled?" Guardian Life Insurance Company of America, brochure entitled "The Golden Eggs . . . or the Goose. Which Would You Insure," page 5.

Setting Your Goals and Analyzing Your Resources

Without adequate planning, few people confronted by a serious long-term disability will be able to maintain their current lifestyles, let alone

WHAT'S MORE LIKELY, DEATH OR DISABILITY?

| At Age | Disability Is This Many Times More Likely than Death | |
	Men	Women
22	2.0	4.7
27	1.7	4.1
32	1.5	4.0
37	1.4	4.3
42	1.3	3.9
47	1.3	3.7
52	1.4	3.7
57	1.7	3.4
62	1.5	2.4

Ratio of disability rate to death rate per 1,000 covered lives in group plans. Adapted from 1987 Commissioners Group Disability Table and 1983 Group Annuity Mortality Table.

accomplish other goals such as paying for college or enjoying a comfortable retirement. The first step is to compare your current living expenses and other financial commitments with the likely changes in those categories resulting from disability. For example, job-related expenses would be eliminated, and your outlays for clothing, auto expense, and recreation might decline. Premiums for life and disability insurance would be eliminated if your policies contained disability premium waivers. Other costs, on the other hand, would likely increase, chief among them medical expenses.

If you become disabled and can't work, the amount of financial support available to you will depend to a great extent on the benefits your employer provides. Sick leave and salary continuation programs represent the first line of defense, enabling your income to continue from your first day of absence. After a month or so, your salary may be covered by a short-term disability plan. Should the disability continue, your employer's long-term group disability coverage will take over, replacing perhaps 60 percent of your original salary. If you are age 50 or older, your employer may arrange for early retirement on disability, with your pension benefit payments commencing at a lower rate than they would have if you left the job at the normal retirement age.

Virtually all large employers offer disability benefits like these. Most small ones do not, however. So if you don't work for a large employer, it will be particularly important for you to explore an individual or supplementary disability policy.

The most important of those other sources is likely to be Social Security, which offers an important level of disability protection to eligible workers. Social Security benefits are indexed to inflation, so they will maintain their long-term purchasing power. After two years on Social Security disability benefits, you automatically become eligible for Medicare and receive the same medical benefits provided to those 65 and older.

HOW LONG WILL YOUR DISABILITY LAST?

Likelihood That a 90-Day Disability Will Continue for Various Periods of Time for a 35-Year-Old Male Professional

	Probability of Continuing
To month:	
4	79%
5	63
6	51
9	33
12	26
To year:	
2	16%
3	14
4	12
5	11
10	9

Source: *The Individual Investor's Guide to Low-Load Insurance Products: How, What, Where to Buy Insurance Wholesale* by Glenn S. Dailey, International Publishing Corp., 625 N. Michigan, Chicago, IL 60611, (312) 943-7354, 507 pp.

WILL YOU GO BACK TO WORK AFTER BEING DISABLED?

Return-to-Work Potential of Disability Cases

Of Those Disabled	% Did Not Return to Work
Age	
16–34	24%
35–44	26
45–54	48
55–64	64
Marital status	
Single	37%
Married	52
Cause of disability	
Cardiovascular	46%
Pulmonary	68
Gastrointestinal	8
Musculoskeletal	29
Neurological	77
Other physical	34

Source: "Will You Go Back to Work after Being Disabled?" *Source Book of Health Insurance Data,* page 146.

The maximum benefit is now about $1,300 a month for an individual. That is the amount you would receive if your earnings have met or exceeded the Social Security wage base in recent years. The wage base, or the maximum amount of earnings subject to Social Security Old-Age, Survivors and Disability Insurance, increases each year. In 1995, for example, the maximum was $61,200. That compares to $60,600 in 1994, $51,300 in 1990, and $25,900 in 1980. If your earnings have been less than the maximum, your Social Security benefit will be somewhat lower, although it is not reduced proportionately. For example, if you earned $30,000 in 1995, or roughly half the Social Security wage

ELIGIBILITY FOR SOCIAL SECURITY DISABILITY BENEFITS

If disabled in 1995, you would need to have worked under Social Security coverage for a certain minimum number of years, depending on your age, to qualify for disability benefits.

Age	Length of Employment Required to Qualify for Social Security Disability Benefits
Under 24	1½ years in past 3 years
24 to 30	Half of years since age 21
31 to 42	5 years
43	5¼
44	5½
45	5¾
46	6
47	6¼
48	6½
49	6¾
50	7
51	7¼
52	7½
53	7¾
54	8
55	8¼
56	8½
57	8¾
58	9
59	9¼
60	9½
61	9¾
62 or over	10

base amount, you would be eligible for a monthly disability benefit of about $1,000, or roughly three-fourths of the maximum benefit.

Your family members may also be eligible for Social Security benefits if you are disabled. Each disabled worker's child up to age 18, or to age 19 if the child is still in high school, is entitled to a payment equal to half the worker's benefit. In addition, the worker's spouse is eligible for the same amount if caring for a child under age 16. When the spouse reaches age 62, he or she is eligible for a monthly payment equal to 37.5 percent of the disabled worker's benefit. That payment rises to 50 percent of the worker's benefit when the spouse reaches age 65.

There's a catch, however. Social Security imposes a cap on the total combined individual and family benefit that can be paid per month. That cap is equal to 150 percent of the disabled worker's individual benefit. Thus, if you were eligible for a $1,400 monthly payment, your maximum family benefit (including the $1,300) would be 150 percent of $1,400 or about $2,100.

Let's look at how your Social Security family benefit would be calculated, assuming your spouse cares for two children ages 15 and 16 in the year when your disability starts. Figures are approximate for 1995 and assume you are eligible for the maximum benefit. Actual payments would be adjusted each year for the cost of living.

Year 1

You	$1,400
Child age 15	700
Child age 16	700
Spouse	700
Total of family benefits	3,500
Maximum family benefit	2,100
Actual benefit amount	$2,100

In Year 1, your spouse and both children would be eligible for payments equal to one-half your disability benefit. However, the total family benefit, including the amount you receive, is capped at $2,100.

Year 2

You	$1,400
Child age 16	700
Child age 17	700
Spouse	0
Total of family benefits	2,800
Maximum family benefit	2,100
Actual benefit amount	$2,100

In Year 2, your spouse would lose eligibility for one-half of your benefit because he or she would no longer be caring for a child under age 16. Family benefits would then total $2,800 a month but continue to be limited by the $2,100 cap.

Year 3

You	$1,400
Child age 17	700
Child age 18	0
Spouse	0
Total of family benefits	2,100
Maximum family benefit	2,100
Actual benefit amount	$2,100

In Year 3, the older child would be age 18 and not receive a benefit unless still attending high school. Your total family benefit would drop to $2,100, the same amount as the cap.

Year 4

You	$1,400
Child age 18	0
Child age 19	0
Spouse	0
Total of family benefits	1,400
Maximum family benefit	2,100
Actual benefit amount	$1,400

Likewise for the younger child in Year 4, so the actual benefit you receive from Year 4 onward would be your own individual benefit of $1,400.

Eligibility rules for Social Security disability benefits are strict. You must be so severely impaired physically or mentally that you cannot perform any type of gainful work. In addition, the impairment must be expected to last at least a year or to result in death in less than a year's time. Most initial applications for benefits are denied, although a portion of those turned down file appeals and eventually obtain benefits. The wait-

The unfortunate truth is that most of us don't have adequate protection against the possibility of long-term disability.

ing period for Social Security benefits after your disability begins is five calendar months, meaning you must be disabled for that full time before you can be approved to receive a benefit. Because of the time it takes to have your application processed and approved, the earliest you could receive a Social Security disability check is likely to be eight months from the date you are disabled. As a result, it is probably unwise to count on receiving Social Security benefits when planning for your disability income needs.

One challenge to planning for disability is the fact that some benefits, such as sick pay, may be offered for a limited time only while others, such as an early retirement pension, may not be available for months or years. And some expenses may change significantly after you become disabled. Work-related expenses may disappear but other costs, such as rehabilitation therapy or in-home care, may be incurred for short- or long-term periods. As a result, your plan should calculate needs and financial

Disability planning worksheet   ESTIMATING FINANCIAL NEEDS

Estimate Your Monthly Spending and Savings Needs

	Current	If Disabled
Mortgage or rent	$	$
Utilities		
Home upkeep, property taxes		
Food		
Clothing		
Insurance—Health		
Life		
Disability		
Auto expenses		
Medical and dental		
Education		
Retirement		
Recreation and travel		
Other expenses		
Total monthly needs if disabled		

resources on a month-by-month basis for a period of one year after a disability, and then recalculate it each year thereafter until you reach age 65.

The worksheet above shows how you would record current expenses and estimate what changes might occur for each expense category in the event of your disability. The next worksheet, pages 350 and 351, enables you to figure your monthly income and expenses for the first year of disability and on an ongoing basis. The example shown is for a worker with after-tax income of $5,500 a month whose spouse now works part time earning $1,500 a month after taxes. For planning purposes, we will assume the worker becomes disabled and see what will happen to income and expenses on a monthly basis during the first year.

Month 1: The worker becomes disabled at the beginning of the first month and receives full pay for 60 days under a salary continuation/ short-term disability plan. The worker and spouse shift their investments away from long-term growth toward current income, intending to raise their income from savings from the current $400 a month.

Month 2: As a result of the disability, the worker needs in-home care for part of each day and the family's net monthly expenses rise from

$6,000 to $7,000. Current income from savings increases to $500 for the month.

Month 3: After 60 days, the worker is paid two-thirds of salary under the short-term disability plan, causing monthly pre-tax income to fall to $3,670. The spouse decides to return to work full time, and expenses rise from $7,000 to $8,000. Current income from savings increases to $600 a month.

Month 4: The spouse starts bringing home $2,500 a month after taxes.

Months 5 and 6: No changes in income or expenses for the month. The worker applies for Social Security disability payments after being disabled for five months.

Month 7: The worker is transferred to the company's long-term disability plan at 50 percent of salary, or $2,750 a month after taxes, less any disability payments received from Social Security or other government sources.

Month 8: The worker starts receiving $1,300 a month in Social Security disability payments, with a corresponding reduction in monthly long-term disability benefit. The spouse is not eligible for a family benefit because there are no children aged 16 or under at home.

Month 9: No changes.

Month 10: The family manages to reduce monthly expenses from $8,000 to $7,000 because the worker no longer needs in-home care for part of the day.

Months 11 and 12: No changes.

As the worker's income and expenses stabilize toward the end of the first year of disability, there appears to be a monthly shortfall in income of about $1,150. This would be the minimum monthly benefit needed from an individual disability income policy.

Disability Income Insurance

Disability income policies are intended to replace a certain portion of your earnings when you can't work as a result of sickness or injury. To collect a benefit, you must be disabled and also have suffered a loss of earned income. Premiums are based on the amount of monthly benefit and a variety of other factors, including how soon benefit payments start after you become disabled, how long benefits continue, and how disability is defined by the policy.

Terms and conditions for policies issued by different companies tend to be much less standardized than those used on other types of personal

Disability planning worksheet   ESTIMATING MONTHLY RESOURCES AND EXPENSES DURING DISABILITY

For Your Own Worksheet, See Page 350.

	Month of Disability					
	1st	2nd	3rd	4th	5th	6th
Employer short-term disability	$5,500	$5,500	$3,670	$3,670	$3,670	$3,670
Employer long-term disability						
Social Security						
State disability program						
Workers' compensation						
Spouse's income	1,500	1,500	1,500	2,500	2,500	2,500
Income from savings	400	500	600	600	600	600
Other income						
Total monthly income	7,400	7,500	5,770	6,770	6,770	6,770
Total monthly expenses	6,000	7,000	8,000	8,000	8,000	8,000
Total monthly excess/ shortfall	+1,400	+500	−2,230	−1,230	−1,230	−1,230

insurance policies. They typically feature many coverage options and riders that add to the cost of basic income protection.

Some of these options merit consideration. One is a provision that raises benefits along with inflation once you become disabled and start to receive monthly checks. Another attractive option is the right to convert

Disability planning worksheet
concluded

For Your Own Worksheet, See Page 350.

Month of Disability

	7th	8th	9th	10th	11th	12th	Ongoing
Employer short-term disability	$	$	$	$	$	$	$
Employer long-term disability	2,750	1,450	1,450	1,450	1,450	1,450	1,450
Social Security		1,300	1,300	1,300	1,300	1,300	1,300
State disability program							
Workers' compensation							
Spouse's income	2,500	2,500	2,500	2,500	2,500	2,500	2,500
Income from savings	600	600	600	600	600	600	600
Other income							
Total monthly income	5,850	5,850	5,850	5,850	5,850	5,850	5,850
Total monthly expenses	8,000	8,000	8,000	7,000	7,000	7,000	7,000
Total monthly excess/ shortfall	−2,150	−2,150	−2,150	−1,150	−1,150	−1,150	−1,150

your disability income policy at a certain age into a long-term care policy that will provide benefits if you must enter a nursing home.

Other provisions, however, are not necessarily a good deal. One example is known as the return-of-premium rider. This provision offers a rebate of a portion of the premiums you have paid, say 60 percent, if you have no disability claims over a certain time, typically five years. The idea may sound appealing but most insurance professionals would advise caution. The extra cost of the return-of-premium rider can make it a bad investment. All these varied policy features and options mean that disability income policies are complex and difficult to compare.

They also can be difficult to buy. The same company that is happy to sell you as much life insurance as you want will be wary when you apply for disability insurance. You will have to take a medical examination and answer questions about your medical history. Your application may be rejected because of an existing medical condition that could lead to disability. Or the company may issue the policy but exclude coverage for disability caused by an existing medical condition. In addition, the insurance company will want to confirm the amount of your earned income at the time you apply for the policy and your record of steady employment over the years. If you make a claim, the company will require proof of your loss of income before it pays. This caution reflects the real concern among insurance companies that some policyholders can find it more attractive to try to collect disability benefits than continue working.

Here are the key features of individual disability income policies:

Definition of Disability
A key element of this type of policy is its definition of what constitutes a covered disability. Typically, the disability must be caused by sickness or injury, must begin while the policy is in force, and must require the care of a physician. In turn, each of those requirements may be defined further. For example, sickness might be defined as a disease that *first manifests* itself after the policy's issue date or, alternatively, one that is *first contracted* after the issue date. With the latter definition, the insurer could deny coverage for a condition discovered after the issue date if it could prove the condition existed before that date.

To receive a benefit, the policy may require you to be totally disabled, but the definition of that condition will also vary among policies. Total disability may be defined as (1) the inability to engage in any gainful occupation; or (2) the inability to engage in any occupation for which you are reasonably qualified by training, education, and experience; or (3) the inability to engage in the material and substantial duties of your own occupation. Some policies define total disability on an "own-occupation" basis for the first two years of disability and on an "any-occupation" basis thereafter. A policy with an "own-occupation" definition of total disability will be more attractive if you are a specialist such as a surgeon, musician, or microbiologist. However, such policies are significantly more expensive than the "any-occupation" variety. The extra cost may not make sense for someone in a more generalist occupation such as sales or general management.

One common policy clause is known as presumptive disability. You are presumed to be totally disabled if you suffer a loss of two limbs, or loss of sight, speech, or hearing. In such instances, you would qualify for the policy benefit whether or not you continued to earn income. Definitions of presumptive disability will vary. For example, one policy may say you are presumed to be totally disabled if you lose the use of two limbs, while another may require the limbs to be severed for a presumption of total disability to be made.

> **Without adequate planning in advance, few people confronted by a serious long-term disability will be able to maintain their current lifestyles, let alone accomplish other goals.**

In addition to covering total disability, many policies also offer benefits in instances where disability is not complete. In some cases, for example, a disabled individual later returns to work full time but is unable because of the disability to earn as much income as he or she earned previously. This difference in earning power is known as a residual disability, and coverage is available to make up the shortfall through what is called a residual benefit. If the total disability benefit is $5,000 a month and the policyholder is able to earn only 80 percent of his or her former income, the policy would pay a benefit equal to 20 percent of $5,000, or $1,000 a month.

Some policies require you to be totally disabled for a period of time, known as the qualification period, before residual benefits can begin. Policies with this requirement should be avoided; they can be highly disadvantageous, for example, if you contract an illness that is progressively debilitating but does not cause total disability at the onset.

Finally, some policies offer coverage for partial disability in cases where the insured is recovering from a total disability and has begun to work part time. Benefits are paid pro rata, depending on the amount of time spent at work, and usually only for a limited time, such as six months. Extra premiums generally are charged for coverage of residual disability and partial disability as extra-cost options.

Benefit Period The time period over which benefits will be paid if you remain disabled typically runs until age 65. Shorter benefit periods, such as a five-year maximum, are available at lower premium rates. Some insurance companies offer lifetime coverage for policyholders disabled before age 65, or for those who are disabled while continuing to work after age 65. Either alternative will add to the cost of your policy.

Elimination Period The elimination or waiting period is the length of time between the onset of disability and the start of benefit payments. In effect, the elimination period is a deductible, similar to an auto insurance deduction where the policyholder pays the first $500 in collision damage expense and the insurer pays the remainder. Disability income policyholders "self-insure" themselves for loss of income during the elimination period before benefits begin. Elimination periods range from 30 days to one year. The longer the elimination period, the lower the policy premium.

Inflation Adjustments During a lengthy disability, inflation can significantly reduce the purchasing power of fixed-level disability benefits. Two different options are available to help your policy keep pace with inflation. They are offered separately and at extra cost.

The first, known as a future purchase option, a benefit increase option, or guaranteed insurability, gives you the right to purchase additional amounts of insurance coverage on a regular basis, often annually, without a medical examination. The company, for example, may offer once each year to increase your monthly benefit by 5 percent in return for a higher premium. You can accept or reject the offer and be presented with the same choice again in another year.

The second option, a cost of living adjustment, provides that once you are disabled and benefits begin to be paid, they will be increased each year according to a formula to keep pace with inflation. Both options are attractive. If you can afford only one, the cost of living adjustment provides the cheapest long-term protection.

Renewability and Rates Disability income policies are intended as long-term protection. That means you want to avoid a policy cancellation or an unexpected price increase. Make sure that any disability policy you consider is noncancelable and guaranteed renewable until age 65. This means the policy cannot be canceled and the premium won't be increased except as specified in the policy.

Social Security Supplement   This provision coordinates part of your disability benefit with Social Security disability benefits, and perhaps with other types of government benefits as well. If you are able to obtain Social Security disability benefits, the monthly benefit from your disability income policy is reduced by a like amount. If you can't get Social Security benefits, the policy pays the full face amount. Often, this benefit is coordinated with other Social Security and government programs as well. Thus, your monthly disability check may also be reduced by the amount of any benefits you receive from the Social Security retirement program, from workers' compensation, or from a state disability insurance program.

Recurrence of Disability   This clause prevents you from having to wait through the elimination period when you have a relapse from a

---

RANKING DISABILITY POLICY FEATURES

Essential

1. Noncancelable and guaranteed renewable.
2. Benefits for residual disability. No qualification period.
3. Benefit period to age 65.
4. Insurance company is highly rated for claims-paying ability by several rating agencies, such as A.M. Best Co. (A+ or better), Standard & Poor's Corp. (AA or better), and Moody's Investors Service (Aa or better).

Attractive but More Costly

1. Cost of living adjustment.
2. Future purchase option.
3. Option to convert to long-term care policy.
4. Benefit period for life.
5. "Own-occupation" definition of total disability.

Will Reduce Policy Cost

1. Elimination period of six months or more.
2. Social Security supplement.
3. "Any-occupation" definition of total disability.

Not Necessary

1. Elimination period of less than six months.
2. Return of premium rider.

CHECKLIST FOR COMPARING
DISABILITY INCOME INSURANCE POLICIES

1. Is the policy noncancelable and guaranteed renewable?

   Yes _____   No _____

2. What is the policy's benefit period?
   Ends before 65 _____
   Ends at 65 _____
   Lifetime _____
   Coverage provided after age 65 if disability occurs while you are still working

   To age: _____

3. Does the policy offer residual benefits?   Yes _____   No _____
   If so, is there a qualification period?   Yes _____   No _____
   What percentage of income must be lost before residual benefits are paid? _____ %

4. Does the policy offer an annual cost of living adjustment once benefits commence?   Yes _____   No _____
   If so, what is the formula for the adjustment?
   Same % as CPI change up to a maximum of _____ %
   Other _____

5. What is policy's definition of total disability?
   Own occupation _____
   Reasonably qualified occupation _____
   Any occupation _____

6. What is the policy's elimination period, or waiting period?
   30 days _____
   60 days _____
   90 days _____
   180 days _____
   1 year _____
   Other _____

7. What is included in the policy's definition of income?
   Salary _____
   Commissions _____
   Deferred compensation _____
   Pension, profit-sharing contributions _____

8. Maximum benefit available as % of income? _____ %

9. Is there a future purchase option or guaranteed
   insurability option?   Yes _____   No _____
   If yes, how often is the future purchase option offered?   _____
      Annually   _____
      Other   _____
   How will the premium rate be set for future purchases?
      Rates in effect at policy issue date   _____
      Rates in effect at purchase date   _____
   What is the limit on amounts of future purchases?
      Same total benefit as % of income in original policy?   _____
      Other limit?   _____
10. Is a Social Security supplement available?   Yes _____   No _____
11. Can the policy be converted to a long-term care
    policy?   Yes _____   No _____
12. Is there a waiver of premium in event of disability?   Yes _____   No _____
13. What is the annual premium cost per $1,000 of
    monthly disability benefit for policy with standard
    features? (Example: $3,000 annual premium for
    $4,000 monthly benefit = $3,000/$4,000 × $1,000
    or $750.   _____

previous disability. Typically it provides that if the same disability recurs
within six months, it will be considered a continuation of the previous
disability and no elimination period will be required before monthly
benefits start.

Return of Premium Rider   As mentioned previously, this provision
offers a rebate of a portion of the premiums you have paid if you have
no disability claims over a certain time.

Waiver of Premium   This clause provides that no premiums are due
as long as the insured is disabled.

Long-Term Care Insurance

Long-term care insurance can be considered another form of disability
protection. Rather than covering the loss of income from disability, long-
term care insurance protects against the costs associated with disabilities
caused by age and infirmity. The biggest of those costs is nursing home

care. Neither Medicare nor Medicare supplement insurance covers basic nursing home care. About 40 percent of those age 65 can expect to spend some time in a nursing home, although the odds that women will require nursing home care are much greater than they are for men. The cost of nursing home care, now averaging about $40,000 a year, can quickly drain a family's assets.

To protect themselves, many people now buy long-term care insurance. These policies pay a certain dollar amount per day for covered care during the policy's benefit period. For example, you might select a long-term care policy paying a $150 daily benefit for a five-year benefit period. The maximum amount the policy would pay, assuming no benefit increase as a result of inflation adjustment or other factors, would be about $275,000 ($150 × 365 × 5). The older you are, the greater your annual premium for a given amount of long-term care coverage. Premiums for a 70-year-old are roughly three times those charged a 50-year-old for comparable benefits.

Most long-term care insurance uses what is called an indemnity policy model. Indemnity plans are similar to most health insurance policies in that the insurance carrier will pay the care provider (or reimburse the claimant) for actual charges up to the policy's coverage limits. Another, less common, type of long-term care plan has more similarity to disability income insurance. Instead of covering or reimbursing for actual charges, a disability model plan pays daily benefit amounts directly to the claimant to be spent for any purpose. Disability model plans are more costly than indemnity model plans but offer added flexibility in paying for home care and miscellaneous expenses and pose less claims-related paperwork.

Here are the key features of long-term care insurance policies:

Qualification for Benefits   To receive benefits, you typically must either suffer serious cognitive impairment or be unable to perform one or more functions known as "activities of daily living," or ADLs, without physical assistance. Serious cognitive impairment will be defined as deterioration or loss of memory, orientation, or ability to reason and may specifically apply to Parkinson's and Alzheimer's diseases.

The definitions of ADLs are not standardized among policies but generally include such activities as dressing, eating, mobility, toileting, and maintaining continence. With some policies, inability to perform two ADLs will trigger eligibility for benefits; other policies require three. Policies that cover both nursing home care and home care may pay nursing home benefits if the claimant can't perform three ADLs, while requiring only two ADLs for home care benefits. Some policies will pay benefits when custodial care is determined by a claimant's doctor to be medically necessary, whether or not the other two conditions apply. Finally, avoid policies that require a hospital stay before you can qualify for benefits.

Benefit Period   The period during which benefits will be paid ranges from one year to lifetime. It generally makes sense to purchase at least three years of coverage. You will save money in premiums and still cover the likely length of a nursing home stay with three to five years of coverage.

Level of Care   Most policies cover all three levels of care (skilled, intermediate, and custodial care) at a nursing home. Home care may also be covered as part of the basic policy or offered as an extra-cost option. Additional features may include coverage for adult day care, assisted living facilities, or hospice care for the terminally ill.

Elimination Period   The number of days you must wait after becoming eligible for benefits before coverage actually begins typically ranges from 0 to 90 days, with some policies offering elimination periods of up to one year. The longer the elimination period, the lower the policy premium.

Renewability and Rates   Most long-term care policies are guaranteed renewable. Premium rates, however, generally are not guaranteed. Insurance companies can raise premiums for a class of policyholders subject to approval from state insurance departments. Because long-term care is a relatively new type of coverage, insurance companies can be expected to adjust premiums as they gain experience with the claims these policies will generate. However, the risk of sharply rising premiums for existing policyholders seems relatively small. Benefits are fixed in dollar terms, so premiums will not be driven up by rising prices for care, as has happened with health insurance. As a result, where long-term care insurance is concerned, the risk posed by rising premiums seems much smaller than the risk that fixed benefits will not keep pace over time with the rising costs of long-term care.

Inflation Adjustments   If you purchase a long-term care policy at age 60, you expect to rely on it for 25 or 30 years. Over that time, nursing home bills will double if costs for long-term care increase at 3

RANKING LONG-TERM CARE
POLICY FEATURES

Essential

1. Benefits paid if you can't perform two of the activities of daily living.
2. No hospital stay required to receive benefits.
3. Coverage specifically includes Parkinson's and Alzheimer's diseases.
4. Benefit period is at least three years.
5. Insurance company is highly rated for claims-paying ability by several rating agencies, such as A.M. Best Co. (A+ or better), Standard & Poor's Corp. (AA or better), and Moody's Investors Service (Aa or better).

Attractive but More Costly

1. Coverage for home care in addition to nursing home care.
2. Longer benefit period for women.
3. Daily benefit that exceeds current average per-diem nursing home costs to help cover future inflation.
4. Inflation adjustment.

Will Reduce Policy Costs

1. Elimination period of 60 days or more.
2. Shorter benefit period for men.
3. Spousal discount for joint coverage.

Not Necessary

1. Waiting period of less than 30 days.
2. Return of premium rider or nonforfeiture clause.

percent a year; at 4 percent they will triple. Without inflation protection, a fixed-benefit policy will lose much of its effectiveness as a means of protecting you against the risk of needing long-term care. One strategy to cover future inflation is simply to purchase a daily benefit that exceeds current average per-diem nursing home costs. Several others are available at extra cost. Known as benefit increase options, they take three common forms:

- **Simple interest benefit increase option.** This option increases the policy's daily benefit once a year by a certain percentage, usually 5 percent. For example, the first year's $100 daily benefit rises to $105 the second year, $110 the next year, then $115, and so forth.

- **Compound interest benefit increase option.** The annual increase is compounded instead of being raised on a simple interest basis. Thus, the first year's $100 benefit rises to $105 in the second year, $110.25 ($105 × 1.05) the next year, then $115.75, and so forth. The compound interest option will do a better job than simple interest of keeping up with inflation. Over 25 years, $100 a day increased on a simple interest basis at 5 percent becomes $225 a day; on a compound interest basis it becomes $340. This option also costs more than the simple interest option.
- **Index-based increase option.** This option increases the daily payment based on the annual change in some measure of inflation, such as the consumer price index.

Return of Premium or Nonforfeiture Clause   A portion of the premiums you have paid is returned to you if you stop paying premiums and let the policy lapse. In effect, this option creates a residual policy value, somewhat like the cash value in permanent life insurance policies. These options will raise your premiums by 20 to 30 percent or more.

Waiver of Premium   This clause provides that no premiums are due when the policyholder is receiving benefits. Restrictions will vary. In some cases, the waiver will take effect not with the commencement of benefit payments but rather 60 or 90 days later. Often, the waiver applies only when you are receiving benefits for a nursing home stay; if benefits are being paid for home care, premiums are still due.

Resources

Books and References

The Complete Book of Insurance: Protecting Your Life, Health, Property and Income. Ben G. Baldwin. Chicago: Probus Publishing Co. 1991.

The Consumer's Guide to Long-Term Health-Care Insurance. Washington, DC: Health Insurance Association of America.

Disability Income Insurance: The Unique Risk. Charles E. Soule. Burr Ridge, IL: Irwin Professional Publishing. 1994.

Guide to Low-Load Insurance Products. Glenn S. Daily. Chicago: International Publishing Corp. 1990.

Long-Term Care: A Dollar and Sense Guide. Washington, DC: United Seniors Health Cooperative.

Planning for Long-Term Health Care. Harold Evensky and Deena Katz. Boston, MA: Houghton Mifflin Co. 1992.

Smart Questions to Ask Your Insurance Agent: A Guide to Buying the Right Insurance for Your Family's Future. Dorothy Leeds. New York: Harper Paperbacks. 1992.

Understanding Long-Term Care Insurance. Washington, DC: National Association of Health Underwriters.

Your Money or Your Life: How to Save Thousands on Your Health-Care Insurance. Donald Jay Korn. New York: Collier Books. 1992.

Hotline

The National Insurance Consumer Helpline (800-942-4242). Sponsored by the American Council of Life Insurance, the Health Insurance Association of America, and the Insurance Information Institute.

PLANNING FOR YOUR SURVIVORS

The chapter begins with a discussion of some fundamental truths about planning for your survivors in the event of your death. The view we take is that family comes first and estate tax issues come second. The chapter covers preparing and executing a will and providing for guardianship of minor children. It also describes the features of a living will and the durable power of attorney and analyzes their pros and cons.

The chapter also helps you analyze and project your family's income replacement needs. It describes the various types of life insurance policies and offers advice in analyzing typical policy illustrations offered by insurance agents. Finally, the chapter offers a basic discussion of estate and gift taxation and describes ways to reduce the tax bite on your estate.

Myth vs. Reality

Myth: My spouse will outlive me.

Reality: That may turn out to be the case. But it can be a mistake to plan for your survivors on the assumption that a particular spouse will die first.

Myth: My family knows my wishes in case of my death or incapacity.

Reality: Unless you express your wishes in the appropriate legally recognized forms—such as a will, trust, living will, and power of attorney for health care—they may not be binding on your heirs or legally enforceable.

Myth: I don't need a will. My financial affairs are simple.

Reality: Dying without a will is known in legal terms as dying intestate. In such cases, a court will appoint an administrator for your estate, and your property will be divided among your heirs according to state law. This arbitrary division will be made regardless of what your wishes might have been. In addition, your estate may have to pay taxes that could have been avoided.

Myth: I can do it myself.

Reality: You should actively participate in your estate planning by setting goals and thinking of your survivors. But sometimes it takes a professional financial planner/estate planner to help you identify issues you hadn't thought of. Since document drafting is a complex specialty, you should consult an attorney to prepare wills and trusts.

Myth: I have plenty of time to plan my estate. I'll get to the documents when I can do everything right.

Reality: Your survivors are younger and less secure financially today than they will be in the years to come. That means planning for your survivors is more crucial for them now than it will be in the future.

Myth: Estate planning is for wealthy people who want to minimize their taxes. I don't have enough assets to worry about it.

Reality: Wealth adds complexity to planning for your survivors, but the need to plan should carry the same amount of urgency no matter how big your bank account.

Myth: I can save a bundle in taxes by setting up a revocable living trust.

Reality: A revocable living trust may be an appropriate means to help you implement your estate plan. However, it offers no savings on either income taxes or estate taxes.

Myth: Life insurance is a rip-off.

Reality: Not if you need it to provide income for your survivors or help pay the taxes on your estate. Because people are living longer, the price of basic life insurance protection has actually been dropping.

Myth: My wife is a full-time mom with no current plans to return to work outside the home. So we don't need much insurance on her life.

Reality: In most cases, a husband and wife with minor children both need life insurance coverage, regardless of their individual earnings. If your wife died, you would need extra income to pay for child care, and perhaps to make up for a drop in your earnings caused by the need to spend more time at home.

Myth:	I drew up a will several years ago and there's no need to do a new one.
Reality:	An outdated will can be worse than no will. Your will becomes outdated when there is a change in your life such as marriage, divorce, birth of a child, or death of a designated heir. Buying or selling property, starting a business, or moving to another state can also cause your will to become outdated. By changing the tax laws, Congress can also make your will obsolete.

Some Fundamental Truths about Planning for Your Survivors

Though the likelihood is probably small that you will die next month or next year, the financial impact of your death on your family and dependents can be devastating if you have not taken a few simple steps to protect them. Unfortunately, planning for survivors frequently gets put on the back burner. The reasons are understandable. Dealing with the prospect of death is unpleasant. If death is not likely to come until you're 80, you may assume that waiting until 65 or 70 to plan for it will still leave plenty of time. The fact is that you may not live to 80, or even 65. Providing effec-

> **Providing effectively for your survivors means that you must plan as if you were going to die tomorrow, however unlikely that may be.**

tively for your survivors means that you must plan as if you were going to die tomorrow, however unlikely that may be.

Once you get started, you will find that planning for your survivors is not morbid or depressing. Rather, it's a positive and constructive thing to do. Once you have accomplished it, you will feel good about having provided in advance to help your loved ones continue their lives comfortably in the event of your death.

The subject of this chapter is often described as estate planning. We choose not to use that term because it tends to focus the discussion on how your assets will be taxed and distributed at the time of your death. It also carries an implication that only people with sizable estates—those who are older and have accumulated property over a lifetime—need to plan for the event of death. In truth, planning is much more important for those who are younger and have less wealth. Our focus is to deal first with decisions relating to your survivors. Decisions about property and estate taxes are important, but they should take a lower priority.

Planning for Your Survivors: A List of Priorities

- Selecting a guardian to look after minor children.
- Replacing the income that your earnings would have provided.
- Setting out your intentions in the event of your incapacity.
- Distributing your property according to your wishes.
- Maximizing wealth transfer.
- Minimizing death taxes.

Elements of a Plan for Your Survivors: The Necessities

Will   Your will is the key legal document in planning for your survivors. You and your spouse should have wills prepared by a qualified attorney and updated periodically. Your will names a guardian to oversee the interests of minor children and an executor to administer your estate. It also serves as the vehicle to transfer your property and carry out other instructions at death. If you die without a will, a court will substitute its judgment for yours in making these decisions. The court will also distribute your property according to state law, which may be contrary to your intentions.

Durable Power of Attorney   Your durable power of attorney can designate someone (normally your spouse) as your attorney-in-fact to manage your financial affairs in the event you become incapacitated or mentally incompetent. You may authorize your attorney-in-fact to handle routine matters such as paying your bills and depositing checks you receive in the bank. Or you may provide broader authority to dispose of property or make gifts to your designated loved ones. If you are incapacitated and have not executed a durable power of attorney, your family will have to go to court and seek appointment of a guardian or conservator to handle your affairs.

Living Will   This document declares your wishes regarding medical measures that might be taken to prolong your life in the event of grave illness or injury. A living will provides guidance and much-appreciated comfort to family members and your doctors if they should have to make decisions regarding medical treatment on your behalf.

Health Care Proxy, or Durable Power of Attorney for Health Care Decisions   Your health care proxy appoints an attorney-in-fact to make health care decisions for you if you are incapacitated. You can establish the extent of the attorney-in-fact's powers and include guidelines about what medical treatment would be acceptable or unacceptable to you. In some states, the living will is effectively included in the health care proxy.

(For more on the decisions relating to a living will and a health care proxy, see page 269.)

Letter of Instructions   This letter specifies your wishes for funeral arrangements and provides guidance for your executor or your survivors in settling your estate. It should identify the location of your will, your inventory of important papers and documents, and the key to your safe deposit box. You may also want to use it to make a final personal statement to loved ones and to bequeath your personal effects. Your letter should also list the names, addresses, and phone numbers of your lawyer, accountant, insurance agent, financial planner, and any other key advisers. Update this document regularly and keep it in an accessible location that is known to your executor or survivors.

Inventory of Important Papers and Documents   This list should describe and tell the location of all information relating to your financial affairs. It should include detailed data about all your property and personal finances, including bank accounts, insurance policies, brokerage and investment accounts, mutual funds, individual retirement accounts, and pension and employee benefit plans; real estate deeds, car titles, mortgages, loan agreements; records related to a business or partnership, including stock certificates and any buy–sell agreement; tax returns and related records; birth and marriage, and divorce papers; military service and discharge documents.

Elements of a Plan for Your Survivors: Some Optional Extras

Life Insurance   Life insurance provides survivor income if you have minor children or your spouse depends on your earnings. It may also be used to generate cash to pay estate taxes on the death of your surviving spouse. (For more on the decisions relating to how much additional life insurance you might need and purchasing a life insurance policy, see pages 279 and 288.)

Revocable Living Trust   A revocable living trust enables you to leave assets to your beneficiaries outside of your will, thus avoiding probate, the court-supervised process of distributing your property. You select the beneficiaries in the event of your death, just as you would in a will, and you designate a trustee to be responsible for the trust property in the event of your death or incapacity. (For more on revocable living trusts, see page 298.)

> **Among the most important decisions you will make in planning for your survivors is to pick the people who will look after your minor children, make medical care decisions for you if you are incapacitated, and distribute your assets to your beneficiaries.**

Irrevocable Trust   An irrevocable trust provides a way to remove assets from your estate and thus reduce estate taxes. An irrevocable trust can be established during your lifetime or through your will at death. Such trusts can be used to keep life insurance proceeds or your residence out of your estate. They are also useful in providing bequests to a child or charity. (For more on the decisions relating to irrevocable trusts, see pages 313 and 315.)

10 Decisions in Planning for Your Survivors

Decision No. 1   What advance directives will you make regarding medical treatment in the event you become incapacitated?

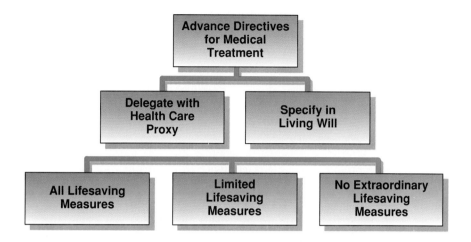

Advances in health care technology have brought us medical miracles—and nightmares as well. Doctors can now sustain life artificially in many situations where death would otherwise occur without mechanical support systems, such as feeding tubes and respirators. As a result, patients can exist indefinitely in a coma or persistent vegetative state with no hope of recovery. If that were to happen to you, what would you want your doctor to do?

You have an opportunity to make your wishes known in advance by executing a living will and/or a health care proxy, also known as a durable power of attorney for health care. The living will sets out your desire not to receive life-sustaining medical treatment if you are terminally ill or in an irreversible coma. The health care proxy names an attorney-in-fact to make health care decisions for you and to serve as your advocate in making sure that your wishes are carried out. It also allows you to state your wishes about accepting or refusing life-sustaining treatment. Unlike a living will, a health care proxy can be used to state your desires about your health care in any situation in which you are unable to make your own decisions, not just when you are in a coma or terminally ill. These two documents can help your loved ones get through the agonizing family decisions when a terminally ill patient lingers on a life-support system with no hope of recovery.

Do you need both a living will and a health care proxy? In many states, a health care proxy is the only document needed because it appoints a representative and declares your wishes. But these documents are governed by state law and there is not yet uniformity among the states. It is essential that your documents be prepared under the laws of your state of residence.

To prepare your advance directives, follow these steps:

- Examine your own personal beliefs regarding the use of artificial means to prolong your life. Get advice in preparing your advance directives from family members, your friends, your doctor, and your clergy.
- Decide what life-sustaining treatment alternatives are acceptable to you. Do you want all available medical treatment in accordance with accepted health care standards? Do you want to be sustained artificially with nourishment and fluids, but have no other extraordinary measures taken? Do you want no life-sustaining treatments?
- Discuss this issue with your doctor and determine whether he or she will be willing to carry out your wishes regarding life-sustaining treatment if you are incapacitated. If the doctor is not willing, you might arrange for treatment by another doctor who will follow your instructions.
- Require a second medical opinion for every important issue that arises in your treatment. That means your family or attorney-in-fact won't be relying on one doctor's determination of whether or not you are terminally ill, or what your prospects might be for regaining consciousness.

Our suggestion: Think of the emotional and financial consequences on your survivors if you were to become terminally ill. Prepare your advance directives with your survivors in mind.

Decision No. 2   Who will you name to carry out your intentions as guardian for your minor children, executor of your will, trustee, or attorney-in-fact?

Among the most important decisions you make in planning for your survivors is to pick the people who will look after your minor children, make medical care decisions for you if you are incapacitated, and distribute your assets to your beneficiaries.

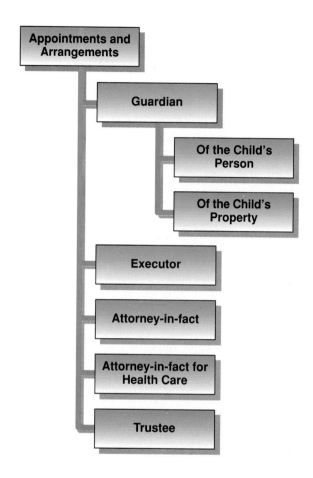

Guardian

A guardian has the responsibility to care for your minor child if you and the child's other parent die, leaving the child an orphan. The responsibility involved in assuming the role of guardian is a major one—the same as the responsibility of being a parent. The guardian makes decisions for the child regarding living arrangements, schooling, medical care, and other matters normally attended to by parents. The person you select as guardian should be loving and responsible, with a demonstrated ability to develop a warm relationship with your child. The best choice is likely to be a close relative, such as one of the child's aunts or uncles. Don't assume the guardian must be married or have children of his or her own at home. A single person who is committed to fulfilling the duties of guardian will generally do just fine. If one of your children has reached the age of majority, you can appoint him or her as guardian of your minor children.

Select at least two candidates and discuss the matter with both of them to make sure they are willing to take the responsibility. Seek advice from your children as well. They may be too young to be asked directly about their feelings toward someone who might be chosen as guardian if they are orphaned. If so, you still may be able to determine their feelings about the individuals you are considering and factor that into your decision. You should expect to come up with two acceptable candidates who are willing to do you and your children this greatest of kindnesses. Decide which one you want as guardian and which as successor guardian in case the other can't or won't serve, and then name them in your will.

A guardian's duties involve more than just personal matters. There are financial considerations as well. Will the person to whom you give custody of your child also be able to handle custody of any assets you will leave to the child? If you are not sure, the law allows you to name two guardians, one to be guardian of the child's person and the other to be guardian of the child's property. Is the guardian able to comfortably meet any extra cost that may be involved in adding your child to his or her household, above and beyond the expense of actually caring for the child? Any money you leave to the child must be used exclusively for the child's expenses by the guardian. That doesn't provide for the cost, say, of adding a bedroom for your child to sleep in or buying a bigger car so there will be a seat for your child. In recognition of these kinds of expenses, you should consider providing funds to the person who becomes guardian for your child, either from a bequest in your will or as beneficiary of a life insurance policy. The extra payment also can provide equal treatment for the guardian's children in the event he or she could not afford to provide it, such as paying for private school tuition.

Executor

The role of the executor, known in some states as the personal representative, is to gather and account for your assets, pay your debts and estate taxes, and distribute the property in the estate according to your will. If you die without a will, a court will appoint an administrator to handle those duties. Who should be your choice as executor? Normally it will be your spouse if your estate is small. Next in line might be an adult child, a sibling, or the person who will receive the largest bequest from your estate. You may also want to name an attorney or a bank, either as executor or co-executor to serve with your spouse or other relative. Many states require that your executor be a resident of the state where your will is being probated.

In any case, you want an executor who is diligent, trustworthy, and comfortable with financial and tax matters. The role of your executor is a short-term responsibility that ends with the distribution of the property in your estate. Avoid choosing an executor who might have a conflict of interest, such as a business partner or someone who owes you an outstanding debt. As with the selection of a guardian, pick at least two candidates to nominate as your executor and discuss the matter with both of them to make sure they are willing to take the responsibility.

Attorney-in-Fact

Your attorney-in-fact will be designated in the document you execute known as a durable power of attorney. The attorney-in-fact will manage your financial and business affairs in the event you become incapacitated or mentally incompetent. The issues involved in selecting an attorney-in-fact are similar to those involved in selecting an executor. However, the responsibilities of an attorney-in-fact are likely to be of an emergency, short-term nature without all the financial, tax, and estate settlement issues that would concern an executor. In general, you should choose your spouse or other close relative who lives nearby to handle this responsibility.

Attorney-in-Fact for Health Care

Your attorney-in-fact for health care makes medical treatment decisions for you in the event you are incapacitated. He or she will be guided by the terms of your living will and durable power of attorney for health care decisions or health care proxy. In most states, you can choose any adult as your attorney-in-fact to hold your health care proxy, except for a physician or health care provider who is caring for you while you are incapacitated. Normally, you will want to choose your spouse, adult child, or close friend to assume this role.

You can designate successors to serve as attorney-in-fact in the event that your original choice has died or is unable or unwilling to perform the required duties on your behalf once you are incapacitated. This is a wise precaution because your designated attorney-in-fact may be emotionally unable to make a decision to terminate life-supporting medical treatment for you, even though it would be your wish to have it done. Also consider whether to name someone as attorney-in-fact if you plan to make a substantial bequest to that person in your will.

Trustee

A trustee will be responsible for managing the assets you transfer to a trust and for looking out for the interests of the trust beneficiaries, whether they are your spouse, children, grandchildren, or favorite charity. Selecting a trustee is an important decision whose effect will be felt for years, so give it careful consideration. The decision has less consequence in the case of a revocable living trust; in most states, you can name yourself as the initial trustee. Normally, you will want to designate your spouse as successor trustee in case of your death or incapacity. If you believe your spouse will need help handling the duties of trustee, you might also provide for a financial institution such as a bank or trust company to be named successor co-trustee. In any case, with a revocable trust you are free to alter your trustee selection during your lifetime.

The rules are different for an irrevocable trust, however, and selection of a trustee becomes a much weightier decision. For a trust to qualify as an irrevocable trust, you must give up ownership and control. That usually includes giving up any power to remove a trustee and appoint a new one. As a result, your selection of a trustee becomes irrevocable, so you will want to choose carefully. As mentioned above, you might want to consider appointment of a co-trustee if, for example, the person you want to look after your beneficiaries would need help managing investments. If the trustee or co-trustee you select is a financial institution or a professional with whom you do not have close personal ties, you may want to give authority to an individual, such as a family friend, to oversee the trustee's activities. That individual may also have authority to select a new trustee under certain circumstances you specify in advance. You may even consider giving your beneficiaries the right to change trustee if the trustee's investment performance fails to meet some reasonable standard.

Final Arrangements

Your wishes for final arrangements, including a funeral, should be contained in your letter of instructions. Don't put them in your will, which may not be opened and read immediately after your death. Identify any burial plot you may own and give the location of the cemetery deed. If you have made advance arrangements with a funeral home, describe them and say where a copy of the contract can be found. Setting out your preferences regarding a funeral or memorial service, organ donations, and burial will lift the burden of decision making from your survivors and help them feel confident that they have been faithful to your preferences.

Decision No. 3   What are your financial goals for your survivors?

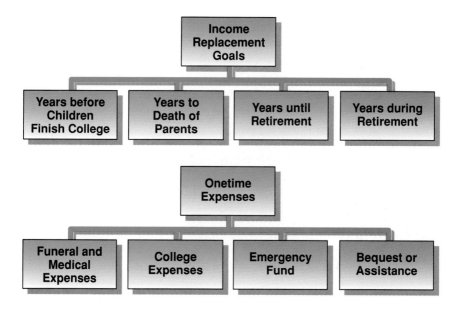

If you have dependents, particularly if they are young children, you should be concerned about providing for their future financial needs in the event of your death. But what if you have no one who qualifies as your legal dependent? That doesn't mean you will have no survivors when you die. Think of the people who are close to you and consider what their needs might be.

Your parents, for example, might look to you in the future for financial assistance or even regular support. What is the likelihood of that happening? If you think the chances are good, you should take their potential needs into account.

Consider also your spouse or companion. Even if both of you have jobs, how would your death and the loss of your income affect your partner's standard of living? Are there financial obligations, such as mortgages, leases, or car loans, that both of you have undertaken with the assumption that the bills will be paid out of two incomes? In the long term, is your partner's earning potential sufficient to support him or her adequately as a single-earner household? Depending on the answers to these questions, you may want to plan to pay off those financial obligations or supplement your partner's future income in the event of your death.

Finally, is there someone you know—perhaps a close friend, a niece/nephew, or a child with a single parent—in financially precarious circumstances who seems likely to need your help some day? Maybe, if it's a child, you have thought about contributing toward college expenses or providing some kind of support in case of an emergency. If you feel you are likely to help, don't let the possibility of your death prevent you from doing so. Instead, consider some kind of financial assistance as one of your goals while you plan for your survivors.

Considerations in Survivor Planning

Your survivors will face two types of financial needs, ongoing living expenses and onetime cash needs.

- **Income to cover ongoing living expenses after the loss of your paycheck.** These expenses can be expected to vary, but will probably continue for many years. For example, your basic household living costs may stay essentially the same (in today's dollars) for a period, then decline after your children finish college and become self-sufficient.

- **Cash needs for major obligations or onetime expenses, some of which will come up immediately.** For example, your survivors can probably expect substantial medical and funeral bills after your death. Other needs in this category will not arise until later. An example would be the cost of college for your children.

Your first emphasis should be on income replacement goals. They warrant a much higher priority because they represent the fundamentals: food, shelter, clothing, medical care, and other basics. Without income to support them, your survivors might literally be out on the street. Cash needs for major obligations or expenses, while important, should get a lower priority. Let's start with income replacement, where the decision is what percentage of your current income you want to replace. The answer is probably less than 100 percent of your current pretax earnings because the expenses faced by your survivors are likely to decline. There are several reasons for this:

- **Savings.** Your survivors will need to set aside less in the way of household savings each year because their long-term goals will be partially or fully funded at the time of your death.
- **Spending.** Some portion of your current household spending is attributable solely to you: the food you eat, the clothing you buy, the cost of the car you drive, what you spend for yourself on entertainment, and the premiums for your life and disability insurance.
- **Debt.** If you purchase sufficient life insurance to retire your mortgage and other debts at your death, your household's monthly living costs will probably drop significantly.

Not all expenses will decline when you die. Some may rise. For example, your spouse or companion may have to get a new job or work longer hours, increasing the cost of child care or after-school programs for your children. If you now handle home maintenance chores and your spouse or companion won't have the time or skills to take them on, someone will have to be paid to do so.

All told, your household should be able to sustain its standard of living after your death with 60 to 90 percent of current pretax income. If you have insurance to pay off all debts, it may be closer to 60 percent. If not, the required replacement ratio will probably be more like 80 or 90 percent. Use this worksheet to develop an estimate of how much your household expenses will change and come up with a desired replacement ratio.

You can expect living expenses for your survivors to vary in the future depending on their stage in life. Income needs may stay at roughly their current levels in today's dollars, for example, until the children finish college and begin to live on their own. Then they may go down, only to rise years later when your spouse or companion retires.

After you have developed and refined your income replacement goals, decide what will be your goals in terms of future cash needs for major obligations or expenses. In general, goals that will reduce fixed household living costs immediately after your death should get the highest priority. They might include paying off or refinancing your home mortgage and other debts. Retiring some or all of your home mortgage debt is much more beneficial to your survivors than is financing future costs such as

Survivor income planning worksheet

ESTIMATE YOUR HOUSEHOLD'S MONTHLY SPENDING NEEDS

	Current Amount	Addition or Reduction	Amount Needed If You Die
Mortgage or rent	$	$	$
Utilities			
Home upkeep, taxes			
Food			
Clothing			
Insurance—Health			
Life			
Disability			
Homeowner			
Auto expenses			
Medical and dental			
Recreation and travel			
Child care			
Education			
Other expenses			
Total monthly expenses			

the expense of a college education in 5 or 10 years. Of course, it may require significantly more in the way of financial resources to pay off your mortgage immediately after your death than to pay for future college tuition.

In planning for your survivors, don't forget about the need to weather financial setbacks. That means your goals should provide for enough money to establish a "rainy day" emergency fund of 6 to 12 months of living expenses.

Our suggestion: Think about the standard of living you want for your survivors. As you consider their needs in the event of your death, you will realize once again the importance of trying to strike a balance with your finances between current and future consumption. The lower your fixed living costs and the greater your savings, the more secure your survivors will be no matter how much life insurance you purchase.

Survivor cash needs planning worksheet

ESTIMATE YOUR
HOUSEHOLD'S CASH
NEEDS FOR ONETIME
EXPENDITURES

	Amount (Today's $)	When Needed (Years from Now)
Funeral costs	$ _____	_____
Mortgage principal	_____	_____
Other loan balances	_____	_____
Emergency fund	_____	_____
Year 1 of college costs	_____	_____
Year 2 of college costs	_____	_____
Year 3 of college costs	_____	_____
Year 4 of college costs	_____	_____
College costs (etc.)	_____	_____
Bequest or assistance	_____	_____

Decision No. 4   How much additional life insurance do you need to meet your financial goals for your survivors?

Unlike other financial goals, which are funded over long periods through savings, the goals you develop for your survivors will be funded at your death in large part from the proceeds of life insurance. Assuming for a moment that you have no investments or other financial resources, the proceeds from your insurance policy if you die would have to be large enough to equal the present value of:

1. The future income stream you have set as a goal to replace your paycheck, starting at the time of your death and continuing through your spouse's retirement; and
2. The onetime expenses among your survivor goals, such as paying off the mortgage or meeting future college tuition bills.

The sum of these two items, and thus your need for life insurance, may be substantial. That need will be reduced somewhat by the value of your current resources, including your retirement and college investments, and any death benefits offered by your employer. You can also count on Social Security to provide survivor income until your children reach age 18 and after your surviving spouse retires. Nonetheless, the younger you are, the greater will be your survivors' future income needs and the less you will have in the way of resources to provide for those needs. The only way to make up for that difference is through life insurance.

When you have refined the goals for your survivors and stated them in terms of amounts in today's dollars, you are ready to use the worksheet on pages 353 and 354 to figure out how much additional life insurance you need. Our assumption, once again, is that future income will remain constant in today's dollars and retain its purchasing power. Thus you will be planning for sufficient insurance to provide your survivors with an income stream that increases each year at the rate of inflation.

Planning for Your Survivors—Richard Powers

Richard Powers, 42, wants to determine if he has sufficient life insurance to meet his goals for his family in the event of his death. His wife, Jill, is 40, and they have two children, Melissa, 9, and Jonathan, 6. Richard's salary as a marketing manager is $75,000 a year, and Jill earns $35,000 as a teacher. They have $57,000 in investment assets.

Richard figures his family could live on about 60 percent of their present total income if the mortgage were paid off at his death. He wants life insurance to provide funds to pay for college costs of the children (four years at $15,000 per year in today's dollars). He also wants to supplement his wife's Social Security income once she reaches age 65. While Jill is currently employed, she only recently returned to work after staying home with the children until Jonathan started first grade. As a result, she

SURVIVOR PLANNING INFORMATION

Richard Powers

1. Current age of spouse or companion	40
2. Years until youngest child reaches age 18	12
3. Retirement age of spouse or companion	65
4. Years in retirement for spouse or companion	25
5. Your annual income (today's dollars)	$75,000
6. Annual income of spouse or companion (today's dollars)	$30,000
7. Total household income (today's dollars)	$105,000

Needs

8. Household income replacement goal (today's dollars)	$65,000
9. Funeral cost and estate settlement cash needs	$35,000
10. Mortgage and debt retirement cash needs goal	$110,000
11. Annual college cost goal for Child 1 (today's dollars) Years until freshman year: 9	$15,000
12. Annual college cost goal for Child 2 (today's dollars) Years until freshman year: 12	$15,000
13. Other cash needs goal (today's dollars) Years until cash needed:	0

Resources

14. Lump-sum death benefit from your employer (today's dollars)	$150,000
15. Total investment assets including 401(k), IRAs, college accounts	$57,000
16. Total death benefits from current life insurance policies	$300,000
17. Estimated Social Security family survivor benefits to age 18 of youngest child (today's dollars)	$25,000
18. Estimated pension income of spouse or companion (today's dollars)	0
19. Estimated Social Security retirement benefit of spouse or companion (today's dollars)	$14,000

does not expect at this time to receive a pension of her own. She will be eligible for about $36,000 from Social Security at age 65 in the event of Richard's death. He wants to supplement that amount with an extra $36,000 of retirement income for her, for a total of $50,000.

Richard estimates funeral and estate settlement costs of $35,000, and the couple owes about $110,000 on the mortgage for their home. In the event of his death, Richard's survivors will receive a benefit from his

HOW MUCH LIFE INSURANCE DO I NEED
TO MEET MY SURVIVOR GOALS?

1. Household income replacement goal for preretirement
   period of spouse or companion (today's dollars) — $65,000

2. Annual income of spouse or companion until
   retirement (today's dollars) — $35,000

3. Income replacement needed from investments
   (today's dollars) (Line 1 – Line 2) — $30,000

4. Capital required to fund income replacement for prere-
   tirement (today's dollars) (Line 3 × Factor from Table 1)   Factor: 20.02 — $600,600

If you have minor children, otherwise skip to Line 7

5. Estimated annual Social Security survivor benefits
   (today's dollars) (see Table 5) — $25,000

   Number of years benefits paid: 13

6. Reduction in amount of capital needed because of Social
   Security survivor benefits (Line 5 × Factor from Table 1)   Factor: 11.57 — $289,250

Retirement income for spouse or companion

7. Retirement income goal for spouse or companion (today's dollars) — $50,000

8. Estimated pension income at retirement of spouse
   or companion (today's dollars) — 0

9. Estimated Social Security benefit of spouse or
   companion (today's dollars) — $14,000

10. Income needed from investments at retirement
    (Line 7 – Line 8 – Line 9) (today's dollars) — $36,000

11. Income needed from investments at retirement
    adjusted for inflation (future dollars)
    (Line 10 × Factor from Table 2)   Factor: 2.67 — $96,120

12. Capital required at retirement to fund investments
    (Line 11 × Factor from Table 1) (future dollars)   Factor: 20.02 — $1,924,322

13. Capital required today to fund retirement income (Line
    12 divided by Factor from Table 3) (today's dollars)   Factor: 4.29 — $448,560

14. Capital required to fund income replacement
    (today's dollars) (Line 4 + Line 13 – Line 6) — $759,910

15. Funeral cost and estate settlement cash needs (today's dollars) — $35,000

16. Mortgage, debt retirement cash needs goal (today's dollars) — $110,000

17. College cost goal for Child 1 (today's dollars)
    (Annual cost × Number of years × Factor from Table 4)   Factor: 1.20 — $72,000

18. College cost goal for Child 2 (today's dollars)
    (Annual cost × Number of years × Factor from Table 4)   Factor: 1.27 — $76,200

19. Other cash needs goal (today's dollars) × Factor
    from Table 1 — 0

20. Capital required to fund all cash needs (today's dollars)
    (Sum of Lines 15–19) $293,200

21. Total capital required to fund survivor income
    and cash needs (today's dollars) (Line 14 + Line 20) $1,053,110

22. Lump-sum death benefit from your employer (today's dollars) $150,000

23. Total investment assets including 401(k), IRAs,
    college accounts (today's dollars) $57,000

24. Total death benefits from current life insurance policies
    (today's dollars) $300,000

25. Total capital available to fund survivor income
    and cash needs (today's dollars) (Sum of Lines 22–24) $507,000

26. Write in amount from Line 21 $1,053,110

If Line 25 is greater than Line 26, you do not need additional life
insurance at this time. If Line 26 is greater than Line 25, enter
difference between the two on Line 27.

27. Additional life insurance coverage needed (Line 26 – Line 25) $546,110

Social Security survivor benefit planning worksheet   RICHARD POWERS

To estimate average benefit, add eligible benefit amounts for each year, then divide by
number of years.

Children are eligible for survivor benefits until age 17, or until 18 if they are in high
school. A spouse or divorced spouse is eligible for a separate survivor benefit if caring for
an eligible child up to age 15.

	Years after Death					
	1st	2nd	3rd	4th	5th	6th
Child 1						
Age	6	7	8	9	10	11
Benefit	12,360	12,360	12,360	12,360	12,360	12,360
Child 2						
Age	9	10	11	12	13	14
Benefit	12,360	12,360	12,360	12,360	12,360	12,360
Spouse						
Benefit	12,360	12,360	12,360	12,360	12,360	12,360
Total benefits	—	—	—	—	—	—
Maximum family benefit	28,800	28,800	28,000	28,800	28,800	28,800

Social Security survivor benefit planning worksheet *concluded*

	Years after Death					
	7th	8th	9th	10th	11th	12th
Child 1						
Age	12	13	14	15	16	17
Benefit	12,360	12,360	12,360	12,360	12,360	12,360
Child 2						
Age	15	16	17	18	19	20
Benefit	12,360	12,360	12,360	12,360	0	0
Spouse						
Benefit	12,360	12,360	12,360	12,360	0	0
Total benefits	—	—	—	—	12,360	12,360
Maximum family benefit	28,800	28,800	28,800	28,800	—	—

	Years after Death					
	13th	14th	15th	16th	17th	18th
Child 1						
Age	18	19				
Benefit	12,360	0				
Child 2						
Age	21	22				
Benefit	0	0				
Spouse						
Benefit	0	0				
Total benefits	12,360	0				
Maximum benefit	—	—				

Total benefits = $325,000

Total years = 13

Average annual benefit = 325,000/13 = $25,000

employer equal to twice his salary. Richard also has two insurance policies on his life with combined death benefits of $300,000.

The sample worksheet shows that Richard needs about $546,000 in additional life insurance coverage at this time. That may sound like a large amount, but he could purchase the additional coverage at his age for about $1,200 a year.

Decision No. 5   What type of life insurance policy should you purchase?

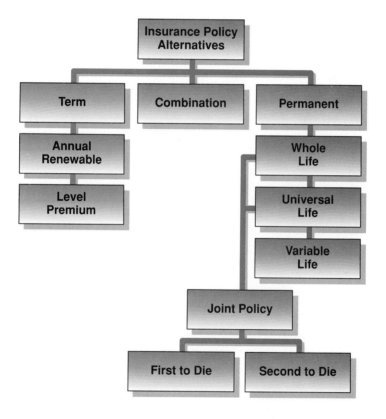

Life insurance offers important advantages as a way to protect your survivors from the loss of your earning capacity. First, the payment of a death benefit is guaranteed by the life insurance company, meaning you can be assured that the money will be there when you die. The insurance industry is heavily regulated and insurance companies have an excellent record for reliability in paying death benefit claims.

Focus on...

WHAT YOUR SURVIVORS CAN EXPECT FROM SOCIAL SECURITY

If you die with young children and you are covered by Social Security, they will be eligible for survivor income benefits. Children can get survivor benefits until age 17, or 18 if they are in high school. A spouse or divorced spouse is eligible for a separate survivor benefit if caring for an eligible child under age 16.

The benefit for each eligible child and for a spouse caring for an eligible child is 75 percent of your primary insurance amount, up to a maximum limit per family. Your primary insurance amount is what you would receive in today's dollars as a retirement benefit if you were to retire at age 65. The maximum primary insurance amount for retirement is $14,388 in 1995. Depending on the age when you die, a higher primary insurance amount may be used to calculate benefits for your survivors. The maximum amount per family will range between one-and-a-half and two times your primary insurance amount, depending on your age and your earnings record. The Social Security Administration will provide you with an estimate of your survivor benefits when you request a personal earnings and benefit statement (see page 280).

Let's look at how Social Security survivor benefits would be calculated, assuming you die at age 40 and your spouse cares for your two children, ages 10 and 12. This also assumes that your earnings have consistently equaled or exceeded the Social Security wage base. The wage base, or the maximum amount of earnings subject to Social Security Old-Age, Survivors and Disability Insurance, was $61,200 for 1995.

Estimating Social Security Survivor Benefits

Child age 12	$12,400
Child age 10	12,400
Spouse	12,400
Total of family benefits	37,200
Maximum family benefit	28,800
Actual benefit amount	$28,800

In this example, the spouse and two children would receive the maximum family benefit until the seventh year after your death. At that time, the older child would be age 19 and have graduated from high school, and thus no longer be eligible. Likewise, the spouse would no longer be eligible because the younger child would have reached age 16. The younger child's benefit of $12,400 would continue until age 18.

Second, the cost of life insurance protection is likely to be small at the time you need it most—when your family is young. Depending on your age, the annual premium for life insurance can be as low as a small fraction of a penny per dollar of coverage. That means buying life insurance for risk protection is a highly efficient use of your money.

Third, life insurance proceeds are free of income tax. If your spouse is the beneficiary of your policy, the proceeds are also free of any estate tax at your death. With no tax bite taken from the policy proceeds, all your insurance dollars go to work providing support for your survivors.

Life insurance offers important advantages as a way to protect your survivors from the loss of your earning capacity.

The advantages of life insurance for survivor protection—low cost and guaranteed, tax-free death benefits—make it essential if you have dependents. Remember, however, that not everyone should buy life insurance. An individual with no dependents and enough money to meet funeral expenses probably doesn't need it. You also may not need life insurance if you already have sufficient resources to support yourself and your spouse or companion in retirement—and no other dependents. Although life insurance can be used for purposes besides survivor protection, its advantages in these instances may be less compelling. For example, insurance can provide cash to help your family pay taxes on your estate, or it can serve as a long-term tax-deferred investment. But before buying life insurance for these purposes, consider alternatives that might be cheaper. You may be able to plan for sufficient estate liquidity in a more cost-efficient way than purchasing insurance. Likewise, you may find that the cost of investment-oriented life insurance outweighs its tax advantages.

Be sure to review your insurance policies periodically to determine if you have the appropriate amount of coverage. As your circumstances change, your needs for insurance will change. If your income and basic living costs have gone up, you may need to purchase more insurance. After your children finish college and become self-sufficient, your life insurance needs may be less. Your goal should always be to purchase only the amount and type of insurance coverage that you really need.

Selecting a Life Insurance Policy

Life insurance comes in two basic varieties, term and permanent. Term insurance provides pure no-frills protection for a particular period of time, usually a year. The price, or premium, reflects the risk to the insurance company of your death during that period. When the term is over, the price of renewing the insurance policy goes up. That's because the likelihood that you will die—and thus the likelihood that the insurance company will have to pay—has increased with your age. Term insurance offers no buildup of cash value, no matter how long you continue to renew the policy. By its nature, term insurance is cheap for younger people but grows very expensive after you reach age 60.

In contrast, permanent insurance, also known as cash value insurance, is designed with the assumption that you will keep the policy for life. The insurance company sets a fixed annual premium much higher than what is needed to cover the risk of your death in the initial years of the policy. The excess amount is used to fund a cash value that grows over the life of the policy. You can take out the cash value in the form of policy loans or by surrendering the policy and canceling your coverage. Compared to term insurance, permanent insurance is more expensive at any given age. As you get older, however, the annual cost of retaining your fixed-premium permanent insurance policy eventually will become less than the premium you would have to pay for a comparable amount of term insurance.

Term Insurance

Term policies are straightforward and fairly easy to evaluate based on their premium per $1,000 of death benefit. The two major types of policies are annual renewable term and level term. Annual renewable term premiums increase each year. Level term, in contrast, charges a rate that is initially higher than the rate for annual renewable term. However, the level term rate remains fixed for a term of 5, 10, 15, or 20 years. At the end of that time, the cost of reentry, or renewing for another fixed term, rises significantly. That increase may be reduced somewhat through a conditional exchange option if you can demonstrate that you are still in good health. You can compare the cost of level term vs. annual renewable term by summing the present values of the annual premiums for each policy over a particular period. (See checklist on page 291.) In recent years, many insurance companies have priced level-term policies very

Focus on...

No-Load and Low-Load Life Insurance

A small but growing number of life insurance companies offer policies without traditional sales charges. They may sell insurance directly to consumers over the telephone, through salaried agents who are not paid commissions, or through fee-only financial planners or insurance advisers.

These no-load or low-load policies can offer significantly better financial performance in their early years for a simple reason. The traditional agent's commission, plus related initial costs, often exceeds the amount of premium you pay for the policy during the first year. "Trailing" annual sales-related expenses of up to 10 percent of the premium may continue for several years.

As a result, traditionally "loaded" policies build up little or no cash value during the initial few years after they are purchased. In contrast, a substantial share of the typical no-load or low-load policy's premium goes to work right away building a cash value.

The difference can be seen by comparing projected cash value growth for a traditional policy and for a no-load or low-load policy with the same annual premium. To make up for this initial disadvantage, a traditionally loaded policy must generate significantly better financial performance in future years than the no-load or low-load policy, which may or may not be achievable.

In a sense, the question of buying traditional vs. no/low-load insurance is similar to the question of whether to buy a mutual fund through a broker and pay a sales charge or to purchase a no-load fund directly from the fund sponsors. An insurance agent may provide you with valuable assistance in selecting the right policy with the right features for you, and the traditional commission represents a reasonable way to compensate the agent for those services. On the other hand, if you are able to analyze and select a policy on your own, the no-load/low-load alternative may be more attractive.

attractively as compared to annually renewable term. If you know you want coverage for a particular period, say 10 years, a level-term policy for that period may be your best choice.

One important feature offered by many term policies is convertibility. This allows you to convert the policy to permanent (usually whole life) insurance without the need for a medical examination. If your health deteriorates in the future, the convertibility feature can assure that you have access to permanent insurance at reasonable cost. Another feature is

COMPARING TERM INSURANCE AND
PERMANENT INSURANCE

Term Insurance	Permanent Insurance
Features	
"No-frills" death benefit	Death benefit plus cash value
Better If You Need Protection	
For 10 years or less	For more than 10 years
Annual Premium	
Lower but will increase	Higher but generally fixed
Insurance Company Financial Strength	
Less important	Very important
Commissions and Sales Costs	
Not significant	It pays to shop

the waiver of premium in the event of disability. You pay extra for this feature and it may or may not be worth the money, depending on the insurance company's definition of disability (see Chapter 9).

Although term insurance is a standardized commodity, don't assume all insurers will charge the same prices, or that group rates are necessarily better. In some instances, coverage under a group policy may cost more than an individual policy sold through an agent. The insurance company needs to price the policy based on the mortality experience of the group; if you are younger and healthier than the average group member, you may be able to do better purchasing an individual policy.

There are exceptions. Some group policies offer favorable rates and, in addition, offer you the opportunity to buy coverage above the basic level. If you need additional insurance, you should first check the rates and terms of your group policy.

Permanent Insurance

Whole Life   Whole life is the traditional form of permanent insurance and remains the largest-selling policy of this type. The premium and death benefit typically are guaranteed, although the death benefit may increase over time. Whole life gradually builds a cash value that can be borrowed against or withdrawn if you cancel your policy. The insurance company usually guarantees a certain minimum level of dividends or earnings credited to the policy, but in most cases they will exceed the guaranteed level.

CHECKLIST FOR COMPARING TERM LIFE INSURANCE POLICIES

1. What is the policy's renewal period?
   Annual _____
   Five year _____
   10 year _____
   15 year _____
   20 year _____
2. Is the policy guaranteed renewable?   Yes _____ No _____
3. To what age is the policy renewable?
   65 _____
   70 _____
   95 _____
   99 _____
   Other _____
4. What is the rating or risk class? Do you qualify for a preferred nonsmoker rating? _____
5. If the policy is annually renewable, what is the schedule of both current and guaranteed premiums until age 65, or to whatever age you will need the coverage?
   Face amount of coverage _____

	Age	Current Premium	Cost per $1,000 Coverage*	Guaranteed Premium	Cost per $1,000 Coverage*
Year 1	_____	_____	_____	_____	_____
Year 2	_____	_____	_____	_____	_____
Year 3	_____	_____	_____	_____	_____
Year 4	_____	_____	_____	_____	_____
Year 5 etc.					

6. If the policy is a level-term policy, will premiums be reset and then fixed for the full period of each future term, or will they begin to increase on an annual basis at some point?
   Fixed for each future term _____
   Eventually reset annually _____
7. If the policy is a level-term policy, is there a conditional exchange option that will provide a lower premium at renewal if new medical evidence of insurability is submitted?   Yes _____ No _____

*Example: $500 annual premium for $250,000 face amount of coverage. Cost per $1,000 = $500/$250,000 × 1,000 = $2.00.

8. If the policy is a level-term policy, what is the schedule of premiums (current, guaranteed premiums, and guaranteed under a conditional exchange option, if any) until age 65, or to whatever age you will need the coverage?

Face amount of coverage _____

	Age	Current Premium	Cost per $1,000 Coverage*	Guaranteed Premium	Cost per $1,000 Coverage*	Cond. Option Premium	Cost per $1,000 Coverage
Year 1	____	_____	_____	_____	_____	_____	_____
Year 2	____	_____	_____	_____	_____	_____	_____
Year 3	____	_____	_____	_____	_____	_____	_____
Year 4	____	_____	_____	_____	_____	_____	_____
Year 5 etc.							

Years current premium guaranteed _____

Maximum premium _____

9. Is the policy convertible to permanent insurance?   Yes _____   No _____

If yes

To what age is the policy convertible?

Convertible to age: 60 _____

65 _____

70 _____

Other _____

In what face amounts can policy conversions be made?

Minimum conversion amount _____

Is a conversion credit offered that reduces the premium when the policy is converted?   Yes _____   No _____

Amount of credit _____

For how many policy years is the conversion credit offered?

Number of policy years offered _____

10. Is there an optional waiver of premium if you become disabled?   Yes _____   No _____

If yes

Does the waiver of premium continue for life or terminate at the end of the current policy term?

Continues for life _____

Ends with term _____

Can the policy be converted while premiums are being waived for disability?

Conversion permitted during waiver _____

Conversion not permitted during waiver _____

*Example: $500 annual premium for $250,000 face amount of coverage. Cost per $1,000 = $500/$250,000 × 1,000 = $2.00.

What is the cost of the waiver-of-premium rider?

	Age	Cost of Waiver
Year 1	_____	_____
Year 2	_____	_____
Year 3	_____	_____
Year 4	_____	_____
Year 5 etc.		

11. What is the present value of the policy's premium cost?
(This figure can be useful when comparing level term and
annually renewable policies. Table uses a discount rate of 6%.)

	Premium	Factor	Premium Divided by Factor
Year 1	_____	1.00	_____
Year 2	_____	1.06	_____
Year 3	_____	1.12	_____
Year 4	_____	1.19	_____
Year 5	_____	1.26	_____
Year 6	_____	1.34	_____
Year 7	_____	1.42	_____
Year 8	_____	1.50	_____
Year 9	_____	1.59	_____
Year 10	_____	1.69	_____
Year 11	_____	1.79	_____
Year 12	_____	1.90	_____
Year 13	_____	2.01	_____
Year 14	_____	2.13	_____
Year 15	_____	2.26	_____

Total = Present value of future premiums

Universal Life   This type of policy offers flexible premiums and, in
turn, flexible death benefits. Universal life returns are sensitive to changing interest rates. Rates offered by the company are changed annually and
guaranteed for the next year. If you like the current rate of return, you
can invest more in the policy. If you don't, you may be able to skip the
premium or pay only a minimal amount. However, the policy may lapse
if you have not paid sufficient premiums to keep the cash value greater
than the periodic charges for expenses and mortality costs.

Variable Life   These policies amount to mutual funds with a life insurance wrapper. They typically offer several fund-like investments with stocks, bonds, and money market funds as alternatives. Premiums are generally fixed and a relatively small death benefit is guaranteed. Returns—and thus growth of cash value and the death benefit—depend on the performance of the underlying funds, not on the insurance company's overall investment performance.

Joint Policies   These policies insure the lives of two or more persons. They can be attractive because their premiums are often less than the total premiums for separate insurance policies on each individual. First-to-die policies pay a benefit on the first death among the covered individuals. They are used by two-income couples who need survivor income replacement in the event of either spouse's death. Another use is for business partners who want the death benefit to provide cash to purchase the ownership interest of any partner who dies. Second-to-die policies, also known as survivorship insurance, pay a benefit on the death of the second of two covered individuals. They are used most often by couples to cover estate taxes on the death of the second spouse.

In General

For any type of permanent insurance, the attractiveness of a particular policy depends on the insurer's investment returns, sales and administrative costs, mortality experience (the longer its policyholders live, the better), and its lapse rate (the more policyholders who cancel, the worse). To project the future performance of a policy you are considering, an insurance agent will prepare a policy illustration using assumptions about each of these variables. Because insurance companies invest primarily in bonds, the cycles of interest rates and bond returns are particularly important in determining their investment performance. (In the case of a variable policy, returns depend on performance of the underlying investment funds.)

If the assumptions are all reasonable, the projection can give you a good picture of how the policy will perform at different levels of interest rates. (Always ask to see what would happen if rates dropped.) However, if the projections are based on guesses that mortality experience or investment returns will improve, the policy illustration may be nothing more than wishful thinking.

CHECKLIST FOR COMPARING
PERMANENT LIFE INSURANCE POLICIES

1. What is the type of policy?
    Whole life
    Universal life _____
    Variable life _____
    Other _____

2. What is the rating or risk class? Do you qualify for a preferred nonsmoker rating?

3. What ongoing annual reports and performance illustrations will be provided after this policy is purchased?

4. What are the financial strength ratings for this insurance company?

Rating Agency	Rating
A.M. Best Co.	_____
Duff & Phelps Credit Rating Co.	_____
Moody's Investors Service	_____
Standard & Poor's Corp.	_____
Weiss Research Inc.	_____

5. Does the policy qualify as life insurance under Internal Revenue Code Section 7702? (If not, policy loans and withdrawals may be subject to tax and penalties.)   Yes _____ No _____

6. Is there an optional waiver of premium if you become disabled? If so, what is its annual cost?   Yes _____ No _____
    Cost _____

If this is a whole life policy

7. Is this a participating policy?

8. At what age does the policy mature or endow?
    65 _____
    70 _____
    95 _____
    100 _____
    Other _____

9. What is the guaranteed minimum rate of credited interest?
    Guaranteed rate _____

10. What interest rates has the insurance company credited for each of the past 10 years?

Year 1 _____	Year 2 _____	Year 3 _____	Year 4 _____
Year 5 _____	Year 6 _____	Year 7 _____	Year 8 _____
Year 9 _____	Year 10 _____		

11. What are the projected cash value and death benefit based
   on the company's current insurance charges and dividends?
   What are the guaranteed cash value and death benefit?

   Face amount of coverage _____

	Premium	Dividend	*Cash Value*		*Death Benefit*	
			Projected	Guaranteed	Projected	Guaranteed
Year 1	_____	_____	_____	_____	_____	_____
Year 2	_____	_____	_____	_____	_____	_____
Year 3	_____	_____	_____	_____	_____	_____
Year 4	_____	_____	_____	_____	_____	_____
Year 5 etc.						

12. Are the projections of cash value and death benefit based on
   the company's current mortality and policy lapse experience
   or improvements in mortality and policy lapse experience?

13. If premiums are projected to vanish, what happens to the number
   of premiums required under various interest rate scenarios? What
   happens if interest rates drop after premiums have vanished?

14. Is all of the death benefit provided through the base policy, or
   is part of the death benefit provided by a term rider?

If this is a universal life policy

15. What is the minimum initial premium
   and for how long must it be paid?   Minimum _____ Years _____

16. How long does the surrender penalty last?   Years _____

17. How does the policy perform under different future
   interest rate scenarios?

If this is a variable life policy

18. What is the minimum guaranteed death benefit, and
   what premium is required to maintain that benefit?

19. What investment funds are available?

20. What has been the investment performance of each fund
   for the past five years in comparison to a benchmark index?

	Total Return		*Total Return*		*Total Return*	
	Fund 1	Benchmark	Fund 2	Benchmark	Fund 3	Benchmark
Year 1	_____	_____	_____	_____	_____	_____
Year 2	_____	_____	_____	_____	_____	_____
Year 3	_____	_____	_____	_____	_____	_____
Year 4	_____	_____	_____	_____	_____	_____
Year 5	_____	_____	_____	_____	_____	_____

	Total Return		Total Return		Total Return	
	Fund 4	Benchmark	Fund 5	Benchmark	Fund 6	Benchmark
Year 1	_____	_____	_____	_____	_____	_____
Year 2	_____	_____	_____	_____	_____	_____
Year 3	_____	_____	_____	_____	_____	_____
Year 4	_____	_____	_____	_____	_____	_____
Year 5	_____	_____	_____	_____	_____	_____

21. What are the investment advisory fees and operating expenses of the funds?

22. What is the policy's current mortality and expense charge? What is the guaranteed maximum charge?

Joint policies

23. If this is a first-to-die policy, what are the provisions to maintain coverage after the first death?

24. If this is a second-to-die policy, does the cash value increase when the first death occurs?   Yes _____   No _____

More important than illustrations are a company's past history of performance and its claims-paying ratings. Because you expect to own a permanent life insurance policy for many years, you want the insurer to be financially sound. (This may be less of a consideration with a variable life policy because the fund assets are legally separate from the insurance company's own portfolio and not generally affected by its financial soundness or overall investment returns.) Look for policies from companies that are highly rated for claims-paying ability by several rating agencies, such as A.M. Best Co. (A+ or better), Standard & Poor's Corp. (AA or better), and Moody's Investors Service (Aa or better).

Our suggestion: Buy convertible term insurance to cover your basic survivor protection needs. In future years, you may find it attractive to convert some or all of your coverage to a permanent insurance policy.

Insurance Rating Agencies

- A.M. Best Co., Ambest Rd., Oldwick, NJ 08858 (908-439-2200).
- Duff & Phelps, 55 E. Monroe St., Suite 36, Chicago, IL, 60603 (312-368-3157).
- Moody's Investors Service, 99 Church St., New York, NY 10007 (212-553-1658).

- Standard & Poor's Corp., 5 Broadway, New York, NY 10004 (800-221-5277).
- Weiss Research, P.O. Box 109665, Palm Beach Gardens, FL 33410 (800-289-9222).

Decision No. 6   Should you establish a revocable living trust?

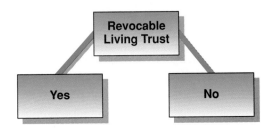

A revocable living trust, or inter vivos trust, as the name indicates, is one that you create during your lifetime (rather than through your will) and can alter or revoke. It enables you to control the trust assets during your lifetime, then pass them to your beneficiaries outside of your will, thus avoiding probate. You select the beneficiaries in the event of your death, just as you would in a will, while naming yourself as beneficiary during your lifetime. In most states, you can also designate yourself as trustee but you will also need to pick a successor trustee, who takes responsibility for managing the trust assets in the event of your death or incapacity.

Revocable living trusts are not tax shelters. You must pay income tax on the trust's earnings while you are alive. After your death, the trust assets are included in your estate and are subject to death taxes. But even without any special tax advantages, revocable living trusts offer a number of benefits. For example, if you were seriously disabled by a sudden illness, your spouse or some other relative would normally have to seek court appointment as your guardian or conservator to handle your financial affairs. With a revocable living trust, your trustee or designated successor trustee would be able to step in immediately to manage your finances while you are incapacitated.

A revocable living trust avoids the cost, potential delays, and public disclosure of probate. Such a trust can also make it easier to administer your property after your death. In some states, your executor must go through a time-consuming process of collecting your assets from financial institutions where they are held and transferring ownership from you to your estate. In contrast, assets placed in a revocable living trust are immediately available. After providing for any debts and taxes that are due, your successor trustee can disburse the funds according to the terms you established in the trust document before your death. A living trust can also be useful if you own real estate in more than one state. By deeding over the property to the trust, you avoid the expense and trouble of having your estate go though probate in each state where you own property.

What is involved in establishing a living trust?

- **Setup costs.** You will likely need an attorney to draft the trust document.
- **Transfer of assets.** Establishing a living trust is just the first step. You must legally transfer title to property to make the trust effective. Generally, there is little cost and no other impact to the property transfers. However, watch for wrinkles that may come into play. A mortgage on property, especially commercial property, may require immediate repayment on transfer from you to the trust.
- **Ongoing administration.** During your lifetime, as long as you are the trustee, there are no special administration requirements for the trust. No separate books need be maintained and no tax returns are required.

Not all assets belong in a revocable living trust. Individual retirement accounts, for example, shouldn't be held in such a trust. IRAs pass directly to the designated beneficiary, so unless you name your estate as beneficiary, the money in the IRA will avoid probate anyway. Property held jointly with the right of survivorship automatically goes to your co-owner at your death, also bypassing probate. You will still need to provide in your will for any property held outside the trust. One alternative is to direct that such property be transferred to the trust at your death in what is called a pour-over provision. These assets will probably have to go through probate first, however.

Our suggestion: A revocable living trust can be a useful estate planning tool. However, it is not appropriate for all circumstances. You should discuss the concept of a revocable living trust with your attorney.

Decision No. 7   To whom, when, and how do you plan to distribute your property?

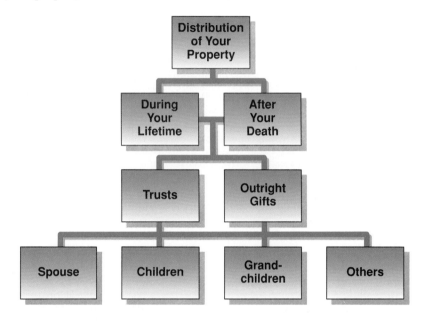

In Chapter 1 we looked at the trade-offs between current consumption and future consumption. Throughout your life, you make choices between consuming now and consuming in the future. But the future consuming doesn't necessarily have to be done by you. You can give away your financial resources, if you choose, so they can be consumed by others, perhaps years or even generations in the future. That's your choice, but in another sense you don't have a choice: Ultimately you *will* give away your financial resources, either during your lifetime or at death. The real choice you face is not *whether* to transfer your assets to others. Rather, your choice will be to *whom*, *when*, and *how* those transfers will be made.

To the extent that you make gifts of your assets during your lifetime, you will have the opportunity to watch them bear fruit and to receive thanks for your generosity. Give away assets at death and you will not be able to draw any satisfaction from the responses of your beneficiaries, unless you disclose your intentions in advance.

If you die intestate (without a will) you give away your assets, but you won't be choosing who gets them, when, or how. Your estate will be distributed to family members and relatives, some perhaps quite distant, according to state law.

Why should you be concerned about the disposition of your assets when you die? For the same reasons you are concerned about planning for your survivors and taking steps to see that they are adequately provided for. You will want to see that the resources you have accumulated are not squandered or subjected to needlessly high estate taxes.

DISPOSING OF YOUR ESTATE

Some Step-By-Step Considerations

* Assuring sufficient life income for your spouse, partner, or other dependents.
* Providing for any minimum spousal share of your estate required by state law.
* Minimizing death taxes.
* Distributing assets that remain after the death of your surviving spouse or partner.
* Disposing of personal property.

In deciding how to dispose of your assets, you should first consider the needs of your spouse or partner and other dependents. Generally, you will not want to transfer income-producing assets to other beneficiaries unless you are certain your dependents have sufficient resources to generate income and cover emergency needs. In addition, some states may require you to provide a certain percentage of your estate to your spouse. One option is to establish a trust to provide life income for your spouse, with the remaining assets going to your children or other beneficiaries at your spouse's death. (See section on QTIP trusts on page 308 and credit shelter trusts on page 304.) If you have minor children, generally you will want to provide for them by giving assets to your spouse, but again you have the option of establishing a trust for them in your will.

Your will does not have to direct the disposition of every dollar of assets you own at the time of your death. After the subtraction of taxes, expenses, and specific bequests ($5,000 to your cousin June) from the assets of your estate, what remains is known as the residue. Your will should specify how that residue will be shared among your beneficiaries, that is, what percentage will go to each. If your combined assets are less than $600,000, you will probably want all your residuary estate to go to your spouse.

A Primer on Gift and Estate Taxes

The federal tax on gifts and estates is unified. That means for tax purposes that transfers of assets during your lifetime and transfers at death

GIFT AND ESTATE TAXES

For Amounts Over	Tax Rate
$ 600,000	37%
750,000	39
1,000,000	41
1,250,000	43
1,500,000	45
2,000,000	49
2,500,000	53
3,000,000	55
10,000,000	60*
21,040,000	55

*Reflects 5 percent surcharge in this bracket to eliminate the benefits of lower marginal rates in previous brackets.

are seen as essentially two sides of the same coin. You can choose one or the other but you will pay taxes on all transfers at the same graduated rates. In keeping with this approach, a unified credit eliminates the first $192,800 in gift or estate tax that you would incur by transferring property during your lifetime or at death. That translates into $600,000 that an individual can give away free of gift tax or bequeath free of estate tax. Transfers above that amount are subject to tax beginning at the rate of 37 percent and rising to 55 percent on transfers above $3 million.

Federal tax law allows you to give up to $10,000 tax free each year to each of your children—or to any other person, for that matter. If your spouse joins in the giving, the amount the two of you may annually bestow rises to $20,000 per recipient. This means a couple with two children may make tax-free gifts to their children of up to $40,000 a year, a couple with four children, $80,000 a year, and so forth.

Gift giving makes for good tax planning, if you can afford it. By disposing of your assets while you are living, you save a considerable amount of estate tax. Let's look at an example. Say you add up your taxable estate and the total comes to $2.4 million. You know you should distribute a portion of your assets before you die. Otherwise, your estate will face an enormous death tax bill. So you and your spouse begin to make annual $20,000 gifts to each of your three children. At the end of 10 years, you've given away $600,000 tax free. The amount of estate tax saved is $286,000. This assumes the $600,000 would not have grown in value had you kept it, and you would have spent, rather than saved, any earnings on the principal amount. With your gift strategy, you have accomplished two key objectives: You've divided your wealth among your family members and saved a considerable amount in estate taxes.

Should you give someone more than the annual tax-free amount? Yes, if you are wealthy enough to be financially secure and you want your family to have substantial gifts during your lifetime. Gifts that top the annual exclusion use up your lifetime unified credit. So you can

Focus on...

TAX BASIS OF TRANSFERRED PROPERTY

Another difference between the treatment of gifts and the treatment of transfers made at death comes in figuring the new owner's basis in the property after the transfer. Basis is the cost of an asset for tax purposes. When the asset is sold, the gain or loss is figured by subtracting the basis from the sales price.

For gifts, the donee generally keeps the donor's basis. For example, if you purchased shares of stock for $25 and gave them to your nephew when the shares were worth $100, his basis in the shares would be $25. If he sold the shares for $100, he would have a taxable capital gain of $75. If you had paid gift tax on the transfer, your nephew's basis would be increased by the amount of the gift tax, subject to certain adjustments.

For transfers at death, the beneficiary gets a "step up" in basis to the market value of the transferred property at the time of the donor's death. Let's take the case of the stock you purchased for $25. Say you decide to leave it to your nephew in your will and the stock is worth $100 at your death. That becomes his basis in the stock. When he sells it for $120, his taxable capital gain is $20.

Because of the step up in basis applied to transfers at death, it can make sense to give high-basis assets (those that have not appreciated in value) to your beneficiaries by gifts during your lifetime and to give low-basis assets in your will. By doing so, the gains from appreciation on low-basis assets will escape income taxes.

---

make gifts of up to $600,000 ($1.2 million for a married couple) more than the annual exclusion before paying any gift tax. You must file a gift tax return for gifts greater than the annual exclusion. When your cumulative gifts over the annual exclusion exceed $600,000, gift tax will be due.

The estate tax is levied at your death on the total value of your assets less any liabilities. You are also allowed deductions for charitable bequests and estate administrative expenses. One other important deduction is the unlimited marital deduction.

You can transfer any amount during your lifetime or at death to your spouse and pay no tax (only if your spouse is a U.S. citizen; see page 304). However, transfers to your surviving spouse will be subject to estate tax when he or she dies (unless gifted or consumed by the survivor).

If you plan to make transfers to your grandchildren (grand-nieces and nephews count, too), you should be aware of the generation-skipping transfer tax. The tax is applied at a flat rate of 55 percent whether the transfers are made directly or through trusts. Two major exceptions: First, there is a $10,000 per donee annual exclusion, identical to the exclusion for gift tax. Second, there is a $1 million per donor exemption (for gifts above the annual exclusion) before generation-skipping transfers are subject to the tax.

Credit Shelter Trust

While the law allows you and your spouse to leave all your property to each other at death without incurring any tax, doing so isn't always a good idea. If your combined estates total more than $600,000, the first one of you to die will lose the benefit of some or all of the unified credit that enables anyone to transfer up to $600,000 with no federal gift/estate tax.

One common way to avoid this problem is to use a credit shelter trust, also known as a bypass trust. A credit shelter trust is created by your will and funded with an amount of assets that will exhaust whatever remains of your unified credit exemption, up to the $600,000 maximum. The assets must be held in your name, not in joint tenancy with your spouse, for you to be able to convey them to a credit shelter trust.

Typically, your surviving spouse (and possibly your children) will receive income from the trust until your spouse dies, then the remaining assets will pass to your children or other beneficiaries free of federal estate tax. The surviving spouse may have limited access to the trust funds for support, maintenance, health, and education.

Let's look at the example of a couple with $1.2 million in assets, each spouse owning half.

WHAT HAPPENS TO A COUPLE'S $1.2 MILLION COMBINED ESTATE IF ALL ASSETS ARE TRANSFERRED TO THE SURVIVING SPOUSE

1.   Spouse   Spouse
     $600,000 $600,000

2. One spouse dies, leaving all assets to the other.
   Federal estate tax   = 0
   Transfer of assets to survivor = $600,000

3.   Surviving spouse
              $1,200,000

4. Surviving spouse dies, leaving all assets to children.
   Federal estate tax   = $235,000
   Transfer of assets to children = $965,000

5.   Children
             $965,000

WHAT HAPPENS TO A COUPLE'S $1.2 MILLION COMBINED ESTATE WHEN FIRST SPOUSE TO DIE ESTABLISHES A CREDIT SHELTER TRUST

1.
Spouse	Spouse
$600,000	$600,000

2. One spouse dies, leaving all assets to a credit shelter trust. Trust income goes to surviving spouse for life.

   Transfer of assets to survivor = 0

   Transfer of assets to trust   = $600,000

   Federal estate tax   = 0

3.
Credit shelter trust	Trust income	Surviving spouse
$600,000	⟶	$600,000

4. Surviving spouse dies, leaving assets to children. Trust assets are transferred to children.

   Transfer of assets to children from second spouse = $600,000

   Federal estate tax   = 0

   Transfer of assets to children from trust = $600,000

   Federal estate tax   = 0

5.
Children
$1,200,000

One spouse dies and leaves everything to the other, without the use of a credit shelter trust. There is no federal estate tax because of the unlimited marital deduction, but the value of the first spouse's unified credit has been lost. When the second spouse dies, the assets are still valued at $1.2 million (assuming neither appreciation in value nor any depletion of the assets), and $235,000 in federal estate tax is due. That leaves $965,000 remaining for the children or other beneficiaries.

What if the couple's wills had each called for the creation and funding of a credit shelter trust at death? The $600,000 in assets of the first spouse to die would be transferred to a trust, avoiding estate tax, while income from the trust would go to the survivor. At the death of the second spouse, the trust's $600,000 in assets (plus any appreciation) and the second spouse's $600,000 in assets would pass to the children without tax, for a savings of at least $235,000 in federal estate tax.

Same Rates, Different Taxes

You don't have to wait until you die to begin distributing assets to your beneficiaries. In fact, there may be good reasons to consider disposing of some assets while you are living. Keep in mind that while the rates are the same for gift taxes and estate taxes, the amount of tax is figured dif-

HOW ESTATE AND GIFT TAX AMOUNTS COMPARE ON $1 MILLION TRANSFER

At Death		By Gift	
Amount in estate	$1,000,000	Amount of gift	**$667,000**
Tax	500,000	Tax	333,000
Proceeds to beneficiaries	**$500,000**	Total transfer	$1,000,000

In the case of the transfer from your estate, the beneficiaries receive $500,000, while beneficiaries of your gift transfer get $667,000.

ferently for each. As a result of this difference, estate taxes will always be higher than gift taxes. Here's why.

Estate taxes are calculated on a gross basis, before any bequests are made from the estate. Let's say you have $1 million you want to transfer to someone. Assume you have already used your annual gift tax exclusion of $10,000 and your entire $600,000 unified credit exemption. Also assume that a tax rate of 50 percent will apply to the entire amount. If you make the transfer from your estate, the tax (.50 × $1 million = $500,000) will be collected before the bequest is made, so the after-tax amount of your transfer will be $500,000.

In contrast, gift taxes are calculated on a net basis, depending on the amount actually given. Your $1 million, therefore, would provide for an after-tax gift of $667,000, with the remaining $333,000 going to pay the 50 percent tax on your gift (.50 × $667,000 = $333,000). One caveat: to realize the savings, you must live for at least three years after the gift transfer. If you die within that time, the amount of the gift tax will be included in your estate.

Our suggestion: Give first consideration to lifetime financial security for you and your spouse or partner before thinking about gifts or bequests to others. If you have enough wealth to be able to make substantial transfers to your children or other beneficiaries, consider the impact the money will have on them. You may want to delay the transfers, for example, until your children reach an age when they are likely to be mature enough to take responsibility for wealth.

Decision No. 8 How will you title or register ownership of your property?

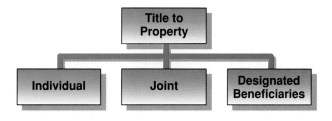

The ownership structure of your property will affect what happens to it in the event of your death. Property you hold as sole owner is disposed of in your will. Assets owned jointly with rights of survivorship pass to the other joint tenant automatically when you die. In other words, your will does not affect the disposition of joint ownership assets. That includes real estate as well as bank or brokerage accounts. For accounts where you must designate a beneficiary, such as individual retirement accounts, the property also passes automatically to your beneficiary. Therefore, beneficiary designations are an important part of overall planning.

The structure of your property ownership should be consistent with the intentions expressed in your will and in any living trust you execute. Problems are likely to arise, for example, if you intend to leave your share of an asset to someone but you are a joint owner of that asset. Joint tenancy property cannot be conveyed by the will of the first joint tenant to die; only the survivor can do so. In such cases, the law may take precedence over your wishes and automatically transfer your share to the other joint owner, not your intended beneficiary, when you die.

If you and your spouse will have a combined estate of more than $600,000, you should be sure to maintain separately owned assets to be able to make use of your individual $600,000 unified credit exemptions for federal estate tax purposes. This may require you to transfer ownership of joint interests so that each spouse has solely owned property. Transfer of assets or ownership interests between spouses should be documented so that sole ownership can be legally proven if necessary. For advice, see your attorney.

Our suggestion: Don't assume joint ownership is the best way to structure ownership of your property.

Decision No. 9   Are there family or personal circumstances, such as a second marriage, incapacitated heir, or noncitizen spouse, that require special planning consideration?

Special circumstances can complicate planning for your survivors. You may have divorced and remarried, for example, and want to provide lifetime income to your spouse but leave the remainder of your assets to your children from your first marriage. Or you may be married to someone who is not a U.S. citizen, meaning transfers to your spouse are not eligible for the unlimited marital deduction. Here are some suggestions for dealing with such circumstances.

Children from a Previous Marriage

The unlimited marital deduction can be used to leave property to your spouse, but you can also specify to whom the property will pass when your spouse dies. The vehicle employed for this particular transfer is called a qualified terminable interest property trust, or QTIP. You may want to consider a QTIP, for example, if you have children from a previous marriage and you want to make sure they will get some or all of your property at your spouse's death.

To meet tax law requirements, your surviving spouse must be entitled to all income from the trust at least annually, and no other beneficiary can have an interest in the trust during your spouse's lifetime. When

Focus on...

IN COMMUNITY PROPERTY STATES

Special considerations will apply to the ownership of your property if you are married and live (or previously lived) in a community property state. Currently, there are nine community property states: Arizona, California, Idaho, Louisiana, Nevada, New Mexico, Texas, Washington, and Wisconsin. Property that each spouse brings to the marriage, as well as certain other assets received after marriage such as gifts, inheritances, and damage awards, can be individually owned. However, the law in these states generally defines as community property (owned by both spouses) all of the following:

• Earnings of both spouses during the marriage.
• Assets acquired with the earnings of both spouses during the marriage.
• Income on assets acquired with the earnings of both spouses during the marriage

Some community property states also treat the following as community property:

• Income from property owned individually by the spouses.
• Any increase in value during the marriage of individually owned property.

During both spouses' lifetimes, there are no appreciable tax advantages to be gained from having property classified as either community or separate property. However, major differences in tax planning after a spouse's death hinge on the proper classification of an asset. It is beneficial to determine the character of assets during your lifetime while you're available for consultation. Further, once a determination is made, record-keeping can be done in a way that supports the classification of the property.

There is an important difference between community property and joint tenancy property. Both halves of community property get a step up in basis at the time of the first spouse's death. Only one-half of joint tenancy property owned by a couple is stepped up when the first spouse dies.

your spouse dies, the trust assets are included in his or her estate, although they will be transferred to the beneficiaries you have designated.

To minimize estate taxes, a QTIP trust is typically used in conjunction with a credit shelter trust (see page 304). You would place an amount equivalent to your remaining unified credit allowance ($600,000 less any previous taxable transfers) in the credit shelter trust, with the trust income going to your spouse and/or children for life. Assets in excess of your unified credit amount would be placed in the QTIP trust. At your spouse's death, assets in both trusts would go to your heirs. Incidentally, the QTIP trust may look similar to a credit shelter trust, that is, the income goes to your spouse and the remainder to your children at your spouse's death. In fact, the provisions may be identical. A key difference allows the QTIP trust to qualify for the marital deduction: a written election filed by your executor with the estate tax return.

An Incapacitated Heir

Special steps are required to plan for the needs of a handicapped child, an aged parent, or another family member who might be incompetent. If your heir is a minor child, you should name a guardian and successor guardians in your will. If the child is incapacitated when he or she reaches the age of majority, a court may have to approve continued guardianship, and if so your will should anticipate that contingency.

Often, the best step is to establish a trust and give the trustee the power to distribute income to your heir, to the guardian, and to care-givers, as needed. If you will be funding the heir's support needs through life insurance, you may want to consider the use of a life insurance trust for this purpose (see page 312). You should also consider the requirements of any government assistance programs for which your incapacitated heir might be eligible. Special provisions may need to be added to the trust so your heir retains eligibility for such assistance programs.

You may want to take precautions in leaving money to an adult child who is financially irresponsible or who may be suffering from addiction to alcohol or drugs. Again, this may be best accomplished by using a trust and giving the trustee authority to withhold or vary distributions to the heir as the trustee sees fit. The trust document should include a "spendthrift" clause to help shield the trust assets from potential creditors by preventing the beneficiary from using income or assets of the trust as collateral for a loan.

Spouse Is Not a U.S. Citizen

The unlimited deduction from gift and estate taxes does not apply to transfers of property to a noncitizen spouse. However, you can give up to $100,000 a year to a noncitizen spouse without any gift tax impact. In addition, you can use your lifetime unified credit equivalent to protect $600,000 of gifts from gift and estate taxes. But there is another approach that enables you to defer estate tax on transfers until the death of the surviving noncitizen spouse. An unlimited marital deduction is available if the property is left to the noncitizen spouse in a qualified domestic trust, sometimes known as a QDOT. These trusts function similarly to QTIPs in that the surviving spouse receives income from the trust and estate taxes are paid at his or her death. Here are the rules regarding QDOTs:

- The trustee must be a U.S. citizen or a corporation based in the United States.
- The surviving spouse must be entitled to all of the income from the trust at least annually.
- The executor must make a QDOT election on the estate tax return.
- The assets in the trust at the death of the second spouse will be taxed as if they had been included in the estate of the first spouse to die. As a result, the effective tax rates on assets in a QDOT will be higher than the rates that would have applied had the surviving spouse been a U.S. citizen.
- Principal distributions other than on account of hardship are subject to estate tax.

Decision No. 10 If you expect to have a large estate or own a business, what steps should you take now to reduce death taxes?

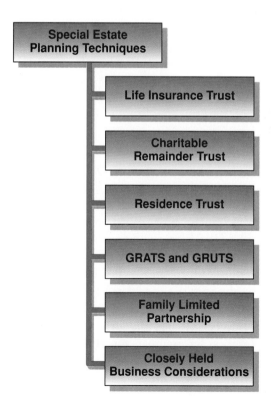

Special Estate Planning Techniques

Life Insurance Trust

Charitable Remainder Trust

Residence Trust

GRATS and GRUTS

Family Limited Partnership

Closely Held Business Considerations

Estates of even a moderate size face a substantial bite from taxes. Remember that federal estate tax rates begin at 37 percent on estates exceeding $600,000. State death taxes may increase that amount. Through careful planning, you can minimize the tax on your estate and provide more money for your heirs. Typically, this planning involves the use of specialized trusts as a means of transferring assets in tax-advantaged ways. Such trusts, for example, may be able to "leverage," or magnify, some advantage in the tax law, primarily unified credit for gift/estate taxes and annual gift tax exclusion, by transferring assets out of your estate at a discount. Here are some approaches for you to consider.

Life Insurance Trust

Life insurance can be used as a financial tool to generate cash to pay estate taxes. Extra cash is essential when a major portion of an estate's value consists of illiquid assets such as real estate or a family business. Otherwise, those assets might have to be sold to pay the estate tax bill.

Although life insurance proceeds are free of income tax, they are not free of estate tax. Insurance proceeds from a policy you own are included in your estate and are subject to federal estate tax. For this reason a life insurance policy purchased to help pay estate taxes may not provide the help you expect. For example, proceeds from a $1 million life insurance policy payable to your children might add $500,000 or more to your estate tax bill, making this a costly way to raise extra cash.

One way to avoid this problem is to establish a trust that owns life insurance covering you and your spouse. The proceeds from an insurance policy owned by a life insurance trust can be kept out of your estate, and out of the estate of your spouse as well. Your spouse, children, or other heirs are beneficiaries of the trust. When you die the trust receives the life insurance proceeds without tax. The trust can (but cannot be specifically directed to) use the proceeds to help pay estate taxes by purchasing assets from or lending cash to your estate. The premiums you pay on policies owned by the trust are considered gifts to your beneficiaries. But, if structured properly, the gifts will qualify for the annual exclusion of $10,000 per beneficiary ($20,000 if your spouse joins in the gift). If you have three beneficiaries, for example, you and your spouse could pay annual insurance premiums of up to $60,000 for a policy in a life insurance trust without incurring gift tax.

Here are some of the rules:

- To qualify, the trust must be irrevocable.
- You can have no control or ownership in the insurance policy, including no right to borrow from it or surrender the policy for cash.
- If you transfer an existing life insurance policy to the trust, the transfer must be completed at least three years before your death for the insurance proceeds to be excluded from your estate.
- The trust document should not be explicit as to the use of funds. For example, it should not specify that the proceeds from the insurance policy be used to pay estate taxes.
- To qualify your insurance premium payments for the gift tax exclusion, the trust must be structured so that your beneficiaries have a "present interest" in the gifts. That means they must have a limited right to withdraw the amounts from the trust, although you will not want them to make any withdrawals.

Charitable Remainder Trust

Charitable remainder trusts offer a means to reduce both income and estate taxes as well as to benefit a qualified charitable organization. You and your spouse would transfer assets to the trust and receive income from the assets for a certain period or for life. (Typically, low-basis assets are transferred because there is no tax paid by the trust when they are sold.) You get an income tax deduction for part of the value of your transfer. The value is discounted to reflect the fact that you will be getting income from the assets and so are actually giving the charity only a remainder interest. Estate tax savings result since the trust assets are excluded from your estate.

Charitable remainder trusts come in two varieties. An annuity trust requires a fixed annual income payout set at no less than 5 percent of the initial fair market value of the trust assets. If the trust does not generate that amount of income in any year, principal must be used to make up the difference in the required payout. A unitrust allows income distributions to vary and to be based on the annually revised market value of the trust assets. The actual distribution can be limited to the lesser of a required annual amount or the net income generated. This form of unitrust is frequently used as a retirement planning vehicle.

A possible disadvantage to charitable remainder trusts is that, on your death, the assets do not pass to your children or other heirs. One remedy is to establish a life insurance replacement trust at the same time the charitable remainder trust is set up. The combination may be the right solution for both your family and your favorite charity.

Qualified Personal Residence Trust

You can transfer ownership of your house to a trust, name your children as beneficiaries of the trust, and continue to use the house during the term of the trust. You are subject to gift tax on the value of the house when you establish the trust. But tax rules allow you to discount that value significantly before the gift tax is applied because you still retain the right to live in it. And future growth in the value of the house is also excluded from your estate. When the trust expires, the residence becomes the property of your beneficiaries.

The trust used for this purpose is known as a qualified personal residence trust (QPRT), or personal residence trust (PRT). This example shows how the discounted value allowed in such transfers can reduce gift or estate taxes. Let's say a 65-year-old owns a residence worth $300,000 and transfers it to a qualified personal residence trust for a 10-year term. Under recently allowable Internal Revenue Service interest rates, the value of the gift to the trust beneficiaries would be approximately $90,000. Assuming estate taxes of 50 percent and a 3 percent annual increase in the value of the residence, the individual would save about $150,000 in estate taxes using this transfer if he or she survives the term of the trust.

Here are some of the rules for a qualified personal residence trust:

- Only a personal residence (principal residence, second residence, or both) is eligible for this arrangement.
- After transferring the residence to the trust, you retain the right to live there for a certain period, say the next 10 years.
- If you die before the term of the trust expires, the fair market value of the residence is included in your estate. But the net tax position is no worse than if you never made the gift.
- If you continue to live in the residence after the term of the trust expires, you must pay the trust beneficiaries a fair market rent.

GRAT and GRUT

These similar types of trust are known as a grantor retained annuity trust (GRAT) and grantor retained unitrust (GRUT). Both offer a special opportunity to transfer assets to family members with little or no gift tax while retaining the income from the asset for a specified term. To create a GRAT or GRUT, the donor transfers assets to an irrevocable trust and retains an annuity interest for a specified number of years. The retained annuity interest is defined either as a dollar amount or a percentage of the initial value of the trust assets (a GRAT), or as a fixed percentage of the annual value of the trust (a GRUT). The value of the annuity as a percentage of the assets transferred is established by IRS tax tables, depending on the specified number of years.

To illustrate how a GRAT works, let's assume you make a gift of stock worth $600,000 to a trust. The stock yields 3.5 percent and the trust term is 15 years. The federal rates prescribed by the IRS are assumed in this example to be 6 percent. Under the GRAT, you would transfer the $600,000 of stock to the trust and receive $21,000 every year for the next 15 years. The IRS tables would value the annuity interest at $174,500. Thus, the present value of the remainder interest is $425,500. The gift would either utilize a portion of your $600,000 unified credit exemption or be subject to the gift tax. If, in this example, the stock appreciates 3 percent per year, it will be worth $934,000 in 15 years. Thus, $509,000 will have escaped estate taxation, saving $225,000 in estate tax.

These planning techniques are generally considered "no lose" propositions. If you outlive the trust period, the principal goes to the beneficiaries and escapes taxation. If you should die during the trust period, the assets revert to your estate, which is where the assets would have been had you done nothing.

Family Limited Partnership

Family limited partnerships enable parents to transfer ownership of a business or other assets to their children at a discount while maintaining control of those assets. The partnership is established with the parents as general partners. They transfer assets to the partnership and over time give limited partnership interests to their children. Because the interests represent minority ownership shares in the partnership and carry no control, they are valued at a discount from their pro-rata percentage share of the partnership's assets. That discount will vary depending on the circumstances, but might typically range from 20 to 40 percent.

The transferred interests are subject to gift taxes but will qualify for the $10,000 annual gift tax exclusion ($20,000 if the spouse joins in the gift). Assuming a discount of 30 percent on partnership shares, a married couple's $20,000 gift tax exclusion could be used to transfer a limited partnership interest with a net asset value of $28,500 to each child annually free of tax. With this discount, a couple could transfer $1 million in partnership interests to three children over a 12-year period and not incur gift taxes. Without the discount, it would take almost 17 years.

Closely Held Business Considerations

If your wealth consists in large part of a closely held business, you face a number of estate planning issues, the two primary ones being business continuity and liquidity. Here are some of the techniques used in planning the estate of a closely held business owner.

Buy–Sell Agreement

This is a legally binding contract to sell your stake in a business—to a co-owner, to the business itself, or to a third party—under specified terms. A buy–sell agreement will either state the repurchase price for the stock in the business or establish a formula for determining the price. From an estate planning viewpoint, a buy–sell agreement is attractive: It guarantees that cash will be available to the estate when the funds are needed to pay federal estate tax. In other words, a buy–sell agreement eliminates the difficulties in selling stock that might otherwise be unmarketable because a buyer has committed to purchase it from your estate.

Stock Redemption

In many cases when stock is redeemed by a family owned corporation and the family continues to control the company, the redemption proceeds would be taxed as a dividend, in other words as ordinary income. Under a special section of the tax code, a post-death stock redemption by a closely held business may qualify for capital gains treatment. The proceeds eligible to be taxed as capital gains are limited to the amount of death taxes and funeral and administration expenses.

Deferral of Estate Tax Payments

For estates that are particularly illiquid because of the inclusion of a closely held business, a special tax code provision allows the deferral of the payment of estate tax to avoid a forced sale of the business. The provision applies when the closely held business accounts for more than 35 percent of an estate's value. Under the provision, estate tax payments can be delayed for up to four years after the normal due date and then paid in 10 annual installments. Interest is due on the unpaid balance, generally at normal IRS rates. (A special rate of 4 percent may be used on a limited portion of the tax.)

Special Property Valuation   This is a special tax relief provision for family farm and ranch property as well as real estate used in other types of family businesses. Importantly, this provision can solve liquidity problems in those situations and prevent a forced sale of the property. The provision operates by allowing the farm and ranch land to be valued at low agricultural value instead of its value for other purposes. Of course, there are a number of strict requirements, the most important of which is that the value of the property must be at least 50 percent of the estate.

Resources

Books and References

The Complete Book of Insurance: Protecting Your Life, Health, Property and Income. Ben G. Baldwin. Chicago: Probus Publishing Co. 1991.

The Estate Plan Book. William S. Moore. Great Barrington, MA: American Institute for Economic Research. 1994.

Estate Planning: Easy Answers to Your Most Important Questions. Alex J. Soled. New York: Consumer Reports Books. 1994.

The Estate Planning Guide. Martin M. Shenkman. New York: John Wiley & Sons. 1991.

The Executor's Handbook: A Step-by-Step Guide to Settling an Estate for Personal Representatives. Theodore H. Hughes and David Klein. New York: Facts on File. 1994.

Federal Estate and Gift Taxes Explained. Chicago: Commerce Clearing House Inc. Revised annually.

First Comes Love, Then Comes Money: How Unmarried Couples Can Use Investments, Tax Planning, Insurance and Wills to Gain Financial Protection Denied by Law. Larry M. Elkin. New York: Doubleday. 1994.

Guide to Low-Load Insurance Products. Glenn S. Daily. Chicago: International Publishing Corp. 1990.

Life Insurance Due Care: Carriers, Products and Illustrations. Richard A. Schwartz and Catherine R. Turner. Chicago: American Bar Association. 1994.

The Life Insurance Kit. Terry R. O'Neill. Chicago: Dearborn Financial Publishing Inc. 1993.

The Rich Die Richer and You Can Too. William D. Zabel. New York: William Morrow and Co. 1995.

Smart Questions to Ask Your Insurance Agent: A Guide to Buying the Right Insurance for Your Family's Future. Dorothy Leeds. New York: Harper Paperbacks. 1992.

Thy Will Be Done: A Guide to Wills, Taxation, and Estate Planning for Older Persons. Eugene J. Daly. Buffalo, NY: Prometheus Books. 1990.

What You Should Know about Buying Life Insurance. Washington, DC: American Council of Life Insurance.

Hotline

The National Insurance Consumer Helpline (800-942-4242). Sponsored by the American Council of Life Insurance, the Health Insurance Association of America, and the Insurance Information Institute.

INTEGRATING YOUR PLANS

BEGINNING THE PROCESS

LIFE EVENT PLANNING

INTEGRATING YOUR PLANS

SAVING AND INVESTING

A REALITY CHECK

So far, we have offered you an overview of the financial planning process and a look at the basics of money and investing. Our chapters on life events discussed college education and retirement, then covered the issues involved in planning for the possibility that you might become disabled or die prematurely.

Now it's time to pause and reflect a little before you get on with your financial plan.

Steps Involved in the Financial Planning Process

Step 1: Committing to the task

Step 2: Developing your goals and setting priorities

Step 3: Assessing your resources

Step 4: Determining what is needed to reach your goals

Step 5: Developing a strategy for each goal

Step 6: Refining your goals

Step 7: Incorporating your strategies into an overall plan

Step 8: Listing and scheduling action steps to implement your plan

Step 9: Putting your plan into effect

Step 10: Monitoring and evaluating the results

Recall the list of steps involved in the financial planning process. You have shown your commitment to the task (Step 1) by reading this book. Now you should be ready to prepare the list of goals that will be the foundation of your financial plan. To get started, it may help to review the decisions presented in the life event planning section—Chapters 7 through 10. They will focus you on what is needed to formulate each particular goal and develop a strategy to accomplish it. Start with a general statement, then refine it, as we did with this example of a retirement goal developed in Chapter 2. Describe each goal in qualitative terms, then make it more specific and measurable.

Retirement Goal

Version 1—Retire with enough money to live comfortably.

Version 2—Retire at age 65 with enough income to maintain our current lifestyle in a less expensive community, and be prepared to retire earlier if necessary.

Version 3—Retire at age 65 with 80 percent of our current income (in today's dollars) for 25 years. Be prepared to retire at age 60 with 70 percent of our income for 30 years.

As you develop and revise your goals, weigh one against another and begin making trade-offs. Here is where the reality check comes into play. Most likely, your resources will not be sufficient to finance every goal to the fullest extent. The process of making trade-offs will bring your goals and resources into focus; each refinement will take you closer to a state of financial equilibrium.

> **As you develop and revise your goals, weigh one against another and begin the process of making trade-offs.**

Take the time now to get started with your plan. Each of your goals requires a strategy to make it happen. And each strategy involves a series of different steps to be implemented. You may want to refer back to the life event chapters for a review of the decisions that will be required to put your strategies to work. If you are preparing your plan yourself, the decisions offer plenty of guidance. If you are using a professional financial planner and have gone through the decisions in those chapters, you are going to be well organized and well prepared for the task ahead. This will pay off through a more efficient relationship with your planner, saving both of you time and allowing the planner to focus more attention on critical issues.

Organizing, making key decisions, developing and refining goals—these are critical steps in the planning process. But you've obviously not finished at that point. You've got to put the plan into effect. Then you will have the satisfaction of seeing the results—control over your finances and achievement of lifetime financial equilibrium. ⚖

STAYING ON COURSE

Some Final Observations

After reading this book, you should be ready to prepare your financial plan, either on your own or with the help of a professional financial planner. The step-by-step advice, worksheets, and checklists provided in the previous chapters will help you ask—and answer—the major questions likely to arise as you map a course to reach your financial goals. We have flagged the important decisions for you, on technical issues ranging from allocating your investment assets to buying life insurance to selecting a pension payout option. And we have offered suggestions to help you make the right choices to make your goals more reachable.

Yet the most important financial planning questions you face will be personal ones, not technical ones. The mechanical details of financial planning have no meaning outside the context of your own goals. Without your personal input, they represent nothing more than pointless number crunching. Keeping that thought in mind, we offer a review of some of our key suggestions to help guide you through the financial planning process.

Emphasize the Personal

Financial planning is a way to incorporate your personal values into your financial future. The personal part of financial planning comes first, and the financial part comes second. It's not an exercise designed to generate an off-the-shelf plan for general use. Because it is personal, financial planning must also reflect the needs and values of your spouse or partner and family, so you should involve them in developing goals and setting priorities.

Done right, financial planning will help you achieve a balance in your life—financial equilibrium. With that balance comes such benefits as greater peace of mind, more control over your own future, and the good feeling from knowing you are using your financial resources in a way that is consistent with your personal goals and values.

Understand the Choices You Are Making

Money decisions involve trade-offs between current consumption and future consumption. Every day, you make choices between alternate ways to spend your money today or to save and invest your money so it can be spent in the future. You can make those choices consciously, with your goals in mind. Or you can go through life making choices without regard to the aggregate impact those trade-offs will have on your future. Financial planning will help you make the trade-offs while keeping your goals in mind.

Look Ahead

Most of financial planning deals with predictable needs. Odds are, for example, that you can estimate your retirement date now with a fair degree of accuracy. Moreover, you can make a reasonable assumption today as to how much money you will need in retirement and the annual savings required to accumulate it. Likewise, if you have young children, you can figure the amount of money that will be needed to start paying college tuition bills when freshman year arrives. The surest way to be able to meet these predictable future expenses is to incorporate them as goals in your financial plan and establish strategies to accomplish them.

> **The most important financial planning questions you face will be personal ones, not technical ones.**

Manage Your Financial Risks

Not all events in life are predictable. Some things, such as disability or premature death, may be highly unlikely. But they nonetheless may pose a meaningful risk to the financial well-being of you and your family. An important part of financial planning involves taking steps to protect yourself and your family from risk. You need to evaluate the risks you face—whether from potential damage to your property or the loss of your ability to earn a living—and determine if you are financially prepared for them. You may need to purchase insurance protection for those risks that are unacceptable.

Plan in Terms of Today's Purchasing Power

You know the purchasing power required today to sustain a certain lifestyle or finance a specific goal, such as a four-year college education. Over time, however, the value of money will change. Trying to figure what you will need in terms of future dollars can be complex and confusing. One way to keep things simpler is to plan in terms of today's dollars, or what something is

> **Financial planning is a way to incorporate your personal values into your financial future.**

worth this year, not what it might cost after 10 or 20 years of inflation. The cost in today's dollars is easy to relate to your present level of income and savings. Future living expenses will climb higher over the years, but so will your income and your capacity to save. By stripping inflation out of the planning equation and concentrating on purchasing power, you will have a more understandable gauge of the real resources needed to meet your goals.

And remember, saving in today's dollars means you want to set aside money with the same amount of purchasing power each year to meet your goals. To do so, you will need to increase your annual savings by the same rate that consumer prices are rising.

Separate Saving from Investing

Saving money simply means not spending it. Investing money, on the other hand, means taking money you have saved and doing something with it to earn a return. Things go much easier when you can separate those two steps. Then saving can be made routine, with automatic deductions from your paycheck. Once saved, the money can wait temporarily in the bank until you decide how to invest it. The investing process requires more time, and possibly help from a professional adviser. By separating saving from investing, you can make sure (1) you are setting money aside in a disciplined, regular way, and (2) your investments are chosen carefully and with due consideration for your overall financial goals.

Let Asset Allocation Drive Your Investments

The key decision in investing is your mix of assets. How you apportion your money among cash, bonds, stocks, and hard assets will determine more than 90 percent of your investment return. Less than 10 percent of your return will be the result of the particular investments you choose within those categories. Therefore, investing should always begin with an asset allocation deci-

> **Done right, financial planning will help you to achieve a balance in your life—financial equilibrium.**

sion. Once that has been made, you can find appropriate investment vehicles within the prescribed asset categories.

Focusing on asset allocation can help you stay the course as an investor. Stock and bond prices, for example, will fluctuate over time. Instead of focusing on these ups and downs, and the emotions of the financial markets that inevitably accompany them, pay attention to maintaining the proper mix among asset categories. Lean against the financial winds by annually rebalancing your portfolio. If stock prices rise, and your portfolio becomes overweighted toward stocks, you return to the right mix by increasing your commitment to bonds. And you thereby reduce the risk of exposure to a fall in stocks. Conversely, if stocks fall and become underweighted in your portfolio, you should increase your commitment to them and position yourself to benefit when stock prices recover.

Understand Investment Risk

To most people, investment risk is the chance that they will lose money if an asset declines in value or becomes worthless. Risk of that nature can be greatly reduced by broadly diversifying your investments, both among and within the major asset categories.

The risk posed by a particular category of investments will depend on your time horizon. Volatile investments—such as stocks, which can be expected to vary substantially in price—are risky for investors with short time horizons. If you have a short-term need for a particular amount of money, invest it in something offering low volatility such as cash equivalents.

For a long investment horizon, volatility is much less of a concern. You can ignore price fluctuations because the money won't be needed for years. Instead, the primary risk you will face is inflation. It represents the risk that your investments will not grow sufficiently to maintain their purchasing power over the long term. To protect purchasing power, be sure to allocate sufficient assets to stocks or mutual funds that invest in stocks.

Let Time Work for You

Financial planning is about money and it's about time. Once you put your financial strategies in place, time will be the most important factor in making them work. The more years that your investments have time to grow through compounded earnings, the more likely it becomes that you will be able to reach your goals. Start early, invest with a plan, and be patient.

Get Help If You Need It

A professional financial planner can help you and your spouse or partner overcome the emotional roadblocks that may be keeping you from making decisions for your future. You may feel uneasy about setting your life's goals down on paper and then dealing with them in dollars and cents. Or you may be reluctant to confront the reality that your financial resources are limited and you must make choices between current and future consumption. Often, spouses or partners have different priorities that may be hard to discuss, let alone reconcile. If you face any of those personal or emotional barriers, an experienced financial planner can help.

Of course, a planner will also assist you with technical advice on such issues as asset allocation, selecting investments, reviewing your insurance needs, and planning for the transfer of your property in the event of your death.

Review Your Progress Regularly

You should check at least once a year to see that your financial plan is on course. Over time, you may need to rebalance your investments or make other changes. Consider a full revision of your plan if there has been a significant alteration in your personal life (e.g., birth of a child, change of career) or in the outside world (e.g., resurgence of inflation, Social Security changes). As part of your periodic review, ask yourself:

- Have any of my goals changed?
- Am I devoting enough resources to each goal?
- Am I investing appropriately?

Be flexible and be ready to make changes if needed. If not, stay the course—and bon voyage.

APPENDIXES

Appendix 1

Some Advice on Recordkeeping

The difference between having your financial affairs neat and well maintained or in a state of disaster is usually a simple matter of organization. To prepare a personal financial summary, you will need to assemble and go through everything from your check register to your credit card statements to your paycheck stubs. Take the opportunity to put things in order and set up an effective system of personal recordkeeping. Once you have finished, you will find that you save all sorts of time and headaches in the day-to-day management of your financial affairs.

First, get a desk, file cabinet, and a supply of file folders if you don't already have them. Keep in the desk the folders for material that you use almost daily—bills to pay, a file for tax receipts—and put the rest in the file cabinet. If you have a home computer, consider one of the many personal financial management or recordkeeping programs that are available. Such a program can help you track spending, monitor performance of your investments, and keep track of tax-related income and receipts. You should also obtain a safe-deposit box at a nearby bank for storage of important papers and valuables.

Folders to Keep in Your Desk

1. Bills to be paid.
2. Documents to be filed, such as insurance policies.
3. Medical bills and receipts.
4. Investment account documents such as trade confirmations.
5. Records of your children's financial affairs (or a separate folder for each child) including custodial account information.
6. Tax-related information for the current tax year, such as receipts for deductible expenses, state and local tax refund information, and forms 1099 for dividends or interest payments.
7. A cash receipts journal to record dividend and interest income, tax refunds, health insurance reimbursements, loan repayments, and other miscellaneous payments you receive.

Folders to Keep in Your Filing Cabinet

1. Household bills paid (by year).
2. Canceled checks, check registers, and bank statements (by year).
3. Credit card statements and account information (by year).
4. Tax returns (by year).

5. Personal financial summaries.

6. Home and home improvement records.

7. Investment account statements, including IRAs and Keoghs.

8. Bank passbooks and certificates.

9. Pension plan documents and benefit statements related to previous employer pension or benefit plans in which you have vested rights.

10. 401(k) statements and plan documents for all employers.

11. Documents related to your current employer's pension plan and other benefits.

12. Business-related documents such as partnership agreements.

13. Copies of your will and these related documents: a letter of instructions, an inventory of important papers and documents, your power of attorney, living will, and power of attorney for health care or health care proxy.

14. Life insurance policies and statements.

15. Health insurance policies and statements.

16. Disability insurance policies and statements.

17. Auto insurance policies and statements.

18. Homeowner insurance policies and statements.

Items to Keep in Safe-Deposit Box

1. Stock certificates

2. Infrequently used jewelry and gold coins.

3. Inventory and receipts (with photos) related to expensive possessions such as antiques and works of art.

4. Copies of your will, living will, durable power of attorney, and inventory of important papers and documents.

5. Deeds, mortgages, and other title documents for real estate.

6. Auto titles.

How Long to Keep Financial Records

You should weed out your financial records periodically and discard documents that no longer need to be retained.

Retain for Three Years

1. Household bills.

2. Expired insurance policies.

Retain for Seven Years

1. Tax returns and supporting documents.
2. Canceled checks, check registers, and bank statements.

Retain Indefinitely

1. Checks and receipts for major purchases.
2. Investment account statements.
3. Home purchase and home improvement documents.
4. Business or income property documents.
5. Gift tax returns.
6. Papers dealing with an inheritance.
7. Nondeductible IRA and all other plan contribution documents.
8. Correspondence and documents related to insurance policies that remain in force.

Appendix 2

Personal Financial Summary Worksheet

Personal financial summary   PART 1, CASH FLOW STATEMENT

Income (Annual)

Income Source 1	_____	$ _____
Income Source 2	_____	_____
Income Source 3	_____	_____
Income Source 4	_____	_____
Income Source 5	_____	_____
Income Source 6	_____	_____
Total income		$ _____

Expenses (Annual)

		% of Total Income
Fixed expenses		
Housing (mortgage, property taxes)	_____	_____
Utilities	_____	_____
Insurance (auto/property/liability)	_____	_____
Insurance (life/disability)	_____	_____
Car loan/lease payments	_____	_____
Other fixed expenses	_____	_____
Variable expenses		
Food and dining out	_____	_____
Transportation and car maintenance	_____	_____
Entertainment and recreation	_____	_____
Medical expenses	_____	_____
Home maintenance, furnishings, and supplies	_____	_____
Clothing	_____	_____
Travel and vacations	_____	_____
Gifts and charity	_____	_____
Other variable expenses	_____	_____
Income taxes	_____	_____
Total expenses	_____	100%
(Income − Expenses) = Savings	_____	_____

Personal financial summary   PART 2, BALANCE SHEET

Category	Amount	*Investment Assets*			
		Cash	Bonds	Stock	Hard Assets
Checking account	————	————	————	————	————
Savings/money market	————	————	————	————	————
Taxable investments					
Account 1	————	————	————	————	————
Account 2	————	————	————	————	————
Account 3	————	————	————	————	————
Account 4	————	————	————	————	————
Account 5	————	————	————	————	————
Account 6	————	————	————	————	————
Tax-deferred investments					
401(k) plan	————	————	————	————	————
401(k) plan	————	————	————	————	————
IRA/Keogh plan	————	————	————	————	————
IRA/Keogh plan	————	————	————	————	————
Annuity	————	————	————	————	————
Total	————	————	————	————	————
Percentage of investment assets	100%	___%	___%	___%	___%

Other Assets

Residence	————————
Car(s)	————————
Furniture	————————
Jewelry	————————
Recreational/electronic equipment	————————
Other personal assets	————————
Total other assets	————————
Total assets	————————

Liabilities

Short-term liabilities	
Bills currently due	————————
Credit card balances	————————
Balance on car loan/lease	————————
Payments due within next year on long-term liabilities	————————

Long-term liabilities
  (Less payments due in next year)   _____
  Balance on mortgage loan   _____
  Balance on home equity loan/2nd mort.   _____
   Total liabilities   _____

Net Worth

(Assets − Liabilities) = Net Worth   _____

Appendix 3

College Planning Worksheet

Section I: College planning worksheet   GATHERING THE
BASIC INFORMATION

	Child's Name	Child's Name
1. Current age		
2. Age at first year of college		
3. Number of years in college		
4. Years until first year of college (Line 2 – Line 1)		
5. Years until last year of college (Line 4 + Line 3)		
6. Estimated annual rate of increase in college costs	%	%
7. Estimated real rate of increase in college costs (Line 6 – 4% inflation rate)	%	%
8. Annual college costs in today's dollars		
9. Student employment, financial aid, and loans per year in today's dollars		
10. Adjusted college costs in today's dollars (Line 8 – Line 10)		
11. Current college investments		
12. Estimated annual investment return	%	%
13. Estimated real annual investment return (Line 12 – 4% inflation)	%	%

Section II: College planning worksheet   ESTIMATING FUTURE COSTS

	Year 1	Year 2	Year 3	Year 4
Years until start of this college year				
	Item 4	Item 4 + 1	Item 4 + 2	Item 4 + 3
Adjusted annual college costs (today's dollars)				
	Item 10	Item 10	Item 10	Item 10
Growth factor for real cost of college (from Table A)				
Growth factor × Adjusted cost = Future costs in today's dollars				
Adjusted total college expense (Sum of future costs for years 1–4 in today's dollars)				

Section III: College planning worksheet   ESTIMATING THE VALUE OF CURRENT SAVINGS

	Child's Name	Child's Name
1. Current college investments (Item 12)		
2. Years to start of college (Item 4)		
3. Estimated real investment return (Item 15)	%	%
4. Growth factor from Table B		
5. Line 4 × Line 1 = Value of current college investments at start of college in today's dollars		

Section IV: College planning worksheet   DETERMINING HOW MUCH MORE IS NEEDED

	Child's Name	Child's Name
6. Adjusted total college expense in today's dollars		
7. Additional capital needed at start of college (today's dollars) (Line 6 − Line 5)		
8. Required annual savings (today's dollars) (Line 7 × Factor from Table D)		
	Factor: ____	Factor: ____

To maintain the constant purchasing power of the amount you save, this should be increased by 4% each year.

9. Required annual savings next year (Line 8 × 1.04)		

Table A—College planning worksheet   GROWTH FACTORS FOR REAL RATE OF INCREASE IN COLLEGE COSTS

Years	5%	6%	7%	8%	9%
1	1.01	1.02	1.03	1.04	1.05
2	1.02	1.04	1.06	1.08	1.10
3	1.03	1.06	1.09	1.12	1.16
4	1.04	1.08	1.13	1.17	1.22
5	1.05	1.10	1.16	1.22	1.28
6	1.06	1.13	1.19	1.27	1.34
7	1.07	1.15	1.23	1.32	1.41
8	1.08	1.17	1.27	1.37	1.48
9	1.09	1.20	1.30	1.42	1.55
10	1.10	1.22	1.34	1.48	1.63
11	1.12	1.24	1.38	1.54	1.71
12	1.13	1.27	1.43	1.60	1.80
13	1.14	1.29	1.47	1.67	1.89
14	1.15	1.32	1.51	1.73	1.98
15	1.16	1.35	1.56	1.80	2.08
16	1.17	1.37	1.60	1.87	2.18
17	1.18	1.40	1.65	1.95	2.29
18	1.20	1.43	1.70	2.03	2.41
19	1.21	1.46	1.75	2.11	2.53
20	1.22	1.49	1.81	2.19	2.65

Assumes 4% overall inflation rate.

Table B—College planning worksheet   GROWTH FACTORS FOR
REAL INVESTMENT RETURN
ON CURRENT COLLEGE
SAVINGS

(Real investment return = Annual % investment return minus Annual % overall inflation [Line 15])

Year	3%	4%	5%	6%	7%
1	1.03	1.04	1.05	1.06	1.07
2	1.06	1.08	1.10	1.12	1.14
3	1.09	1.12	1.16	1.19	1.23
4	1.13	1.17	1.22	1.26	1.31
5	1.16	1.22	1.28	1.34	1.40
6	1.19	1.27	1.34	1.42	1.50
7	1.23	1.32	1.41	1.50	1.61
8	1.27	1.37	1.48	1.59	1.72
9	1.30	1.42	1.55	1.69	1.84
10	1.34	1.48	1.63	1.79	1.97
11	1.38	1.54	1.71	1.90	2.10
12	1.43	1.60	1.80	2.01	2.25
13	1.47	1.67	1.89	2.13	2.41
14	1.51	1.73	1.98	2.26	2.58
15	1.56	1.80	2.08	2.40	2.76
16	1.60	1.87	2.18	2.54	2.95
17	1.65	1.95	2.29	2.69	3.16
18	1.70	2.03	2.41	2.85	3.38
19	1.75	2.11	2.53	3.03	3.62
20	1.81	2.19	2.65	3.21	3.87

Table C—College planning worksheet

GROWTH FACTORS FOR
REAL INVESTMENT RETURN
ON FUTURE COLLEGE
SAVINGS

(Real investment returns [Annual % investment return minus Annual % overall inflation])

Year	3%	4%	5%	6%	7%
1	1.03	1.04	1.05	1.06	1.07
2	2.09	2.12	2.15	2.18	2.21
3	3.18	3.25	3.31	3.37	3.44
4	4.31	4.42	4.53	4.64	4.75
5	5.47	5.63	5.80	5.98	6.15
6	6.66	6.90	7.14	7.39	7.65
7	7.89	8.21	8.55	8.90	9.26
8	9.16	9.58	10.03	10.49	10.98
9	10.46	11.01	11.58	12.18	12.82
10	11.81	12.49	13.21	13.97	14.78
11	13.19	14.03	14.92	15.87	16.89
12	14.62	15.63	16.71	17.88	19.14
13	16.09	17.29	18.60	20.02	21.55
14	17.60	19.02	20.58	22.28	24.13
15	19.16	20.82	22.66	24.67	26.89
16	20.76	22.70	24.84	27.21	29.84
17	22.41	24.65	27.13	29.91	33.00
18	24.12	26.67	29.54	32.76	36.38
19	25.87	28.78	32.07	35.79	40.00
20	27.68	30.97	34.72	38.99	43.87

Table D—College planning worksheet

Years to Start of College	Investment Return			
	6%	8%	10%	12%
1	1.000	1.000	1.000	1.000
2	0.535	0.550	0.565	0.581
3	0.360	0.374	0.387	0.401
4	0.273	0.285	0.299	0.312
5	0.220	0.233	0.245	0.258
6	0.185	0.197	0.210	0.223
7	0.160	0.172	0.185	0.198
8	0.142	0.153	0.166	0.179
9	0.127	0.139	0.151	0.164
10	0.115	0.127	0.140	0.153
11	0.106	0.118	0.130	0.144
12	0.098	0.110	0.122	0.136
13	0.091	0.103	0.116	0.129
14	0.085	0.097	0.110	0.124
15	0.080	0.092	0.105	0.119
16	0.076	0.088	0.101	0.115
17	0.072	0.084	0.098	0.112
18	0.067	0.081	0.094	0.109
19	0.066	0.078	0.092	0.106
20	0.063	0.075	0.089	0.104

Assumes 4% annual increase in amount saved to keep pace with inflation.

Appendix 4

Retirement Planning Worksheet

Retirement planning worksheet	GATHERING THE BASIC INFORMATION

1. Current age
2. Retirement age
3. Life expectancy
4. Years until retirement
5. Years in retirement
6. Current annual income
7. Retirement income replacement ratio
8. Annual retirement income goal (today's dollars)
9. Estimated Social Security benefits (today's dollars)
10. Estimated pension income (today's dollars)
11. Value of investments available to fund retirement

Retirement planning worksheet

HOW MUCH DO I NEED TO SAVE
EACH YEAR TO MEET MY
RETIREMENT GOAL?

1. Annual retirement income goal
   (today's dollars)   _____   _____

2. Estimated Social Security benefits
   (today's dollars)   _____   _____

3. Estimated pension income (today's dollars)   _____   _____

4. Income needed from investments (today's
   dollars) (Line 1 – Line 2 – Line 3)   _____   _____

5. Income needed from investments at retirement
   (Line 4 × Factor from Table 1)   _____   _____

   Factor: _____   Factor: _____

6. Capital needed to fund income from
   investments (Line 5 × Factor from
   Table 2)

   Factor: _____   Factor: _____

7. Income needed to maintain purchasing
   power of pension (Line 3 × Factor from
   Table 1)

   Factor: _____   Factor: _____

8. Capital needed to fund income to maintain
   purchasing power of pension (Line 7 × Factor
   from Table 3)

   Factor: _____   Factor: _____

9. Total capital required at beginning of
   retirement (future dollars) (Line 6 + Line 8)   _____   _____

10. Value (today's dollars) of investments
    available to fund retirement (401(k), IRA,
    profit sharing, deferred compensation, and
    personal investments)   _____   _____

11. Value of investments at retirement (future
    dollars) (Line 10 × Factor from Table 4)   _____   _____

    Factor: _____   Factor: _____

12. Write in amount from Line 9   _____   _____

    (If Line 11 is greater than Line 12, you do not
    need to save any more for retirement. If Line 12
    is greater than Line 11, enter difference between
    the two on Line 13.)

13. Additional capital needed at retirement (future
    dollars) (Line 12 – Line 11)   _____   _____

14. Additional capital needed at retirement (today's dollars) (Line 13 divided by Factor from Table 4)

    Factor: _____   Factor: _____

15. Required annual savings (today's dollars) (Line 14 × Factor from Table 6)

    Factor: _____   Factor: _____

    Each year, to maintain the constant purchasing power of the amount you save, this should be increased by 4%.

16. Required annual savings next year (Line 15 × 1.04)

    _____   _____

Table 1—Retirement planning worksheet   INFLATION FACTOR

Years to Retirement	Factor
1	1.04
2	1.08
3	1.12
4	1.17
5	1.22
6	1.27
7	1.32
8	1.37
9	1.42
10	1.48
11	1.54
12	1.60
13	1.67
14	1.73
15	1.80
16	1.87
17	1.95
18	2.03
19	2.11
20	2.19
21	2.28
22	2.37
23	2.46
24	2.56
25	2.67
26	2.77
27	2.88
28	3.00
29	3.12
30	3.24

Table 2—Retirement planning worksheet

| | Investment Return | | |
Retirement Period	6%	8%	10%
20 years	16.79	14.31	12.38
25 years	20.08	16.49	13.82
30 years	23.07	18.30	14.93
35 years	25.79	19.79	15.76
40 years	28.26	21.03	16.39

Table 3—Retirement planning worksheet

| | Investment Return | | |
Retirement Period	6%	8%	10%
20 years	4.63	3.70	3.00
25 years	6.53	4.96	3.84
30 years	8.48	6.14	4.56
35 years	10.42	7.21	5.15
40 years	12.31	8.15	5.63

Table 4—Retirement planning worksheet

Years to Retirement	Investment Return Factor		
	6%	8%	10%
1	1.06	1.08	1.10
2	1.12	1.17	1.21
3	1.19	1.26	1.33
4	1.26	1.36	1.46
5	1.34	1.47	1.61
6	1.42	1.59	1.77
7	1.50	1.71	1.95
8	1.59	1.85	2.14
9	1.69	2.00	2.36
10	1.79	2.16	2.59
11	1.90	2.33	2.85
12	2.01	2.52	3.14
13	2.13	2.72	3.45
14	2.26	2.94	3.80
15	2.40	3.17	4.18
16	2.54	3.43	4.59
17	2.69	3.70	5.05
18	2.85	4.00	5.56
19	3.03	4.32	6.12
20	3.21	4.66	6.73
21	3.40	5.03	7.40
22	3.60	5.44	8.14
23	3.82	5.87	8.95
24	4.05	6.34	9.85
25	4.29	6.85	10.83
26	4.55	7.40	11.92
27	4.82	7.99	13.11
28	5.11	8.63	14.42
29	5.42	9.32	15.86
30	5.74	10.06	17.45

Table 5—Retirement planning worksheet

Years to Retirement	Present Value Factor		
	6%	8%	10%
1	1.000	1.000	1.000
2	0.535	0.550	0.565
3	0.360	0.374	0.387
4	0.273	0.285	0.299
5	0.220	0.233	0.245
6	0.185	0.197	0.210
7	0.160	0.172	0.185
8	0.142	0.153	0.166
9	0.127	0.139	0.151
10	0.115	0.127	0.140
11	0.106	0.118	0.130
12	0.098	0.110	0.122
13	0.091	0.103	0.116
14	0.085	0.097	0.110
15	0.080	0.092	0.105
16	0.076	0.088	0.101
17	0.072	0.084	0.098
18	0.067	0.081	0.094
19	0.066	0.078	0.092
20	0.063	0.075	0.089
21	0.061	0.073	0.087
22	0.058	0.071	0.085
23	0.056	0.069	0.083
24	0.054	0.067	0.081
25	0.053	0.065	0.080
26	0.051	0.064	0.078
27	0.050	0.063	0.077
28	0.048	0.061	0.076
29	0.047	0.060	0.075
30	0.046	0.059	0.074

Reflects 4% annual increase to keep pace with inflation.

Appendix 5

Disability Planning Worksheet

Disability planning worksheet	ESTIMATING MONTHLY RESOURCES AND EXPENSES DURING DISABILITY					
	Month of Disability					
	1st	2nd	3rd	4th	5th	6th
Employer short-term disability	$ _____	$ _____	$ _____	$ _____	$ _____	$ _____
Employer long-term disability	_____	_____	_____	_____	_____	_____
Social Security	_____	_____	_____	_____	_____	_____
State disability program	_____	_____	_____	_____	_____	_____
Workers' compensation	_____	_____	_____	_____	_____	_____
Spouse's income	_____	_____	_____	_____	_____	_____
Income from savings	_____	_____	_____	_____	_____	_____
Other income	_____	_____	_____	_____	_____	_____
Total monthly income	_____	_____	_____	_____	_____	_____
Total monthly expenses	_____	_____	_____	_____	_____	_____
Total monthly excess/ shortfall	_____	_____	_____	_____	_____	_____

	Month of Disability						
	7th	8th	9th	10th	11th	12th	Ongoing
Employer short-term disability	$ ___	$___	$___	$___	$___	$___	$___
Employer long-term disability	___	___	___	___	___	___	___
Social Security	___	___	___	___	___	___	___
State disability program	___	___	___	___	___	___	___
Workers' compensation	___	___	___	___	___	___	___
Spouse's income	___	___	___	___	___	___	___
Income from savings	___	___	___	___	___	___	___
Other income	___	___	___	___	___	___	___
Total monthly income	___	___	___	___	___	___	___
Total monthly expenses	___	___	___	___	___	___	___
Total monthly excess/ shortfall	___	___	___	___	___	___	___

Appendix 6
Survivor Planning Worksheet

Survivor planning worksheet   SURVIVOR PLANNING INFORMATION

1. Current age of spouse or companion   _____
2. Years until youngest child reaches age 18   _____
3. Retirement age of spouse or companion   _____
4. Years in retirement for spouse or companion   _____
5. Your annual income (today's dollars)   _____
6. Annual income of spouse or companion (today's dollars)   _____
7. Total household income (today's dollars)   _____

Needs

8. Household income replacement goal (today's dollars)   _____
9. Funeral cost and estate settlement cash needs   _____
10. Mortgage and debt retirement cash needs goal   _____
11. Annual college cost goal for Child 1 (today's dollars)
    Years until freshman year: _____   _____
12. Annual college cost goal for Child 2 (today's dollars)
    Years until freshman year: _____   _____
13. Other cash needs goal (today's dollars)
    Years until cash needed: _____   _____

Resources

14. Lump-sum death benefit from your employer (today's dollars)   _____
15. Total investment assets including 401(k), IRAs, college accounts _____
16. Total death benefits from current life insurance policies   _____
17. Estimated Social Security family survivor benefits to age 18
    of youngest child (today's dollars)   _____
18. Estimated pension income of spouse or companion (today's dollars) _____
19. Estimated Social Security retirement benefit of spouse
    or companion (today's dollars)   _____

Survivor planning worksheet   HOW MUCH LIFE INSURANCE DO I NEED TO MEET MY SURVIVOR GOALS?

1. Household income replacement goal for preretirement period of spouse or companion (today's dollars) _____

2. Annual income of spouse or companion until retirement (today's dollars) _____

3. Income replacement needed from investments (today's dollars) (Line 1 − Line 2) _____

4. Capital required to fund income replacement for preretirement (today's dollars) (Line 3 × Factor from Table 1)   Factor: ____ _____

If you have minor children, otherwise skip to Line 7

5. Estimated annual Social Security survivor benefits (today's dollars) (see Table 5)

   Number of years benefits paid: ____ _____

6. Reduction in amount of capital needed because of Social Security survivor benefits (Line 5 × Factor from Table 1)   Factor: ____ _____

Retirement income for spouse or companion

7. Retirement income goal for spouse or companion (today's dollars) _____

8. Estimated pension income at retirement of spouse or companion (today's dollars) _____

9. Estimated Social Security benefit of spouse or companion (today's dollars) _____

10. Income needed from investments at retirement (Line 7 − Line 8 − Line 9) (today's dollars) _____

11. Income needed from investments at retirement adjusted for inflation (future dollars) (Line 10 × Factor from Table 2)   Factor: ____ _____

12. Capital required at retirement to fund investments (Line 11 × Factor from Table 1) (future dollars)   Factor: ____ _____

13. Capital required today to fund retirement income (Line 12 divided by Factor from Table 3) (today's dollars)   Factor: ____ _____

14. Capital required to fund income replacement (today's dollars) (Line 4 + Line 13 − Line 6) _____

15. Funeral cost and estate settlement cash needs (today's dollars) _____

16. Mortgage, debt retirement cash needs goal (today's dollars) _____

17. College cost goal for Child 1 (today's dollars) (Annual cost × Number of years × Factor from Table 4)   Factor: ____ _____

18. College cost goal for Child 2 (today's dollars)
    (Annual cost × Number of years × Factor from Table 4)   Factor: _____   _____

19. Other cash needs goal (today's dollars) × Factor
    from Table 1   Factor: _____   _____

20. Capital required to fund all cash needs (today's dollars)
    (Sum of Lines 15–19)   _____

21. Total capital required to fund survivor income
    and cash needs (today's dollars) (Line 14 + Line 20)   _____

22. Lump-sum death benefit from your employer
    (today's dollars)   _____

23. Total investment assets including 401(k), IRAs,
    college accounts (today's dollars)   _____

24. Total death benefits from current life insurance
    policies (today's dollars)   _____

25. Total capital available to fund survivor income
    and cash needs (today's dollars) (sum of Lines 22–24)   _____

26. Write in amount from Line 21   _____

        (If Line 25 is greater than Line 26, you do not need
        additional life insurance at this time. If Line 26 is greater
        than Line 25, enter difference between the two on Line 27.)

27. Additional life insurance coverage needed
    (Line 26 – Line 25)   _____

Survivor planning worksheet   SOCIAL SECURITY SURVIVOR BENEFIT

To estimate average benefit, add eligible benefit amounts for each year, then divide by number of years.

Children are eligible for survivor benefits until age 17, or until 18 if they are in high school. A spouse or divorced spouse is eligible for a separate survivor benefit if caring for an eligible child up to age 15.

Years after Your Death

	1st	2nd	3rd	4th	5th	6th
Child 1						
Age	_____	_____	_____	_____	_____	_____
Benefit	_____	_____	_____	_____	_____	_____
Child 2						
Age	_____	_____	_____	_____	_____	_____
Benefit	_____	_____	_____	_____	_____	_____
Spouse						
Benefit	_____	_____	_____	_____	_____	_____
Total benefits	_____	_____	_____	_____	_____	_____
Maximum family benefit	_____	_____	_____	_____	_____	_____

Years after Your Death

	7th	8th	9th	10th	11th	12th
Child 1						
Age	_____	_____	_____	_____	_____	_____
Benefit	_____	_____	_____	_____	_____	_____
Child 2						
Age	_____	_____	_____	_____	_____	_____
Benefit	_____	_____	_____	_____	_____	_____
Spouse						
Benefit	_____	_____	_____	_____	_____	_____
Total benefits	_____	_____	_____	_____	_____	_____
Maximum family benefit	_____	_____	_____	_____	_____	_____

	Years after Your Death					
	13th	14th	15th	16th	17th	18th
Child 1						
Age	_____	_____	_____	_____	_____	_____
Benefit	_____	_____	_____	_____	_____	_____
Child 2						
Age	_____	_____	_____	_____	_____	_____
Benefit	_____	_____	_____	_____	_____	_____
Spouse						
Benefit	_____	_____	_____	_____	_____	_____
Total benefits	_____	_____	_____	_____	_____	_____
Maximum benefit	_____	_____	_____	_____	_____	_____

Table 1—Survivor planning worksheet   CAPITAL NEEDED TO FUND INCOME REPLACEMENT

(For Use with Worksheet Line 4, Line 6, Line 12, and Line 19)

Years in Period	
1	.94
2	1.92
3	2.89
4	3.83
5	4.76
6	5.67
7	6.56
8	7.43
9	8.29
10	9.14
11	9.96
12	10.77
13	11.57
14	12.35
15	13.12

Years in Period	
16	13.87
17	14.60
18	15.33
19	16.04
20	16.73
21	17.42
22	18.09
23	18.74
24	19.39
25	20.02
26	20.64
27	21.25
28	21.85
29	22.44
30	23.01
31	23.58
32	24.13
33	24.68
34	25.21
35	25.73
36	26.25
37	26.75
38	27.24
39	27.73
40	28.20
41	28.67
42	29.13
43	29.58
44	30.02
45	30.45
46	30.88
47	31.29
48	31.70
49	32.10
50	32.50

Assumes inflation rate of 4% in annual income, investment return of 6%, and annuitization of principal.

Table 2—Survivor planning worksheet   INFLATION FACTOR

Years to Retirement	Factor
1	1.04
2	1.08
3	1.13
4	1.17
5	1.22
6	1.27
7	1.32
8	1.37
9	1.42
10	1.48
11	1.54
12	1.60
13	1.67
14	1.73
15	1.80
16	1.87
17	1.95
18	2.03
19	2.11
20	2.19
21	2.28
22	2.37
23	2.46
24	2.56
25	2.67
26	2.77
27	2.88
28	3.00
29	3.12
30	3.24

Table 3—Survivor planning worksheet

Years to Retirement	Investment Return Factor		
	6%	8%	10%
1	1.06	1.08	1.10
2	1.12	1.17	1.21
3	1.19	1.26	1.33
4	1.26	1.36	1.46
5	1.34	1.47	1.61
6	1.42	1.59	1.77
7	1.50	1.71	1.95
8	1.59	1.85	2.14
9	1.69	2.00	2.36
10	1.79	2.16	2.59
11	1.90	2.33	2.85
12	2.01	2.52	3.14
13	2.13	2.72	3.45
14	2.26	2.94	3.80
15	2.40	3.17	4.18
16	2.54	3.43	4.60
17	2.69	3.70	5.05
18	2.85	4.00	5.56
19	3.03	4.32	6.12
20	3.21	4.66	6.73
21	3.40	5.03	7.40
22	3.60	5.44	8.14
23	3.82	5.87	8.95
24	4.05	6.34	9.85
25	4.29	6.85	10.83
26	4.55	7.40	11.92
27	4.82	7.99	13.11
28	5.11	8.63	14.42
29	5.42	9.32	15.86
30	5.74	10.06	17.45

Table 4—Survivor planning worksheet   COLLEGE INVESTMENT RETURN FACTOR TABLE

Years to First Year of College	Factor
1	1.02
2	1.04
3	1.06
4	1.08
5	1.10
6	1.13
7	1.15
8	1.17
9	1.20
10	1.22
11	1.24
12	1.27
13	1.29
14	1.32
15	1.35
16	1.37
17	1.40
18	1.43

Assumes after-tax investment return will be 2% less than rate of increase on college costs.

Table 5—Survivor planning worksheet

Years to Retirement	Present Value Factor		
	6%	8%	10%
1	1.000	1.000	1.000
2	0.485	0.481	0.476
3	0.314	0.308	0.302
4	0.229	0.222	0.215
5	0.177	0.170	0.164
6	0.143	0.136	0.130
7	0.119	0.112	0.105
8	0.101	0.094	0.087
9	0.087	0.080	0.074
10	0.076	0.069	0.063
11	0.067	0.060	0.054
12	0.059	0.053	0.047
13	0.053	0.047	0.041
14	0.048	0.041	0.036
15	0.043	0.037	0.031
16	0.039	0.033	0.028
17	0.035	0.030	0.025
18	0.032	0.027	0.022
19	0.030	0.024	0.020
20	0.027	0.022	0.017
21	0.025	0.020	0.016
22	0.023	0.018	0.014
23	0.021	0.016	0.013
24	0.020	0.015	0.011
25	0.018	0.014	0.010
26	0.017	0.013	0.009
27	0.016	0.011	0.008
28	0.015	0.010	0.007
29	0.014	0.010	0.007
30	0.013	0.009	0.006